The Tilapia Trail
– the life story of
a fish biologist

by

Ro Lowe-McConnell

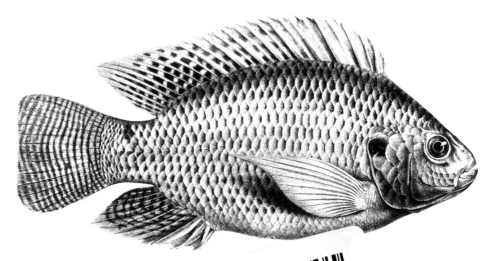

MPM Publishing Ascot

MPM Publishing
West Mains, London Road,
Ascot SL5 7DG

First published 2006
© Ro Lowe-McConnell

Set in Book Antiqua
Typesetting by MPM

Printed in Great Britain by
The Lavenham Press, Suffolk

ISBN   0-9545596-4-9

The Tilapia Trail
– the life story of
a fish biologist

CONTENTS

Tilapia species encountered on The Tilapia trail

Most readers can ignore this page but, for those who are interested: the genus *Tilapia* (and 'tilapia' is still used as a colloquial term for all of them) is now restricted to the guarders i.e. non-mouth brooding species (of which only *T. zillii* and *T. rendalli* are considered here). The remainder are now grouped as either *Oreochromis* (the female mouth-brooders which include most of the East African species considered here) or *Sarotherodon* (the male mouth-brooders of which only *S. galilaeus* in Lakes Albert and Rudolf is considered). The genus *Oreochromis* contains four subgenera: *Oreochromis, Nyasatilapia, Neotilapia* and *Alcolapia*, whose species are listed below for clarification.

O. (Oreochromis) of which the following are discussed in this book:
O. niloticus Nilotic – Lakes George/Edward, Albert, Rudolf, Kivu (introduced to Lake Victoria 1953)
O. esculentus endemic – Lakes Victoria/Kyoga
O. leucostictus Lakes George/Edward, Albert (introduced Lake Victoria 1953)
O. spilurus niger ('*Tilapia nigra*') Sagana ponds
O. karogwe Pangani River and ponds
O. urolepis hornorum (= 'Zanzibar tilapia' used in hybrid experiments)
O. mossambicus. Now circumtropical in fish ponds (Guyana, Trinidad)
O. shiranus Lake Nyasa/Malawi
O. shiranus chilwae Lake Chilwa
O. pangani pangani Pangani River
O. pangani girigan Pangani River
O. jipe Lake Jipe
O. hunteri Lake Chala
O. mortimeri (fish ponds, Central Africa)
O. andersonii (fish ponds, Central Africa)

Subgenus *Nyasalapia*, males with genital tassels:
O. (N.) karongae (now includes *T. saka*)
O. (N.) squamipinnis (Lake Nyasa 'Chambo'species flock)
O. (N.) lidole
O. (N.) karomo Malagarasi River
O (N.) variabilis Lakes Victoria/Kyoga
O. (N.) upembae Upper Congo/Lualaba River (cf *O. malagarasi*)
O. (N.) malagarasi (called '*T.cf nilotica*'in Malagarasi River)
O. (N.) rukwaensis Lake Rukwa
O. (N.) macrochir (Kafue 'cone')
O. (N.) mweruensis ('star' plaques)

Subgenus *Neotilapia*:
O. (Ne.) tanganyikae Lake Tanganyika

Subgenus *Alcolapia*:
O. (Alcolapia) alcalicus (Lake Natron, Kenya alkaline lakes)
O. (A.) grahami Lake Magadi, an alkaline lake (introduced to Lake Nakuru)

Introduction

This book began as a light-hearted narrative of my early explorations of the ecology and evolution of the very abundant and diverse fishes in the African Great Lakes from 1945 onwards (in Chapters 1- 5). Initially one chapter was devoted to 'The Tilapia Trail' as these particular cichlid fishes were most important in the diet of the riparian people throughout much of Africa. Subsequently, tilapia have gained new importance as the best fish to culture throughout the warm waters of the world. This is increasingly imperative as fisheries in both fresh waters and the sea are declining so rapidly. So the whole book came to be called *The Tilapia Trail*, creating a hybrid of research history and personal narrative. It describes studies of these fishes in their natural homes, and my own very enjoyable occupation pursuing them in beautiful places. Unexpectedly, following my years in Africa, the good fortune of marrying Richard McConnell then gave me a new life in South America (Chapter 6), which provided a splendid opportunity to compare the ecology of the floras and faunas of these two continents, before they were despoiled by the needs of rapidly rising human populations.

Readers engaged in field research, or studies of fish elsewhere, may find this background of interest. Perhaps you recognise some of the colourful aquarium fishes exported from both continents and would like to know more about them in their natural habitats. Maybe you know Africa as it was or as it is now and will enjoy sharing my perspectives. So choose which chapters to read. For those desiring further details, notes with references are given for each chapter at the end of the book, together with a list of my relevant scientific papers.

The Tilapia Trail also leads the reader through three recurring themes, which perhaps have wider relevance than just fish biology. First is the crucial importance of social and scientific networks, which not only provide personal and practical support, but are also important test beds for new ideas. Mulling over data with colleagues and friends, especially of an interdisciplinary nature, is highly catalytic in refining thoughts and improving the robustness of hypotheses. I have found my friends and colleagues enormously helpful in so many ways. A second issue concerns the fragility of the scientific edifice. The fish collections I accumulated, and many others like them, made possible the construction of phylogenies and facilitated the taxonomic bedrock for tilapia biology that Trewavas and others provided. But this taxonomy, an important tool for understanding distributions and translocations, may itself be transient. It was based on the techniques of the time and focused on morphology. Species definitions were based on patterns, colour, spine and scale counts, pharyngeal teeth. Perhaps one day animals will be classified by DNA sequencing, like reading bar codes. What then? Will the taxonomic framework be shown to be robust? In any event, the concept of the species is fragile in such a rapidly evolving group as the cichlids.

A third recurring topic is the great change in the art of the possible since my day. All the equipment I needed was bulky and much had to be gathered in the UK and transported thousands of miles by sea. Nowadays, light- weight camping gear, for example, is available almost anywhere, cars can usually be relied on, and roads are often good. In those days, the majority of time in the field was expended in the logistics of living, whereas now a high proportion of field time is available for scientific work. Modern scientific equipment is not only more portable, but makes possible faster data collection and enables new lines of enquiry. Today environmental variables and geographical locations can be measured accurately, almost instantly, using gadgetry that would fit into a pocket. Data can be sent home immediately on the mobile phone network or subjected to rigorous analysis on a laptop the same evening. It was not always thus and one of the objectives of this book is to remember that. Another is to recall the happy discovery that fish biology could be such fun!

Acknowledgements

The book would never have been completed without the help of Mary Burgis, a friend and colleague from Uganda days, who has typeset the whole thing and rearranged some of the technical information into a more accessible format, with valuable editorial assistance from her husband Pat Morris.

This book, the product of more than half a century of field experiences, mainly in Africa and South America, owes its being to so many helpful people of different nationalities that it is impossible to name them all. Some are acknowledged in my previous publications, but throughout the project I have been encouraged by many old friends and colleagues, especially Peggy Varley (née Brown) and Gordon Howes who read many drafts. Gordon also drew most of the pictures of fishes used in earlier publications, some of which are reproduced here. The photographs were mostly taken by me, Peggy, Mary or Pat Morris. Those taken by others are acknowledged in the captions. I wish I had been a better photographer myself.

I would also like to thank the many colleagues all over the world who have continued to send me reprints and reports that have kept me up to date on recent developments, for example on the continuing story of ecological change in Lake Victoria, on developments in cichlid and electric fish research, also the problems arising from man-made lakes and others resulting from the rapid clearance of so much Amazon forest for cattle and soya bean cultivation. Relevant references are listed in the Notes and References for those who want to follow up any of the information and also to help bridge the gap between historical and modern research in this area.

Chapter 1
Liverpool and the Lake District
– an unlikely trailhead

Strange as it may seem, the Lake District was the very best place to prepare for my later African adventures. It was here, in the north-west of England, that I first visited the strange mock-gothic edifice, called Wray Castle, in which the 'Freshwater Biological Association of the British Empire' (the FBA) was then housed. It was during a sunny bicycle ride, escaping from a bombed Liverpool, where I was reading Zoology and Botany at the University in the early years of the second world war. The setting was beautiful, on the west shore of Lake Windermere, England`s longest lake (11 miles long). The Castle is reached by a country road along the base of bracken-clad hills, and looks north to the mountains of the Lake District: the Langdale Pikes to the west, the Fairfield 'armchair' above Ambleside. On impulse I dropped my bike in a field and swam across to an island in the lake. Then, dripping, I continued along the road and arrived bedraggled at Wray Castle to enquire about a water scorpion bug (*Nepa*) needed for an undergraduate thesis. The Director, Barton Worthington very kindly came down from his office to talk with me, and introduced me to the entomologist Noel Hynes. Perhaps next year I would return to an Easter Class? A quarter of a century later, after years spent in Africa and South America, Barton and I became neighbours in Sussex until his death in 2003, which stimulated me to start writing this book.

A drawing of Wray Castle on a Christmas card sent to me by Winifred Frost in 1949.

Africa had been my childhood dream, to be an explorer-naturalist; later, South America was pure bonus. What does it all add up to after fifty years of sheer enjoyment of a life of tropical studies? Much of my life has centred mainly on fishes, birds and other creatures of the lakes and swamps of Africa and the streams and rivers of South America, with holidays snorkelling (goggling) in warm seas to look at colourful fishes in coral reef communities. Should I not try to pass on some of the delights and pay tribute to the many people who had made it all possible – gurus, guardians, colleagues, friends, native fishermen?

I also want to record the huge ecological changes encountered during my life time, induced primarily by rapidly rising human populations and rising standards of living. What were environmental conditions like then? What are they like now? The main scientific themes that developed over the years concern the roles of ecology and behaviour in the evolution of biodiversity. This was aided by the environmental changes caused by introductions of exotic species and the opportunities offered by the vast new man-made lakes regarded as giant experiments. How have our methods and paradigms now changed for the scientific study of these tropical places?

Perhaps it was the pictorial map of Africa given to my brother, while I was fobbed off with Australia, that started it all. It was certainly compounded by a desire to live in a warm climate, with a huge diversity of exotic birds and animals, after having had to play in cold northern gardens as a child. But I had a very happy and stable childhood, growing up in a beautiful sunny house looking out over a walled garden, past old beech trees and fields to the River Mersey, where white 'banana boats' from the West Indies steamed upriver to Garston docks on the high tide. At low tide the shore was frequented by flocks of feeding waders, scurrying dunlin and small ringed plovers, larger redshank and curlew, and in winter grey and golden plovers. Where had they all come from? Where would they go? What were they feeding on? Why were their legs different colours? We had frequent visits to Hilbre Island, in the Dee estuary, which was cut off at high tide bringing the waders right to our feet. At home, the windows of my attic eyrie, looking over fields and river, were open to the prevailing winds sweeping in from the Atlantic bringing sea and shore smells. The starlings chortling on the roof mimicked the cry of the redshanks, and leaf-cutting bees made nests along the roof gutter. So wildlife was part of my life from the start and Daisy Bowker, my godmother, was a biology teacher who encouraged these interests.

To prepare for my hoped-for life in wild places I slept in the garden or on the flat roof. I had inherited a tree seat, built by the young Charles Elton – who became a founding father of animal ecology – high in the gnarled weeping ash tree in our garden when our parents exchanged residences in Liverpool in the 1920s. Growing up there we were very fortunate to have so many interesting and friendly neighbours with tropical connections – including the Director and staff of the Liverpool School of Tropical Medicine. Our donkey was stabled in the garden of Professor Proudman, a world authority on tides, after whom the Proudman Oceanographic Laboratory came to be named. My younger brother and I grew up in a home full of books and were given a splendidly wide education, though our loving parents also subscribed to the view 'what children need is a little healthy neglect' and they took it very well when I did go off to Africa on my own in 1945, aged 24.

Boarding at Howells School at Denbigh, in North Wales, on the other side of the hills we could see across the Mersey estuary from home on clear days, gave me a very sound basis in biology and many life-long friends. School was followed by university but just as I was about to start reading Zoology and Botany at Liverpool University the Second World War was declared – blackout and gasmasks, food rationing, air raid sirens and bombs. This was a time when students had to turn their hands to all kinds of unusual jobs. As Deputy Director for Education my father was deeply involved in the evacuation of all the Liverpool school children to North Wales, which involved arranging foster homes for them for an indefinite period. My mother was an air-raid warden. As an air raid shelter we strengthened the cellars of our house with timbers, beach-combed from the shore, which had floated over from Cammell Laird's shipyards on the other bank of the wide estuary. Here we slept on camp beds in some comfort. Incendiary bombs came first. Later, in a week-long blitz, the daffodils in the park were mown down by the blast, their yellow trumpets protesting to the sky. Merely being alive each morning was exceedingly exhilarating as we cycled the five miles to university, seeing what damage had been done en route. One day the university blood bank was hit – what a mess – broken glass everywhere in the department, where as we swept up we gaily decided which awful objects ought to have been destroyed by the blast. During the blitz the students were used to the full as rescuers and general assistants – budding engineers dug people out of rubble, the medics put body bits in bags in a makeshift mortuary. Others helped to run church halls suddenly full of bombed-out families who needed milk for their children, food and other necessities of life, and to have billets found for them. Despite, or because of, all the horror there was a great camaraderie.

Good friends were also made later during undergraduate Easter classes at the Herdman Marine Biological Station at Port Erin on the Isle of Man and at the FBA in the Lake District. It was good to escape into the country for Easter field classes. At Port Erin we were introduced to a succession of creatures on rocky shores, discovering radially symmetrical echinoderms with their waving tube feet, and the scallops (*Pecten*) dredged from the sea added to our wartime diet. Another year, at Wray Castle, where I had already met Barton Worthington, the FBA Easter Class was run by Philip Moon and Betty Walshe, with Professor Munro Fox who decided to be a co-student among the fifteen or so gathered from various universities. The group included David Le Cren who became a long-term colleague and eventually Director of the FBA laboratory. Wray Castle was already an international centre for freshwater studies, with a marvellous library of reprints. Sitting on the wide oak windowsill, with its view out over the lake to the hills above Ambleside, I chose to devour this feast rather than going with the others to the local pub, the 'Drunken Duck'.

After we graduated, David and I were among those invited back to the FBA to help in various projects aimed at producing wartime food from freshwaters. My allotted task was to study the migrations of silver eels from the many Lake District lakes when setting out on the start of their long journey back to the Sargasso Sea to breed. David started what turned out to be a long-term study of the populations of perch in Lake Windermere, which at that time were being canned for wartime food as 'Perchines'. Among the others helping the eel project (at £4 a week), were Peter Tuft and Jimmy Beament who later became distinguished professors.

Life at Wray Castle was a splendid introduction for an embryonic limnologist/fisheries biologist as limnologists from all over the world visited the laboratory. Since most of us then lived in the ramifying castle, making cocoa over the kitchen Aga stove at midnight, one got to know many of them very well. Furthermore, since the Director, Barton Worthington, was engaged on a wartime survey of supplies for the Middle East, various FBA Council members from different UK institutions took turns to supervise us. As a result we learned many diverse things from a wide variety of people such as, 'Fanny' J.T. Saunders of Cambridge University (of invertebrate textbook fame), Prof. W.H. Pearsall of University College London, who was studying plant successions in the fens at the head of Esthwaite Water, and Prof. Patrick Buxton of the London School of Hygiene and Tropical Medicine, who taught me much that was later of use in Africa. It was here I first met Ethelwynn Trewavas of the Fish Section, British Museum (Natural History) who became a very special guru/colleague, and F.T.K. Pentelow, from the Ministry of Agriculture & Fisheries who, with a wide smile behind his thick pebble glasses, expounded 'Pentelow's Two Laws of Biology': (1) to label everything – before one forgot, and (2) 'knowing when to stop' – i.e. before later results cancelled out earlier ones.

Not only did all these, and later, contacts provide stimulating company at the time but many resulted in life-long friendships. A network of friends with similar interests provides sources of information, ideas and (crucially) food for thought, linking the many interacting facets of biology, geography, chemistry etc. etc. As will be evident, an ever expanding network became a most fundamental aspect of my working life, without which it would have been very different and much less enjoyable.

In all, Wray Castle was a very jolly and formative place for a young biologist. The Aquatic Insect collections from the British Museum (Natural History), the BM(NH), had been evacuated there to avoid being bombed in London. They were curated by experts on particular groups, including W.E. China on aquatic bugs (Hemiptera), D.E. Kimmins on dragonflies (Odonata), mayflies (Ephemeroptera), caddis flies (Trichoptera) and allied groups. We all shared the everyday lunchtime discussions at long dining tables. In later years, Fishery Officers training for overseas posts joined us for a few weeks at a time and many overseas students visited or undertook particular projects. These included Eville Gorham from Canada who had a personal interest in acid water in streams long before 'acid rain' became an issue, whose work thus provided a baseline by which to judge later 'acidification'.

Most of the regular FBA staff were away on wartime jobs, but reappeared at intervals, including the entomologist T.T. Macan who was working on malaria control and Clifford Mortimer, the limnologist, who later directed work on the Great Lakes of the USA. Other resident research staff included the inimitable Winifred Frost who was working on salmonids, including Windermere`s special charr *(Salvelinus)* and eel biology. She later visited the Trout Research Station at Sagana on Mount Kenya to study Kenya`s eels *(Anguilla)*, which migrate into the Indian Ocean to spawn. The algologist John

Life-long friends and colleagues from FBA days at Wray Castle standing on the drive at Ferry House to which the FBA moved in 1950. From left: Charlotte Kipling, Peggy Brown, Winifred Frost, David LeCren and Kate Woolham, who became David's wife. The view behind them is the north basin of Windermere.

Lund was undertaking a long-term study of algal production in the lake and later used experimental tubes in Blelham Tarn. He was visited frequently by Professor Fritsch who curated the National Collection of Freshwater Algae. Winifred Pennington (after her marriage known as Anne Tutin) was studying pollen in cores drilled from the lake sediments which revealed the history of Lake Windermere and other Lake District lakes. The bottom coring apparatus, as well as water sampling bottles, had just been developed at the FBA by 'Pop' Jenkin, father of Penelope Jenkin, one of the first biologists to study an African lake, investigating the feeding habits of flamingos on Kenya's rift valley lakes.

At FBA one learnt to use reversing thermometers, Jenkin water samplers, and other equipment with which limnological results had to be obtained before the development of today's sophisticated equipment. The local laboratory staff, headed by George Thompson, gave skilled help with collecting samples and we all pulled seine nets, set gill nets and lifted fish traps. The eel work involved attempts to use light paths to deflect the very light-sensitive silver eels into traps beside streams as they migrated seawards from the various lakes. This was done on the dark nights of Autumn at the start of their long migration back to the Sargasso Sea. What stimulated them to go? A rising flood after a day of heavy rain was certainly one trigger but also caused debris to block the traps. Manning the eel traps on Cunsey Beck, flowing from Esthwaite Water into Lake Windermere, entailed a five mile cycle ride through dark country lanes under wartime 'blackout' conditions, and working through the night if it had rained all day. A good training! The phase of the moon also played an important role. In the cellar of Wray Castle we built an artificial river ('The Styx') to test eel swimming speeds, and injected them with hormones to try to get them to mature without the long migration.

Barton Worthington, who had led the first exploratory fishery surveys of many East African lakes, was at this time asked by the Colonial Office of the British Government to prepare a memorandum for research and management of freshwater fisheries in East Africa. This was approved by a conference of the three Territories concerned (Kenya, Tanganyika and Uganda) in October 1944. The conference also strongly supported the idea of both a Fisheries Research Station (to be set up on Lake Victoria at Jinja, Uganda) and a Lake Victoria Fisheries Board, both to be financed from the newly formed Colonial Development and Welfare (C.D. & W.) Fund which had been established in 1940 to meet the developing needs of the colonies in the post-war era. Here would come my chance to go to Africa! So I hitched my wagon to Barton's star.

Barton was a pioneer in studying the ecology and biogeography of the East African Great Lakes and their fisheries, based mainly on two expeditions to Kenya and Uganda. Having just graduated from Cambridge University in 1928–29, he accompanied Michael Graham, from the Fisheries Laboratory at

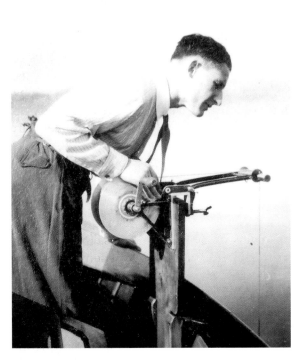

Barton Worthington one of the leading pioneers in the study of African lakes operating a water sampler over the side of a boat in about 1931.

Lowestoft, on the first fishery survey of the huge (69,000 km^2) equatorial Lake Victoria, helping with all the fishery work and taking water and zooplankton samples. When Graham had to return to Lowestoft in 1929, Barton was asked by the Governor of Uganda to make a comparable survey of Lake Albert in the Western Rift Valley and of Lake Kyoga, into which Lake Victoria flows before its waters plunge over the Murchison (Kapegabo) Falls to Lake Albert. The results of these surveys were published in Colonial Office Fishery Reports, followed by a series of papers in scientific journals.

Whilst working up the collections brought from these lakes to the Zoological laboratory in Cambridge and the British Museum (Natural History) in London, Barton planned a Cambridge Expedition to East African Lakes (1930–31) financed mainly by University and research institutions. This time he was accompanied by Leonard C. Beadle, just back from an expedition to the Grand Chaco swamps of South America with George Carter of Cambridge University, and 'Bunny' Fuchs (later Sir Vivian Fuchs of Antarctic fame), to study the geology of the lake basins. Barton`s first wife Stella went with them, as surveyor/geographer. Following trials of their gear from a base camp on Lake Naivasha (where they nearly lost the outboard engine brought with them from the UK, almost the first outboard seen in East Africa), they first studied the lakes in the Kenya Rift Valley, Lake Rudolf (later called Turkana) and Baringo, and with brief visits to the smaller, very alkaline lakes including

Lake Hannington (Bogoria) lying further south. The problems of obtaining, and then transporting a ship's lifeboat, borrowed from the Kenya Marine on Lake Victoria, to Lake Rudolf were vividly and amusingly described in the Worthington`s book '*Inland Waters of Africa*' (1933). The expedition then moved to Uganda to survey lakes Edward and George in the Western Rift Valley, after which Barton and Stella visited some smaller Ugandan lakes. The latter included Lake Bunyoni, a volcanic lake in the southwest, Lakes Kachira, Nakavali and Kijanebalola, a series of shallow swampy lakes lying between Lakes Edward and Victoria, and the small Lake Nabugabo which is cut off by a 4000 year old sandbar from the northwest shore of Lake Victoria. As the Uganda Government had requested a fisheries report, a separate report for the Uganda lakes was published by the Crown Agents, but most of the scientific results from this 1930–31 Cambridge Expedition were published in a series of papers in the *Proceedings of the Linnean Society of London* 1932–33.

Barton had planned to continue biogeographical studies of the fishes with expeditions to the great lakes further south, including Lakes Bangweulu, Nyasa (Malawi) and Tanganyika where Belgian scientists were already at work. In preparation, he had studied the specimens of previous collectors stored at the BM(NH), producing three papers on the non-cichlid fishes of these lakes (Bangweulu, Nyasa, and Tanganyika). The East African Governments financed a student to help Barton sort his collections, thus enabling Kate Ricardo to become involved with African lakes, both with the fishes and vertical migrations of zooplankton from samples collected by Barton from Lake Victoria and other East African lakes.

In 1936–37, Kate and a Cambridge friend, Janet Owen, embarked on their own expedition to study the fish and fisheries of Lake Rukwa and the Bangweulu Swamps, producing a Crown Agent Fisheries Report (1939) and a Linnean Society paper on the fishes of Lake Rukwa. On this expedition, they travelled widely, arriving in Africa via Angola and going home down the Nile, as much later recorded in their delightful book *Letters from the Swamps; East Africa 1936–37* (1991). On their travels Kate had her first view of Lake Nyasa, peering through the reeds at the north end, with marvellous views across the lake to the Livingstone Mountains. This was the lake to which she returned as a member of the 1938–39 Lake Nyasa Fishery Survey described later. On their homeward journey they also travelled on Lake Tanganyika`s famous lake steamer the '*S.S. Liemba*', formerly the *Graf von Gotzen*, which was scuttled off the Malagarasi Delta by the Germans in 1915 to avoid its capture by the British and Belgians in the First World War.

Barton's major scientific achievement at that time was to put together the first picture of the biogeography and ecology of the fishes in these African lakes, as described in general papers that he read to the Royal Geographical Society, London (1929, 1932). These papers take into account contributions

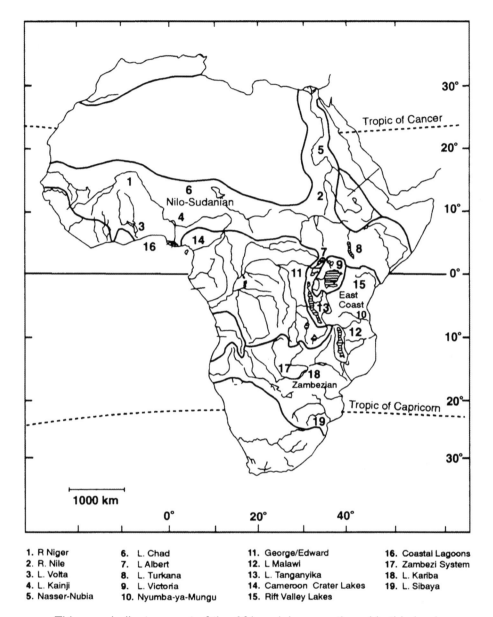

1. R Niger	6. L. Chad	11. George/Edward	16. Coastal Lagoons
2. R. Nile	7. L Albert	12. L Malawi	17. Zambezi System
3. L. Volta	8. L. Turkana	13. L. Tanganyika	18. L. Kariba
4. L. Kainji	9. L. Victoria	14. Cameroon Crater Lakes	19. L. Sibaya
5. Nasser-Nubia	10. Nyumba-ya-Mungu	15. Rift Valley Lakes	

This map indicates most of the African lakes mentioned in this book.

from fellow scientists on the geology of drainage connections, including Fuchs' observations on raised beaches round the lakes and other indications of changed drainage patterns. He also described the discovery of fossil Nile perch (*Lates*) and crocodiles in the Lake Edward beds. The past history of East Africa's pluvial periods, had also been much studied by his Cambridge friends Lewis Leakey in Kenya and E.J. Wayland in Uganda.

Barton was particularly impressed by the contrast between the 'Nilotic' fish faunas found in Lake Albert and Lake Rudolf, later known as the *nilo-*

sudanian fauna of fishes distributed from the Niger to the Nile, which include large predatory fishes such as the Nile Perch *Lates* and Tigerfish *Hydrocynus*, and those of the 'plateau' lakes with their 'Victorian' fish fauna characterised by species flocks of small haplochromine cichlids, that are not found in abundance in the nilotic lakes. In a 1937 paper, Barton discussed present and past barriers to fish movements, geographical isolation and ecological isolation leading to the conditions under which new species have evolved in the various lakes. For example, on the White Nile system the upper reaches of the river have two falls – the Ripon Falls separating Lake Victoria from Lake Kyoga with a drop of only some 15 ft (*c*5m) broken in places, and the Murchison Falls with a vertical drop of 130 ft (*c*40m) or more between Lake Kyoga and Lake Albert. Lakes Kyoga and Victoria have fish faunas which are similar as far as genera and most of the species are concerned (with a few subspecific differences) but the Murchison Falls present a major barrier between these two lakes and Lake Albert and the Nile downstream. Hence many genera of Nile fish (including *Lates* and *Hydrocynus*) occur naturally only in the river below the Murchison Falls. In only three cases were the same species present above and below these falls – and these were mainly fish that can utilise air. In warm climates an ecological factor of great importance is the depletion of oxygen in tropical swamps which presents a barrier to many fish species.

Barton concluded that when geographical isolation is complete, in a high percentage of cases it is accompanied by evident differentiation, but the degree depends on the group of organisms concerned. Among fishes the family Cichlidae tends to differentiate wherever they are isolated in favourable environments, whereas others such as the lungfish, show no disposition to do so. The differentiation of species (or subspecies) tends to be greater if associated with a change in the environment. In a group capable of rapid differentiation (such as the Cichlids), the environmental conditions are all-important in determining the amount of differentiation that can take place. Two especially important conditions are the existence of unoccupied ecological niches, and the absence of large predators. This is brought out clearly in the table comparing cichlids and non-cichlid fish species now known from these lakes.

The importance of predators in controlling cichlid speciation was later questioned by Geoff Fryer but, as I later pointed out, in Lake Tanganyika which has four endemic *Lates* species, piscivores appear to have had an opposite effect in the open water from that in littoral communities. Cichlid speciation in open waters without cover is controlled, but on the rocky shores where the fish had cover, open water living piscivores may present a biological barrier between fish populations, so aiding speciation. The introduction of *Lates* into Lake Victoria in the mid 1950s provided an unintentional experiment, (see Chapter 4) as this introduction was followed by the disappearance of some 200 endemic cichlid species from the open lake, whereas those living with cover along rocky coasts survived.

But all that is for later. While still at the FBA during the War it seemed that I was destined to become an initial member of the staff of the East African Fisheries Organization which Barton was planning to set up on Lake Victoria in Jinja, Uganda, after the war was over. However, since this laboratory would not be ready for a year or so, what should I do in the interim? His suggestion that I should work in Cyprus was not my choice, so it was arranged with the Colonial Office that I should go to Lake Nyasa (Malawi) to continue the Fisheries Survey of that lake started by Bertram, Borley and Trewavas, which had been interrupted by the war. So first I had to prepare for this venture by obtaining all the necessary gear and learning how to use it.

Today when a young scientist can leap into a plane and arrive at a well-equipped laboratory, complete with modern sampling devices and computers, to study some aspect of a specialist subject, it is difficult to realise what was then involved in such a prototype enterprise. There was neither a laboratory nor any fishery department in Nyasaland (now Malawi), so I had to become one. A suggestion that I should be attached to the Department of Agriculture was scotched by the Director of Agriculture not wanting any lone (female) fisheries research officer attached to his department. John Borley was still in Nyasaland but was by then a District Commissioner in Dowa, an upcountry station well away from the lake. So it was necessary to obtain (despite wartime shortages) and take with me by sea, equipment to be self-sufficient for working in remote areas for at least a year.

The number of indigenous fish species in East African lakes. (Cichlids mostly haplochromines except in L. Tanganyika.) Species numbers from Snoeks (2000).

	Cichlid species		Non-cichlid species		Estimated age of lake	Drainage
	No spp.	% endemic	No spp.	% endemic		
Tanganyika	250	98%	75	59%	20my	Congo
Malawi (previously Nyasa)	c800	99%	45	29%	c2my	Zambesi
Victoria	c500	99%	45	16%	400,000y refilled c14,600y	Nile
Edward/ George	60	92%	21	5%		Nile
Albert	11	36%	37	5%		Nile
Turkana (previously Rudolf)	8	50%	36	17%		(Nile)

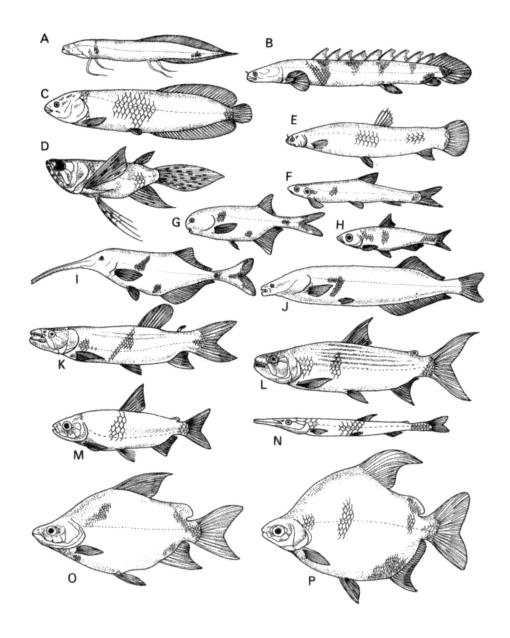

Representative African freshwater fishes I:
(Numbers in brackets are total lengths commonly encountered.)
A. *Protopterus* Lungfish *(100cm);* **B.** *Polypterus (40cm);* **C.** *Heterotis (50cm);*
D. *Pantodon (6cm);* **E.** *Phractolaemus (6cm);* **F.** *Kneria (6cm);* **G.** *Petrocephalus
(15cm);* **H.** *Pellonula (14cm);* **I.** *Campylomormyrus (12cm);* **J.** *Mormyrops (100cm);*
K. *Hepsetus (30cm);* **L.** *Hydrocynus (50cm);* **M.** *Alestes (12cm);* **N.** *Belonophago
(12cm);* **O.** *Distichodus (50cm);* **P.** *Citharinus (70cm).*

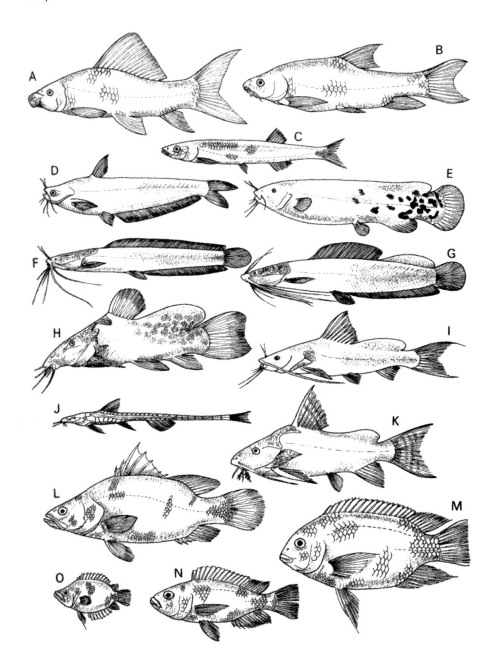

African Freshwater fishes II:
A. *Labeo (50cm);* **B.** *Barbus (50cm);* **C.** *Engraulicypris (10cm);* **D.** *Schilbe (20cm);*
E. *Malapterurus* Electric catfish *(25cm);* **F.** *Clarias (50cm);* **G.** *Heterobranchus*
(120cm); **H.** *Auchenoglanis (80cm);* **I.** *Bagrus (100cm);* **J.** *Belonoglanis (8cm);*
K. *Synodontis (50cm);* **L.** *Lates* Nile perch *(100cm);* **M.** *Tilapia (30cm);*
N. *Haplochromis (12cm);* **O.** *Polycentropsis (6cm).*

Barton was invaluable in advising on equipment needed for African lake research. I would need gill and seine nets, coils of rope, drums of (neutralized) formalin and collecting tanks for preservation of fish specimens plus laboratory equipment – dissecting microscope, fish measuring boards, scales for weighing catches, reversing thermometer, water and oxygen sampling gear. I also had to have camping gear, including folding bed plus mosquito net rods, mosquito net, canvas safari (called ulendo in Nyasaland) gear including table, chair and bath, and suitable clothes (then on coupons). The latter included mosquito-boots and a spine pad and topi (then considered essential for protection from the sun), rescued from a neighbour's dressing-up box. The list went on and on – Tilley and hurricane lamps, shotgun with cartridges of various bores, stationery, torches and a supply of batteries, polaroid glasses for looking into water (no scuba invented then – that came much later and revolutionised such research), camera and films (very hard to get under wartime conditions) plus identification keys and other books. With an outboard engine, all this gear filled fourteen crates which accompanied me by ship from Southampton to Cape Town in South Africa where the ship docked, then by train to Salisbury in Southern Rhodesia (now Zimbabwe), and on by lorry across Portuguese East Africa (now Mozambique) to Nyasaland.

Furthermore , it was necessary to learn how to use (and repair) such gear. The FBA was an ideal place to do so. George Thomson and his merry men taught me how to mount, set, use and mend gillnets and seine nets. Then I had to visit Bridport in southern England to order nets to take with me. 'Wooly' (H. Buchanan-Wollaston), who had been evacuated to Wray Castle from the Lowestoft Marine Fisheries Laboratory, advised on fish measuring equipment including a method of 'pricking' the total lengths of large samples of fish on to water-proof paper. This enables their length frequencies to be easily seen in order to determine their growth rates. A pair of polaroid lenses were to be used to examine growth rings on opercular (gill cover) bones of the tilapia in order to age them – a method David Le Cren was then using to determine growth rates of Windermere perch. I had to learn to handle boat engines and the shotgun 'for the pot if not for defence against wild animals'. I also had to master the rudiments of the language then in use in Nyasaland from a mission book which, to the ribald joy of my colleagues, in its first section 'on engaging labour' started with the memorable Chinyanja phrase 'I want a man not a child'. This phrase did, in fact, became very useful when, on arrival at Lake Nyasa I found I had to start by building huts for the boat boys, the 'capitao' fish recorder called Chigona, and Greniger who was 'lent' to me by the Provincial Commissioner as a stalwart houseboy/camp cook, who looked after me so well throughout my time in that country, and the night watchman. The huts became a row of wattle and daub rondavels, distinguished by grass roofs at a rather jaunty angle and from which a leopard took the night watchman's dog.

What are tilapia?

In addition to what are known as the haplochromine cichlids, the family of fish known as Cichlidae also includes over eighty known species of the important food fish generally called by the common name tilapia. Tilapia are endemic to Africa and the Middle East although a few species are now circum-tropical pond fish. They are all basically herbivores or plankton feeders when adult (some including bottom debris in their diet), while the fingerlings are generally zooplankton feeders. Not more than six indigenous species of tilapia ever occur in one lake, in contrast with the smaller haplochromine cichlids which have radiated to use all kinds of food, enabling many species to live together in one lake.

Tilapia fall into two groups:

Some are herbivorous species with few gill rakers which are substratum-spawners in which both parents guard their young, the *Tilapia zillii* and *T. rendalli* ('*T. melanopleura*') group of the genus *Tilapia*.

The second group are phytoplankton-feeding or bottom-feeding microphagous species with more numerous gill rakers, in which the parents mouth-brood the eggs and young. This group is now divided into two genera, *Oreochromis* species in which males spawn in leks and only the female mouth-broods, as do the majority of eastern African species and those used in pond culture, and *Sarotherodon* species in which both sexes share mouth-brooding, as in some West African species. This latter includes *S. galilaeus* which is also found in the 'nilo-sudanian' lakes Albert and Rudolf (Turkana) in East Africa.

Most African cichlids are female mouth-brooders, those of South America are substratum-spawners. Tilapia are unique in having evolved mouth-brooders of both kinds (i.e. male and female brooders) and substratum spawners.

As part of my training, looked on as a prototype course for Fisheries Officers joining an Overseas Research Service to be developed after the war was over, I was sent to the Torry Research Institute in Aberdeen to learn about how to process fish by cold and hot smoking, since ice was not then available on the African lakes. Most important, in 1945, I had several months in the Fish Section of the British Museum (Natural History) in London with Ethelwynn Trewavas, using their collections to learn how to identify fishes from Lake Nyasa and how to collect further material of fishes and invertebrates on which they might feed (called 'taking advantage of the scientific opportunity` in which Barton was a great believer). A better guide than Ethelwynn I could not have had. I also visited Kate Ricardo (by then married to Colin Bertram a Cambridge biologist with Antarctic experience). She was coping with two young sons in Sussex, at a cold and frosty time, my first ever visit to the county which became my home some twenty years later.

What fishes did Ethelwynn introduce me to? Africa is a very old continent much of it having remained above sea-level since the Precambrian 500 million years ago. It has a rich freshwater fish fauna of about forty families with over 3000 species, representatives of which are shown on the previous pages. Many families occur only in Africa but some families from Gondwanaland times (including the cichlids, characoids and catfish families) are shared with South America. Others such as the cyprinid carps and minnows, are shared with Asia. The spectacular adaptive radiations of the perch-like cichlid fishes in the African Great Lakes had attracted most study, and most communities in these lakes are dominated by these fishes. The riverine faunas are dominated by non-cichlid

Kate Ricardo was another of the early pioneers in the study of fish in African lakes. She first went to Africa in 1936 and later, to Lake Nyasa in 1938.

fishes, including cyprinids, characoids, catfishes and numerous endemic mormyrid species. Representatives of many of these families indicating their bizarre forms, evolved for different ways of life, are shown in the drawings. As cichlids spawn in still water they were well adapted to colonise lakes. In Lakes Tanganyika and Malawi spectacular adaptive radiations have produced numerous endemic genera while Malawi and the younger Lake Victoria have huge species flocks of endemic haplochromine cichlid species.

Riverine faunas are, on the whole, dominated by non-cichlids (characoids and catfishes in South America, cyprinids in Asia), many of them bottom feeders on small invertebrates. The marine family Centropomidae is represented by the large predatory Nile or Niger perch, *Lates niloticus*, which grows to over 120 kg and is widely distributed from West Africa to the Nile (a 'nilo-sudanian' distribution) but absent from Lake Nyasa which has a Zambezi drainage fish fauna. These are the *dramatis personae* on whose stage I was soon to arrive.

Chapter 2
Africa here I come!

Lake Nyasa (now known as Lake Malawi) is one of the most beautiful lakes in the world. A long deep rift valley lake, its clear waters lap on to long sandy beaches alternating with rocky stretches from which fish eagles (*Cuncuma vocifer*) sail out over the lake with fierce haunting cries. It is Africa's third largest lake, over 350 miles long, about 50 miles wide and over 700 metres (about 2100 feet) deep. It lies near the southern end of the Rift valley (9° to 14° S) and, from the eastern arm, where it divides at its southern end, drains through the small Lake Malombe and the Shire River into the Zambezi river system. Some 11,000 square miles (30,044 km²) in area, the lake lies at *c*1500 feet above sea level, the ground on either side rising steeply on the western side to the Vipya and Nyika plateaux and on the eastern side to the Livingstone mountains. The southern part of the lake is relatively shallow. R.S.A. (Bobby) Beauchamp, who was then carrying out work on the hydrography of the lake, discovered a thermocline at 50–200 m, below which the water is deoxygenated.

We now know that this lake has more species of fish than any other lake in the world, though many still await scientific descriptions and names. Many of the very colourful rock-dwelling species, called by the local African name 'mbuna', are now well known to aquarists. The open water is very clear, with surface water temperatures ranging from *c* 21 to 28° C. The lake is far enough south of the Equator to have clearly defined seasons. The strong southeast trade wind, known as 'mwera', blows up the lake for days at a time in the cooler dry months from March to August. This makes the lake very rough in the 'mwera' season, preventing fishing. The temperature then rises giving a hot dry season before the rains arrive in November. They are heaviest from December to February, often with a short sharp blow from the northeast. In addition to an annual variation in lake level of about a metre or so, which greatly affects the riparian agricultural and fishing populations, the lake has also had long-term variations in mean levels which have evidently influenced the evolution of the cichlid fishes.

The Lake Nyasa Fishery Survey 1938–39

The Lake Nyasa Fishery Survey was initiated in 1938 as part of the Nyasaland Nutrition Survey under the leadership of Dr B.S. Platt. This aimed to find methods of improving the health and standard of living of the African population. Since a third of the country was water, and in those days tsetse flies prevented the keeping of cattle, protein from fish was much needed. Members of the nutrition survey already working in Nyasaland included Dr Platt's assistant Dr G.A.C. Herklots, seconded from Singapore to liaise with

A gill net catch from the SE arm of Lake Nyasa 1946.

the fisheries survey, the anthropologist Dr Margaret Mead, Dr Fitzmaurice, the Medical Officer who befriended me on my survey, Dick Kettlewell a Nyasaland Agricultural Officer knowledgeable on what crops could be grown, and Miss Barker who collected dietary information from African families.

The three members of the Fishery Survey were Kate Ricardo from Cambridge who had already made a survey of lakes Bangweulu and Rukwa in Central Africa, John Borley seconded from the Nyasaland Administration, and Ethelwynn Trewavas from the British Museum (Natural History) who wrote the preliminary description of the Nyasa fauna and notes on the tilapia and other cichlid fishes. Financed by the UK's Colonial Development and Welfare Fund, the survey aimed to discover what part fish played in the native economy, to estimate the total fishery resources of the lake and the extent to which they were being utilised, and to see how the resources could best be exploited so that the main stock of fish would not be damaged. To do this they first chartered the UMCA (the Universities Mission to Central Africa) steamer the *SS Malonda* for six months to circumnavigate the lake in order to observe the types of fish and fishing in different parts of this enormous lake. Their report, with its descriptions of the main fish species, keys for their identification, their local names and natural history gleaned from fishermen around the lake, proved a bible for later studies. They recorded the gear used in the native fisheries, carried out some experimental fishing and made suggestions on how to develop the fisheries. Kate was going to study the biology of the main commercial fish, especially tilapia, on her return to the lake, but the war interrupted these plans, so in 1945 I went to complete the job instead of Kate.

Ethelwynn Trewavas (left) at the launch of the boat named after her which was built at Eel Pie Island on the River Thames before being taken out to Lake Malawi.

Ethelwynn on the new research launch, also named the Ethelwynn Trevawas, on Lake Malawi in 1985 with Denis Tweddle, Digby Lewis and a group of local scientists, fishery officers and boat crew.

A typical rocky shore at the south end of Lake Malawi. In places like this the cichlids scrape algae off the rocks.

A typical beach on the shore of Lake Nyasa/Malawi at Senga Bay – a complete contrast to the habitat shown in the photograph above.

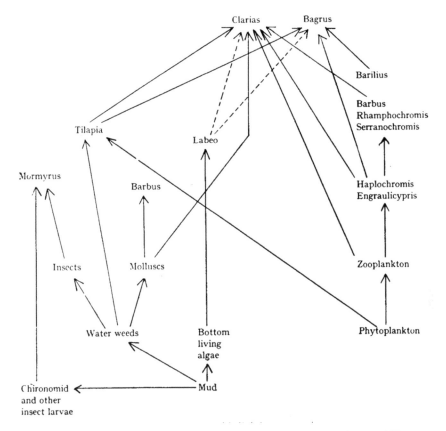

Outline food web for Lake Nyasa published by Bertram, Borley and Trewavas in 1942. "Dotted lines mean that this link is not certain."........ "For the open waters data are scarce, but probably there is a simple food chain from the small fish feeding on the plankton to the larger predators."......"In the shallower water at the edge of the lake, there is more variety in the food supply for the fish."

The 1939 survey had found a fish fauna of 223 species, 194 of which were endemic (found only in this lake) including 178 cichlid species. The glossary of native names given in their report was invaluable to my later survey. The non-endemic fishes showed that the lake had faunal relationships with the Zambezi system. The cichlids included almost every kind of feeding habit. Many 'mbuna' grazed algae off the rocks, others (such as *Lethrinops* species) dug in the sand for small invertebrates including insect larvae and snails. Larger piscivorous species fed on small fish including tilapia. The non-cichlids included the lurking predators *Bagrus* (*B. meridionalis*, known as 'kampango') and a species flock of large clariid catfishes, eel-like *Mastacembelus*, a large mormyrid; the salmon-like cyprinid *Barilius* ('mpasa') and small *Barilius* ('sanjika') migrated up the inflowing rivers to spawn, as did the mud-feeding cyprinid *Labeo*. The open waters were frequented by a small sardine-like pelagic cyprinid *Engraulicypris sardella* ('usipa') which became very abundant in certain years.

From the scientific point of view the Lake Nyasa cichlids offered exceptional opportunities to try to find out why and how so many had evolved within the lake, the subject of an enormous amount of subsequent research. From the fisheries point of view the large cichlid tilapia species supported the main fishery carried out by riparian Africans using home-made seines pulled in from sandy beaches with ropes of plaited palm leaves. The explorer David Livingstone, one of the first Europeans to see the lake, reported such seines in use in 1865. Later the Yiannakis brothers, a family of Greek fishermen had introduced the use of very long seines, and large open water ring nets deployed from two motor launches, as in their homeland around the Aegean islands. The few gillnets in use, made from local plant fibres, and the survey's experimental flax nets, caught mainly non-cichlids. The large piscivorous fishes were caught with hooks on handlines or longlines. Africans made many cunning fish traps, some of which were used in the lake. Others formed barriers across inflowing rivers to catch fish migrating upstream to spawn, including the 'mpasa' (*Barilius*) from the north end of the lake, *Labeo* and *Clarias* which migrated up the less permanent rivers further south.

The first survey had produced an outline food web for the fishes, and described the native fisheries and the role of fish in the local economy. Although interrupted by the war, their report was published in 1942 giving their results obtained in 1938–39. On their trip round the lake they had visited sites that would become bases for further surveys.

The 1945-47 survey

That was the background, so when and how did I get to Lake Nyasa?

On VE day I was one dot in that vast jubilant crowd outside Buckingham Palace, rejoicing that the war in Europe was at last over (and afterwards one of the 22 people packed into an eight-seater railway carriage trying to get home from London). Then, with my fourteen bales of fishing and collecting gear, I sailed to South Africa in a ship carrying war brides to Australia. I was off loaded in Cape Town to take the train to Salisbury in Southern Rhodesia, from where I was to get road transport across Portuguese East Africa to

---

On the opposite page are outline drawings of the more important fish in Lake Nyasa (from Bertram, Borley and Trewavas 1942).
A. Marcusenius   B. Engraulicypris   C. Gnathonemus   D. Alestes
E. Synodontis   F. Haplochromis sp. "Utaka"   G. Lethrinops
H. Tilapia   I. Tilapia   J. Serranochromis   K. Barilius
L. Rhamphochromis   M. Barbus rhoadesii   N. Labeo
O. Barilius   P. Barbus eurystomus   Q. Mormyrops
R. Mormyrus   S. Bagrus   T. Clarias
NB The drawings from A to H are all to one scale and the remainder from I to T are drawn to half this scale.

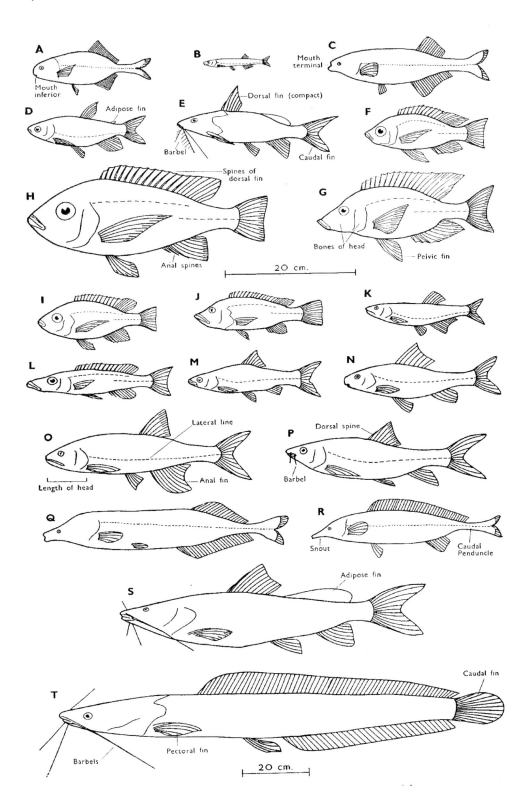

The hand-drawn map of Lake Nyasa which appeared in my final report. Depths are given in fathoms and the locations of my sampling sites are shown with the methods used indicated. Above is a photograph of locals drying fish on the beach at Mvunguti. The one below is looking out into the main lake across Monkey Bay.

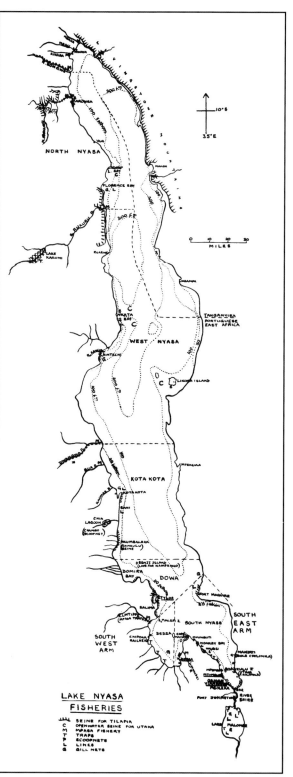

An african seine net nearing the beach.

Nyasaland. While I was on the train, the great news came that Japan had surrendered – VJ day. What rejoicing that World War II was over at last! Local inhabitants flocked to Salisbury to celebrate, with much alcohol and roasted oxen, and I found that I was eighth on the waiting list to sleep on the hotel floor. A helpful local policeman found me a room where the occupant was away and I could stay 'if they could find the key'. He also helped in arranging my journey to Nyasaland by car, if a small boy could sit on my lap for two days. The Afrikaner mother of the small boy took a dim view of me – 'women should not be allowed to travel round Africa on their own – there should be a law against it'. The luggage would have to go by lorry (which broke down in Portuguese East Africa and took weeks to arrive). As we crossed the great Zambezi River at Tete, where we stayed over night in the hotel, a buoy marked where a lorry had fallen off the ferry.

Arriving in Nyasaland I had a great welcome at Ryall's hotel in Blantyre, having shared a cabin on the ship with the owner's daughter who was returning to Nyasaland from England. Then I went up-country by train with a champagne party on the station marking our departure. I was met at Salima by John Borley, now a District Commissioner in Dowa. Both John and the Provincial Commissioner, Bob Kepple-Compton, and their wives were exceedingly helpful. I stayed with John and family to learn something of the ways of the country, not only from his invaluable 'Fisherman's Handy Billy' on weather lore and how to handle boats, but most importantly on the proper etiquette for meeting chiefs in lakeside villages. I should never receive anything with my left hand (the Duke of Windsor had done this on his Nyasaland visit, so a chief I met was not at all surprised that he had had to abdicate from the English throne). I was also told of the need to carry a large sack of salt for buying fish specimens as money was of little use in lakeside villages and it was useful to take a range of fish hooks and sweets for the children, as prizes for helping to catch small fish.

My house on the beach of Lake Nyasa, headquarters of the 1945–47 fishery survey.

Bob K-C very kindly arranged for one of his houseboys, Greniger, to look after me as cook/houseboy, during my eighteen months in Nyasaland. They also arranged for me to use the KotaKota District launch (the *Pelican*) with its crew, until another launch could be hired for the survey, and for me to rent, from an Indian Rahaman, his beach house as the survey base. It was situated right on the lake shore in the southeast arm of the lake between Fort Johnston and Monkey Bay which had the great advantage of being next to 'Dally's Hotel'. This was a very friendly holiday fishing camp consisting of a cluster of rondavels, with an open-sided dining room and bar right on the lake shore. It was run by the very helpful Fred Dally, recently retired from the Public Works Department. Fred could turn his hand to anything. When the diesel engine of the launch misbehaved, when having to build huts for the survey 'boys', or when I needed transport in his old open-backed truck to Fort Johnson, the nearest DC's office, for post, banking, four-gallon tins of petrol (debbies) etc, life would have been very difficult without his help. He also taught me to shoot for the pot. But he had certain rigid beliefs, such as that all elephants cross the road before 9 pm. Not true, as one night we were nearly thrown out of the rush chairs perched in the back of his open truck when passing through a herd on the Monkey Bay road. Dally was called out for most local emergencies, as I witnessed when we went to collect 'murderers' who were being hunted and when found were tied to spiny palm branches. The jolly and motherly Mrs Dally arrived at weekends with all the news from her job in Fort Johnston where Peter Selous, son of the famous hunter, was the District Commissioner.

I used to have dinner at Dally's most evenings, walking with my hissing Tilley lamp along the beach, wary of snorting hippos or crocodiles close to shore. Dinner tables were set out on the sand under the stars, in the warm darkness, accompanied by the glorious cacophony of insect and frog noises from nearby trees, a nightly chorus much missed on my return to England. The bar was a cheerful place, full of tall stories and much laughter, where one caught up with all the local gossip. People from all over Nyasaland and further afield who visited this beautiful lake stayed at Dally's and some of them I got to know very well. We even had some news from the outside world, on an old radio inhabited by a large cockroach that was trundled along by the metal bar as one tried different radio frequencies.

Lake Nyasa was quite the best lake in which to study tilapia biology as it was the only one to have a species flock of tilapia evolved within the lake. In addition, the fish had distinct breeding seasons which permitted growth rates to be determined much more easily than in the equatorial East African lakes, and the clear water allowed direct observations of the fish (an important point in those pre-scuba days). The 1939 survey had found that the main commercial tilapia, formerly thought to be one species under the name of *T. squamipinnis,* was a complex of three, possibly four, closely related species, plus several puzzling forms with distinct native names the status of which was unknown. The difficulty of separating these species in the field when they were not in

The huts we built for my survey assistants, "the boys", and in the foreground their wives pounding maize, or millet, a daily chore.

breeding colours, and the impossibility of distinguishing them among the young stages, complicated the study. Since we found that the different species bred at different times of year, the importance of being able to distinguish them for proper fishery management was obvious. Six tilapia species were recognised in the lake. The main commercial ones were the *T. squamipinnis-saka-lidole-karongae* complex, all of which had evolved in the lake and were known locally as 'chambo'. Their breeding males all developed long genital tassels (characteristic of the tilapia subgenus later called *Nyasalapia* by Trewavas). The endemic *T. shirana* was most nearly related to *T. mossambica* found in the lower Shire River, and the non-endemic substratum-spawning *T. melanopleura* (= *T. rendalli*) was widely distributed elsewhere in Africa.

The tilapia investigation had to be approached from three angles: (i) systematic work to differentiate the separate species; (ii) determining the growth rates of each tilapia species, which was attempted on a large scale because at that time there was almost no information on fish growth rates in natural tropical waters; (iii) a study of the life histories and habits of the different species, their breeding seasons and breeding grounds, food, movements and predators. The effects of fishing on the stocks also had to be

Women preferred to collect water from pools dug in the beach which gave them cleaner water than they would get from the inshore areas of the lake where the wind stirred up the sediment, and where too they might be attacked by crocodiles.

Monkey Bay at the south end of Lake Nyasa/Malawi.
In the distance is a column of emerging lakeflies rising like smoke from the lake.

The RV Usipa anchored in Senga Bay in 1995, the headquarters of the SADC/UK
Pelagic Fish Resource Assessment Project (see Chapter 8) on Lake Malawi.

*Visiting the Ethelwynn Trewavas in Monkey Bay with
Denis Tweddle during my visit in 1991.*

*Examining the catch from the swamp at Senga Bay with Denis Tweddle
1991. Lungfish now occur in this swamp having escaped from an
overturned lorry loaded with fish for export.*

The Yiannakis brothers at home mending fishing nets.

considered and suggestions made for the future development and control of the lake fisheries. The biology of several other species and their fisheries were also investigated, for example, the cyprinids *Labeo mesops* (caught in gillnets) and the large salmon-like *Barilius microlepis*, both of which made seasonal migrations up the inflowing rivers to spawn. Observations were also made on the large predatory fishes *Bagrus meridionalis* ('kampango'), *Clarias* and a species flock of very large *Bathyclarias* endemic to Lake Nyasa which were caught on hooks. Notes were also made of the smaller zooplankton-feeding 'utaka', a group of some six or more cichlid species fished from northern waters by African openwater ('chilimila') seines, and on the little zooplanktivorous pelagic endemic cyprinid *Engraulicypris sardella* ('usipa') which was so abundant in certain years.

For sorting out the tilapia species and determining breeding places and seasons, I visited all the fishing beaches around the south-east arm of the lake, with some longer launch trips north to Kota Kota and the Chia lagoon, where the fishermen used special scoop nets to catch the tilapia, as seen in use by David Livingstone in 1859 when he visited the lagoon. In March 1946 I spent a month at the north end of the lake, based at Karonga. Much of my information came from lively discussions sitting on sandy beaches with the local fishermen while they hauled in their seine nets. This was an operation which would take one or two hours with many people gathered around waiting to buy the catch, while children played and women washed clothes in the lake. This audience was delighted to see the photographs in the 1939

Above: the Yiannakis brothers' ring net being hauled in and, right, their large seine net being prepared for setting from the beach.

report, which stimulated them to illustrate their own observations on the fishes by making drawings in the sand. I was then allowed to identify and measure the fish in the seine catches.

My home base 'laboratory' in the house rented from Rahaman, was next door to the Yiannakis brothers fishery. They very kindly allowed me to measure very large samples of tilapia, caught in their long shore seines and open water ring net which they used all over the southeast arm of the lake south of Boadzulu Island. This close-knit Greek family ran the largest fishery on the lake, three of the brothers and their families living together in nearby houses. Jim, a stocky chap in brief shorts, solar topee firmly strapped to his head, organised the fishing and fish processing (gutting and freezing). Brother Chris ran their lorries which took dried and frozen fish overnight through to Salisbury in Southern Rhodesia. Dark-eyed Stavros was a quieter character who supervised the fishing and had a store of observations on tilapia behaviour. The family was an interesting matriarchy, as I found when they were visited by their elderly mother from their Greek home island who came to arrange the (unwelcome) marriage of their sister to a Greek she barely knew on a tobacco estate.

The brothers had started by catching fish in traps across the Shire River near Fort Johnson in 1933. In 1942 and 1943 they were allowed to use a large seine from various beaches, and in 1943 they also began to experiment with the large open water ring net, as used in their Aegean home island. Worked from two motor launches, this net was more than 1000 feet (*c* 350 m) long and 120 feet (*c* 40 m) deep, and fished from surface to bottom in all the water south of Boadzulu Island which was less deep than the net. Their business had developed enormously during the war (since the 1939 fishing survey) and in 1946 they had bought out a rival firm. The catch records I analysed were chiefly from this source. My presence nearby, with an eye on their catches, was perhaps not altogether welcome. One day they came up with a solution: I was greeted by brother Jim with the bright suggestion 'you get married, you have baby, then you no have to play with fish!' A little further north an Indian, Ibraham Osman, started seining in 1943 for the production of dried fish. An Englishman W.P. Tyler seined for many years from beaches near Salima and Domira Bay, but in 1946, shortly after I had camped in a cloud of mosquitoes in his garden, he died and fishing operations there ceased.

Each month we also set a fleet of experimental 2 inch to 5" mesh gillnets about a mile offshore and in many other places as we travelled around by launch. The gillnet catches were mostly of *Bagrus*, *Clarias*, *Labeo* and large endemic *Mormyrops longirostris*, which was later discovered to use its electric organs to stun cichlid prey at night. We also sampled several African fisheries for tilapia caught with large-meshed shore seines for adult tilapia ('chambo' = *T. squamipinnis* plus *T. saka* and 'dole' = *T. lidole*), and small-meshed 'kambusi'

The survey launch on Lake Nyasa 1945.

or 'utaka' seines which caught juvenile tilapia (known as 'kasawala') along with many smaller cichlid species and juvenile non-cichlids.

The local Africans also used traps in channels in the sudd or amongst reeds or water plants. These large unbaited traps caught *T. shirana* and brooding females of *T. squamipinnis* and *T. saka*. The small-meshed 'kambusi' traps, often baited with maize porridge, caught 'kasawala' and small *T. shirana*. The

The survey team outside my house making string for fishing nets from old car tyres.

African shore seines varied enormously in size depending on the string available (a real problem at that time) and the wealth of the fishermen. Nets became patched and repatched with pieces of netting of different mesh, some large tilapia nets might be 400 yards long, mainly of four-inch stretched mesh, as the lighter the net the more easily it could be hauled. There were many snags from stumps of trees drowned by the rising lake level, and there were crocodiles too. While waiting on the beaches, fishermen rolled net string from local plant fibres on their thighs. A most coveted source of string was old motor tyres, lorry tyres being especially valuable, which were painstakingly taken to pieces for net twine. By obtaining old tyres for them I made good friends among the local fishermen.

At that time there was no general licensing system or collection of statistics from African fisheries, though John Borley had organised African recorders working from four fishing centres in 1941–43. There was also no hard and fast distinction between domestic and commercial fishing and the fishermen also had to tend their gardens in the rainy season. The bulk of their catches was consumed in villages near the lake but large numbers were sold or bartered to middlemen waiting on the beaches, where they purchased tilapia or 'utaka', dried them on the beaches, packed them into long cylinders of bamboo, then carried them as head loads or on bicycles, lorry or train, to the main towns such as Blantyre. In 1945–47 the numbers of buyers exceeded the amount of fish caught and many returned empty handed. In the deeper parts of the lake (eg off Nkata Bay and Likoma Island), where there were few good seining beaches, the 'utaka' caught in African home-made, open water 'chilimila' small-mesh ring nets were more important than tilapia.

The methods I used for estimating growth rates of each tilapia species were mainly tracing the progression of the length frequency modes month by month (Peteresen's method), obtained by pricking the total length of each fish in our samples (generally c 500 fish at a time) on to waterproof paper as I had been taught before I left Wray Castle. Thus the gradual increase in total length of the majority of tilapia in each group could be followed. In an attempt to

Right: Chigona and John lifting a gill net. Below: Sorting the catch on the verandah of my house with Greniger, in his cook's kofia (hat) hopefully awaiting a fish for lunch.

determine the growth rate of the juvenile tilapia ('kasawala') which lived in bands along the sandy beach near the lab, we made routine monthly catches with the 30 yard long seine throughout the year to try and trace their length frequencies progressions. But for two reasons this presented difficulties. We found the breeding seasons of the different tilapia species overlapped, giving a very prolonged season. It was also impossible to distinguish species among these juveniles. 'Kasawala' of comparable size joined this band throughout most of the year, and as they grew in length they moved away from the beach beyond the reach of the seine, biasing the samples. So this method was not as successful as it would have been when applied to fish with a well-defined breeding season in a temperate climate.

For the larger tilapia, caught in large seines and ring nets used by the various fisheries, huge numbers of lengths were measured in the same way to trace length frequency mode progressions amongst the older fishes. Back calculations of growth rates were also made from growth rings on the opercular (gill cover) bones collected from large numbers of tilapia, together with data on their lengths, weights and gonad condition. These opercular bones, when viewed between two polaroid discs (as David Le Cren was using to determine perch growth rates in Lake Windermere) indicated spurts in growth. This was especially evident when, in September 1946, there was an exceptional bloom of *Anabaena* on which all three species were feeding heavily. These growth zones could be used to age the fish, but the marked slowing

The Yiannakis' fish processing shed.

Minimum breeding sizes of Lake Nyasa tilapia at 3 years old		
Species	total body length	body weight
T. squamipinnis	c24 cm	264 gm
T. saka	27 cm	412 gm
T. lidole	28 cm	463 gm

Males and females grew at the same rates and to comparable sizes, except in *T. shirana* in which females started to breed at a small size (probably two years old) and males when 3 years at 22cm.

down of growth in mature tilapia meant they could not be used to calculate mortality rates.

The various lines of investigation suggested that these tilapia all reached their respective minimum breeding sizes when just three years old. But once breeding size had been reached growth in length slowed down and almost ceased. There was a maximum size characteristic of each species, higher in open water than in the inshore species. However, this size was evidently influenced by fishing, as samples of the tilapia caught in Yiannakis' seines in 1941–43 (measured by John Borley's recorders) were significantly larger (mean 28–30 cm) than those (mean 21–27 cm) in our 1945–47 samples at the same site. The tilapia were much more abundant throughout the year in the 1941–43 samples. This suggested that already the population was being too heavily fished.

The six tilapia species in the lake were found to form a series living predominantly from inshore to more offshore open waters where shoals of endemic 'chambo' (*T. saka, T. squamipinnis* and *T. lidole*) could be seen on calm mornings skittering at the lake surface feeding on phytoplankton. From the inshore-living to the open-water-living end of the series the food contained a higher proportion of phytoplankton, instead of bottom diatoms and debris;

A female mouth-brooding tilapia collecting its young into its mouth.

and the tendency to school in small close shoals increased. The amount of movement about the lake also increased. *T. shirana* populations were very localised and *T. lidole* a more far-ranging fish. The young were mouth brooded by the female to an increasingly large size; and growth in length increased but growth in weight decreased, so open water species were lighter at a given length. Each species spawned at the most oligotrophic (clear water) end of the species' range and brooded its young in the most eutrophic (rich water).

The non-endemic *T. melanopleura* lived mainly in lagoons around the main lake, amongst water weeds on which they fed. *T. shirana* also inhabited inshore zones amongst water weeds, *Ceratophyllum*, and off reedy (*Phragmites*), *Typha* or sudd *(Papyrus)* shores, where they grazed on epiphytic algae and bottom debris. The endemic species in the 'chambo' complex were all mainly phytoplankton feeders living in small shoals in the open water. *T. lidole* shoals were caught further offshore. In the 'chambo' both sexes ceased to feed while breeding.

Tilapia (now *Oreochromis*) *saka* were found spawning in 6–9 feet of water off reedy shores near weed beds in August to December in the hot weather before the rains. *T. squamipinnis* spawned deeper during the rains (November to March), and *T. lidole* from October to December in deeper clearer water. Spawning grounds could be detected by the aggregations of males in

The sandy beach in front of my house on a moonlit night.

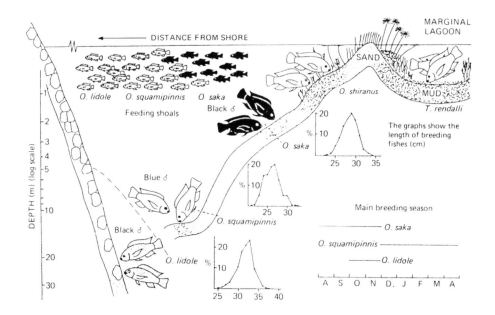

Breeding sites of the five species of tilapia which live at the southern end of Lake Nyasa/Malawi. Breeding sites of all species are shown: other particulars apply only to the three most open-water species, which are by far the most abundant. (From Fryer and Iles 1972, based on Lowe 1952.)

their characteristic breeding colours: blue with a white head in *T. squamipinnis* (clearly visible through the clear water), black with a white tipped dorsal fin in *T. saka* and *T. lidole*. These species all developed a complex lighter-coloured genital tassel when spawning. *T. lidole* evidently spawned off steep rocky or clean sandy shores north of Boadzulu Island. *T. karongae* appeared to be restricted to the northern half of the lake, inhabiting shores where permanent rivers entered the lake (much later George Turner synonymized *T. saka* with *T. karongae*). *T. melanopleura* was a substratum spawner, both sexes caring for the eggs and young in and around a nest hole in lagoons. But in all these other tilapia species eggs and young are brooded in the mouth of the female. She picks up the fertilized eggs from the 'nest', which is a spawning plaque made and guarded by the male on special spawning grounds (leks). The females carry the young to brooding grounds in more eutrophic water and leave them inshore (*T. saka* in reed beds). The fry leave the mother's mouth to feed, but dart back into her mouth (or sometimes into a stranger's mouth) when danger threatens. The most open water-living female *T. lidole* broods young to the largest size (an astonishing 58 mm long compared with up to 24 mm in *T. saka*, and 30 mm in *T. squamipinnis*). Ring net catches showed this species brooded young in the open water, and I watched numerous fry, spat out by the parent fish when caught in the ring net, being gobbled up by piscivorous cichlids. What a waste.

Counts of ripe yellow ova in the ovaries of the females showed that they lay some 250 to 500 eggs in a batch, all at one time, with some residual small ova left in the ovary. Up to 287 eggs were collected from the mouth of a brooding *T. squamipinnis*, and 324 fry, all 15 mm long, from the mouth of one *T. karongae*. It seemed that natural mortality in these tilapia was greatest amongst the juveniles, and the brooded young were much affected by the large scale fishing, especially on *T. lidole* brooding grounds. A typical log entry describes many thousands of spat out 'chambo' fry round the boat, the mouthfuls keeping together in close groups of 100–200 young swimming together in six inch diameter balls. The less developed they were the closer they bunched, a gift to the many shoals of piscivorous cichlids around the boat. In one bucket they tried to get into a *Barbus* mouth.

Brooded eggs hatched in a glass jar in the lab showed that yolk sacs were absorbed in about 5 days, and the young would probably be brooded for another week. So the females might have only one batch of young during the breeding season each year (unlike most tilapia in ponds, and in the equatorial Lake Victoria, which produce several batches of young in succession). *T. shirana* had more ripening ova (500-600) young brooded to only 12 mm and possibly two broods a season.

What were their predators? The pied kingfisher (*Ceryle rudis*) fed on small fish living in the shallows, diving where 'kasawala' were abundant. The fish eagle *(Cuncuma vocifer)* was found to take mostly adult tilapia, but fed on *Clarias* when tilapia were scarce. Other kingfishers and various kinds of heron, pelicans and osprey also fed on fish, but the proportion of tilapia in their diet was not known. There were immense numbers of fish-eating birds living on the lake. These included two species of cormorant, the large white-breasted cormorant (*Phalacocorax carbo lucidus*) which nested in bushes on the islands and shores of the lake (notably on Boadzulu Island and Lake Malombe) and the smaller reed cormorant (*P. africanus*) which was found along reedy shores. Here the snake necked darter (*Anhinga anhinga*) was also numerous. One *P. carbo lucidus* had a ripe *T. squamipinnis* in its stomach, but some shot on Boadzulu Island had been feeding on piscivorous open-water living *Rhamphochromis* cichlids. The reed cormorants fed most heavily on the 'kasawala' and up to 54 of them were found in one darter stomach. South of Boadzulu Island, hundreds of large cormorants used to feed busily at sunrise, had full stomachs again at midday and were often seen feeding again in the evening. Four of them each had half a pound of fish (over 300 g) in their stomach. Crocodiles were also very plentiful, but only three stomachs were examined one of which contained tilapia, another had mammal remains. Apart from eating fish, crocodiles had an important effect on the fishery by increasing the hazards of fishing and destroying much fishing gear.

Of parasites, occasional nematode stages were found encysted as black spots in the tilapia flesh, and an acanthocephalan was found in a *T. lidole* gut. External parasites included the fish louse *(Argulus africanus)* and a copepod *(Lernaea bagrae)* attached to *Clarias* and *Bagrus*. In December 1946 *T. squamipinnis* and *T. lidole* were carrying heavy infestations of another copepod *(Lernaea tilapiae)*. 'Kasawala' in the warm sandy shallows were occasionally infested with an *Ichthyopthirius*-like white spot protozoan parasite.

It would seem that the ancestral species of the T. *squamipinnis-T. saka-T. lidole-T. karongae* flock was an inshore-living form and that these endemic species arose in the lake as they pushed out into open water. Possibly competition for food in times of scarcity and/or for suitable spawning territories may have encouraged the survival of variants best suited for open water life. From his studies in East African lakes Worthington had suggested that the presence of the large fish predators such as Nile perch *(Lates)* and Tigerfish *(Hydrocynus)*, probably restricted the evolution of cichlids, and the absence of such fish from Lake Nyasa was probably important in allowing

tilapia to move out into open water. Interestingly, Lake Tanganyika which has both these large predators has no open water tilapia, and the experimental introduction of *Lates* into Lake Victoria in the mid 1950s, certainly resulted in a huge loss of open water-living cichlid species.

Rodney Wood watching cichlids at Monkey Bay, 1946.

Since David Livingstone recorded seines and scoop nets in use in 1859, man has evidently been an important predator for a long time. Moreover, as nets used from small canoes fished only the inshore waters for tilapia this would encourage the establishment of open water forms. The fluctuations in lake level have also probably played a major part in the evolution of all the cichlid species in Lake Nyasa. Rodney Wood, a noted naturalist with whom I stayed at Monkey Bay, described how, about 1914–18, when the lake was considerably lower both the blue and black male forms (= *T. squamipinnis* and *T. saka*) made sand scrape nests off the reeds on the clean sandy bottom of Monkey Bay, at a depth where they could be watched spawning. At the time of my survey, when the lake was ten to fifteen feet higher and had drowned many of the weed and reed beds, it seemed that the blue male *T. squamipinnis* still spawned in the old places which were now well under water. By contrast, the black male *T. saka* was restricted to places where there were still weed beds off reedy shores, a difference in place and depth of spawning, reinforcing a difference in time of spawning. The inshore-dwelling *T. shirana* probably had several broods a year. Retention of the young by a brooding female to a larger size may have inhibited repeated spawnings, and early and late breeding populations became different species. Geologically, the northern end of Lake Nyasa is older than the southern end and the original lake, which was about 1000 feet higher than the present one, extended southwards in the Middle Pleistocene. It seems likely that *T. saka* may have come from *T. karongae* or an ancestral species (indeed George Turner later regarded these as one species which now has to be called *T. karongae*). The black male of *T. lidole* suggests this came from the black male forms, and not from *T. squamipinnis*. *T. shirana* probably evolved from *T. mossambicus* which is today found in the Lower Shire River.

I analysed the effect of all this fishing by the commercial firms, together with estimates of catches in the African gear used around the lake, and put forward suggestions for development and control of the fisheries. As there was then no Fishery Department I got roped into a Legislative Council meeting in Zomba to discuss the future prospects of the lake's fisheries. Invited to dine at Government House and not used to much alcohol, it was alarming to suddenly catch sight of a large leopard backed by the rising sun behind my chair at table. Fortunately this was only the emblem of Nyasaland!

While in Zomba I was also asked to give a talk on the lake to the redoubtable Nyasaland Council of Women, known locally as the Nagger's Union, which was fun. Another time I passed through Zomba just after a dramatic rainstorm (27 inches in 24 hours) in which part of Zomba Mountain slid on to the tennis court and nearly demolished Government House. A boulder strewn river blocked the road. Very sadly the Chief of Police (who had previously very kindly taken me to the lower Shire River at Port Herald) was drowned in that flood.

As part of this study, catches from the fishing methods, both African and non-African, that were responsible for catching fish at various stages of their life histories, were summarised. In 1945–47 large numbers of 'kasawala' less than 15 cm long were caught in African 'kambusi' seines. Some immature tilapia of 15–25 cm were also taken in African 'chambo' seines, but greater numbers were caught by the large non-African seines and ring nets of both legal and illegal mesh sizes. Spawning *T. squamipinnis* and *T. saka* were taken in both native and non-native seines and ring nets, but many spawning grounds were protected from shore seines by the stumps of drowned trees. *T. lidole* was being caught on the spawning grounds by native seines but had natural protection in the depth and distance from the shore at which they spawned. Newly hatched young were destroyed with the brooding females or abandoned to their fate when brooding fish were caught. Brooding *T. saka* and *T. squamipinnis* were trapped in the reeds between November and March, and the latter with young were also caught in native and non-native seines and ring nets from December to March.

All the evidence available suggested that the effect of the large non-African fisheries on the tilapia had been to catch increasingly more fish to the point at which the total catch remains the same, or falls, however much the fishing effort is increased. Statistics of catches submitted by non-African firms operating south of Boadzulu Island indicated that an average of over two million tilapia were removed each year between 1944 and 1946 from this area by these firms. About two and half times as many tilapia were landed in 1946 as in 1939, but to achieve this increase the fishing effort was probably more than trebled. Since 1944 the total yield had not increased (and may have fallen) in spite of increased fishing effort. An increasing proportion of open water *T. lidole* in the catches had masked the decrease in catch of the more inshore-living species. *T. shirana* recorded by the 1939 survey as being second in commercial importance was now no longer numerous enough to be of any commercial importance in the south-east arm of the lake.

The change in proportions of the different tilapia species had led to increasing use of ring nets rather than shore seines. This in turn led to increased exploitation of the openwater *T. lidole* until about equal numbers of *T. lidole* and 'chambo' (ie *T. saka* and *T. squamipinnis*) were caught in the ring net. The mean length of 'chambo' caught in the southeast arm had decreased very significantly. Non-African seines included 33% immature 'chambo' and 13% immature 'dole' in their catches in 1945–47. Ring nets caught 31% immature 'chambo' and 29% immature 'dole'. Numerous young were destroyed with the brooding females of *T. squamipinnis* and *T. lidole* that were caught in seine and ring nets about December. The seasonal distribution of catches was very affected by the weather, catches being poor in cold or windy conditions.

Until recently fishing had been concentrated on inshore species which aided the present natural tendency, with the high lake level, for populations of inshore species to be low and of open water species to be high. The introduction of the ring net had, however, led to increased exploitation of the open water *T. lidole*. Ring nets also caught higher proportions of immature *T. lidole* than did the shore seines.

The African fisheries affected mainly the inshore-living species of tilapia. Owing to the scarcity of inshore tilapia in the southeast arm in recent years, a flourishing 'kambusi' seine fishery, which caught a high proportion of small immature tilapia ('kasawala') had developed. As the adult tilapia are most easily available to the inshore gear (seines and traps) when the female fish were close inshore brooding young, many offspring were destroyed when the females were caught.

Northern Lake Nyasa

The month of March 1946 was spent at the north end of the lake based at Karonga to see how *Tilapia karongae* fitted into the tilapia series, and to explore the *Barilius* ('mpasa') fishery. Karonga was too far away from base for me to reach with 4 gallon debbies of petrol for the launch, so Nyasaland Railways were approached to see if the *SS Mpasa* could tow the launch up to Karonga. 'Oh yes' was the reply, 'we have done this before'. But when they added that the towed boat had been struck by lightning and went to the bottom, I settled for shipping the launch's dingy and outboard engine together with all the collecting gear. It was an amusing trip round the lake on the old *SS Mpasa* commanded by Capt. Farquharson. With numerous African and Asian passengers camped on deck we called in at many ports, delivering people with vast bundles and all manner of stores from the towed lighters. These ports included Likoma Island, where the Universities Mission to Central Africa had its headquarters and a church with a large walk-in baptismal font. Then back west across the lake to Nkata Bay, which in 1954–55 became the headquarters of the Joint Fisheries Research Organisation survey of Northern Lake Nyasa directed by Peter Jackson. This was where Geoffrey Fryer made his classic study of the 'mbuna' cichlids on the rocky and sandy shores and T.D. Iles studied the biology of the zooplanktivorous 'utaka' group of cichlids, which were caught in small 'chilimila' ringnets by the locals. Peter Jackson investigated the species flock of large *Bathyclarias* catfishes endemic to this lake, and Derek Harding the hydrology.

At a port on the Tanganyika shore we delivered a boat load of 700 watering cans needed by a tobacco plantation. ('Why 700?' – 'Because the other 300 were not obtainable when we left'.) While preparing gear for this trip, a visitor at Dallys had warned me to keep my Tilley pressure lamp 'handy'. This was indeed useful as early in the trip it was taken away by the ship's engineer to aid repair of the ship's engines. The old steam-propelled, 105 foot long *Mpasa*,

The ill-fated S.S. Vipya off Fort Johnson in 1946.

which began to operate on the lake in 1933, also ran aground at the north end of the lake and was towed off the sand bank early one morning amid much clamour. Her long overdue replacement, the *S.S. Vipya* was still being assembled at Fort Johnston, where her 'measured mile' test had taken place in the lake outside my house. The engineers setting up the marker posts on land had been hampered by that pest 'buffalo bean' which has such prickly hairs that it necessitates immediate removal of all one's clothes. Very sadly the *Vipya* sank a few miles off Florence Bay in a storm in July 1946 on her third trip, and her master Capt. Farquharson was among the 145 people drowned. After several court hearings, what really happened on 30 July 1946 still remained something of a mystery.

At Karonga I stayed with the DC, who accompanied me on some of my trips to look at local fisheries. Both blue (= *T. squamipinnis*) and black (= *T. karongae* and *T. saka*) male tilapia were caught in seines and traps, but no *T. lidole* were seen. Some of the black males of *T. karongae* were ripe in March, considerably later than the black males of *T. saka* in the south (and at the same time as the blue males of *squamipinnis* in the South-east arm). Plans to return to the north later in the year never materialised (for lack of transport), so sorting out the relationships of all the tilapias living together here had to await George Turner's studies in the 1990s.

As these northern waters are whipped up by the South-east trade winds they become very rough and fish were most easily cropped in the rivers. As a

Scoop netting 'mpasa' from the North Rukuru River.

result an important African fishery at the north end of the lake was for the predatory salmon-like cyprinid *Barilius microlepis* 'mpasa', which migrated up the large permanent rivers to spawn. Large fish traps were built in fences across these rivers, and scoop nets were also used along the banks. During this survey 'mpasa' were only seen from the North Rukuru River and Lintippe (the latter probably the southernmost river with a regular 'mpasa' run). In these rivers 'mpasa' ran up to spawn between November and April, the time depending on rains in the hills affecting the rivers. These 'mpasa' only migrated up the large permanent, relatively clear rivers to spawn . A smaller species, *Barilius microcephalus*, 'sanjika', and *Barbus eurystomus* also migrated up rivers to spawn. *Labeo mesops* 'nchila', *Barbus rhoadesii* and *Synodontis zambesiensis*, full of spawn were caught further south, in smaller muddier, less permanent rivers. The 'mpasa' fisheries were all African, apart from trolling for sport by a few Europeans. Barriers were built across the main rivers and, despite the fishing laws, a 10% gap was rarely left. Considerable erosion of the banks occurred as a result of the water being dammed by the fish fences, the river forcing its way around the barrier unless it burst the barrier in times of flood. Crocodiles abounded in these rivers, damaging the traps and endangering the lives of the fishermen.

I spent one splendid day cycling along the very narrow rutted red paths through fields of millet and bananas, many miles up the North Rukuru River to examine the 'mpasa' fish trap fences. I was in the good care of the local chief's messenger, clad in a voluminous pair of trousers which he carefully removed to keep them dry as he helped me, and the bicycles, over tributary streams. The removal of the trousers revealed a large banana leaf worn as

Two of the smaller cichlids of
Lake Nyasa/ Malawi:
Aulonocara *(above) dwells
on the sandy areas while*
Pseudotropheus *(right) is a
rocky shore dweller as is the
much larger* Crytocara
(below)

Rhamphochromis lives in the open water of Lake Nyasa/ Malawi.

Home down the Nile: the first stage entailed crossing Lake Kyoga in Uganda where the steamer pushed laden barges ahead of it (above). At the landing stage, passengers waited patiently to go ashore (below).

underpants, which looked most uncomfortable. When, at the end of the day, he took me to visit the chief, the large trousers were explained as the chief was the very large man who had, it seemed, lent his trousers to the messenger to add respectability to our day out. In one place where the hardly visible path had washed away I fell backwards into a camel thorn bush. As the DC's wife was away having a baby, the resultant spines, lodged firmly in my back, had to be dissected out by Karonga's doctor using my dissecting instruments. He was reported to have recently taken a 'pot shot' at my host, the DC. Life in small isolated stations sometimes did strange things to people.

At Karonga in March 1946, despite a local Native Authority rule that seines should not be used near the Rukuru mouth during the 'mpasa' season, many seines were catching 'mpasa'. The larger nets caught up to a dozen per haul, together with 'sanjika', tilapias, and *Barbus*. Any 'mpasa' desirous of ascending the North Rukuru river to spawn was first faced with numerous crocodiles lying off the river delta, then had to escape a number of seines and fishermen with scoop nets chasing them in the shallow water of the delta. Once in the river proper there were fishermen with large scoop nets fishing from platforms built every fifty yards or so along the banks for several miles of the river, plus eight complete barriers of traps spread out over about thirteen miles of river. There were also fish netting parties in which all the men of a village were

seen to form a line across the river with a scoop net in each hand. It is interesting that David Livingstone, who described such fish weirs with basket traps to catch 'mpasa' or 'sanjika' running up the rivers to spawn in August and September 1859, commented that 'it seemed a

'Mpasa' traps used on the North Rukuru River.

The main road from Fort Johnson to Monkey Bay 1946.

marvel how the most sagacious 'sanjika' could get up at all without being taken'. He suggested that a passage up the river was found at night. The fishermen did, however, find it very hard to fish the traps under conditions of very high water and during my time spent at Karonga on many nights the traps were not fished at all. The seining and scoop netting also ceased at night. Sudden changes in water level may damage the traps thus allowing the fish to swim upstream. At certain river levels 'mpasa' may also jump the barriers.

Analyses of the length frequencies of all the 'mpasa' examined from many types of gear in March 1946 suggested that they grew to about 10 cm the first year. The smallest breeding male seen was 32 cm total length (next smallest 41 cm) and the smallest breeding female 29 cm; both then possibly three years old. The data did not suggest that the sexes grew at different rates, but many of the large 'mpasa' (53cm, possibly seven years old) were males. Ideally these 'mpasa' needed to be protected until they were at least 30 cm (12 inches long) to allow them to mature. Small 'mpasa' 4–16 cm long were caught around the outflow of the river, suggesting that they were washed or moved down to the lake, where they became widely distributed.

I get wheels!

At first I only had a bicycle for cycling along the sandy Monkey Bay road (with its notice 'Beware of elephants on this road'). On one occasion, when I was accompanying 'Tommy', a missionary from the UMCA on her rounds, inspecting the very primitive village schools, grunts from the bush alongside the road led to some very rapid peddling. When clear I questioned 'was that grunt imagination?' Answer 'No!'. Fred Dally used to take me out shooting for guinea fowl for the pot and, since the chinyanja terms for guinea fowl and lion were to my ear very similar, on one occasion I misheard a warning and it was a male lion and not a guinea fowl I met round a bush. We also once met a troop of hunting dogs, which were not common in that area. Game was scarce as much of it had been shot to control tsetse flies and sleeping sickness.

Wartime shortages still existed but I did eventually acquire a small and very old Fiat car (milometer: twice-round-the-clock). As the shortages made new tyres difficult to get, the Fiat had oversize tyres precariously fitted over its rims so that they tended to come off if one cornered too smartly. On my initial drive, down a very rough track to visit an agricultural show, when I failed to find the reverse gear, a passenger said 'Never mind, we'll get some boys and lift her round' - which is what we did!

At the beginning of September 1946, at the request of the Government of Nyasaland, I paid a visit to Lake Kazuni some fifty miles up the South Rukuru River to examine the possibility of stocking it with fish for local consumption. This entailed a very long journey on a road which only had about one lorry a week should I break down. The front universal joint of my Fiat (nick- named 'sanjika' or 'the little swift one') had already collapsed on my way home from Zomba. A passing motorist, a Rhodesian visiting the lake to fish, who had kindly cut a pole from the bush with which to tow me home, commented that he 'would not go round the block in it'. But he very kindly fixed it before I ventured forth to Lake Kazuni.

The car was loaded heavily with gear and 4 gallon 'debbies' of petrol. Greniger, who came to look after me while I camped in a tent in a local authority compound, sat in the front seat with the precious Tilley lamp on his knee, giggling 'too few room'. Lake Kazuni, only about five miles long, was really a swelling on the southern Rukuru River about fifty miles up from Lake Nyasa. In September when almost at its lowest, it did not appear to be more than about six feet deep, but would be another six feet higher and cover a considerable larger area in the wet season. A permanent river flowed through it. The water was full of brown mud stirred up by the very numerous hippopotami, one of which charged us in our very decrepit local canoe. Large patches of *Ceratophyllum* and *Trapa* which were dotted over the whole lake provided abundant shelter for fish and an excellent supply of insect larvae and snails as fish food (pH 8.0, water temperature 22.5°C). But the resident fauna comprised only three widely distributed fish species: *Barbus paludinosus*, *Haplochromis callipterus* and larger *Clarias mossambicus* catfish. No sign of 'mpasa', nor any tilapia, although both were known from the lower reaches of the river. Their absence was attributed to 'large rock barriers' lower down the stream. Crocodile traces were found and fish eagles were seen feeding on the catfish. White breasted cormorants, darters and pied kingfishers took the small fish and there were numerous herons. The local Africans fished from a few canoes in a poor state of repair, using hooklines and traps, and reported that they used unbaited traps in the wet season to catch *Clarias*, *Labeo* and small *Barbus* migrating upstream to spawn.

'Fortune favours the brave' they say. On the return journey we reached Lilongwe before Sanjika's 'big ends' went. Lilongwe was then so small that repairs had to be effected in a pit in someone's backyard. During the enforced stay while the car was repaired I took the opportunity to examine the Lilongwe River, as there had been a suggestion that this might be stocked with *T. shirana* to provide sport and food. About sixty five miles upriver from the lake, the river at this low-water season was about ten yards wide. Did the spawning fish, particularly 'mpasa' and 'sanjika' reach Lilongwe when migrating upriver to spawn? I examined fish from African traps and set our three inch mesh gillnet, which caught both *T. shirana* and *T. melanopleura*, and the predatory large cichlid *Serranochromis thumbergi*, with *Clarias mossambicus* and *Barbus rhoadesii*. The African trap catches included a surprise: dwarf, but ripe male and female, 'sanjika'. Was this a local race living in the river? It was later described as a new species by Denis Tweddle.

Another small shallow lake I investigated was Lake Chilwa. This is a lake of very variable area (on average about 1000 km²) near Zomba, around which Dr C.F. Hickling, visiting Fisheries Adviser from the UK Colonial Office, had suggested experimental fish farms might be tried. Lake Chilwa is an inland drainage area without any direct connection to any other lake. All the fish found here were representatives of species widely distributed in central Africa, although a search was made for an undescribed tilapia, found to be a subspecies of *Tilapia shirana* (later named *Oreochromis shirana chilwae*). The small widely distributed *Tilapia sparrmani* were also numerous, together with small *Barbus* of several species, *Haplochromis callipterus*, very numerous *Clarias mossambicus* and rare *Clarias theodorae*, were all caught in African traps. Tilapia and *Clarias* were also taken in gillnets and on longline hooks set in open water near to Chisi Island. On 24 July 1946 a local resident, Robin Thornycroft took me all round the lake, where on the far side of Chisa Island, a 'white woman' proved a novelty for the African children.

Considerable quantities of fish were taken from the lake to Zomba, only twenty miles away and as far as Mlanje tea plantations. All the fishing and marketing was done by Africans, most of the fish being distributed by bicycle to a wide circle of African villages. Plans to develop the road to the lake for export of fish by lorry would, it seemed to me, lead to fish being exported much further afield, so depriving local villages (and about a million people) of the benefits of fish from this lake. In 1947 the lake was visited by Mr Schwarz, a Fish Farming expert from Palestine, who considered that the development of fish ponds there would be too difficult owing to the problem of draining them in such flat terrain. In later years Lake Chilwa almost dried up, but dwarfed tilapia persisted in some small pools and the tilapia populations recovered very quickly when the lake refilled, as investigated by the University of Malawi under Professor Kalk. Morgan (1970) analysed this tilapia fishery.

Home down the Nile

On leaving Nyasaland in April 1947 to complete the Nyasa Fisheries Report at the BM(NH), I travelled homewards via East Africa and on down the River Nile. This enabled me to visit the embryonic East African Fisheries Research Laboratory (EAFRO) in Jinja, where the Nile leaves Lake Victoria on its 4000 mile journey to the Mediterranean Sea.

But first we had to get off the ground. The small plane from Blantyre airport got stuck in the mud and had to be pulled out by a tractor for another go. Then I went on by a larger plane from Salisbury (now Harare) to Nairobi. In Salisbury the barely preserved specimens of Lake Nyasa tilapias, requested by Hugh Copley to make casts for the Nairobi Museum, sadly went astray as the airline attached them to the luggage of a 'Reverend Louw' bound for Johannesburg. I wondered when he would discover them? At Nairobi airport the delightful and ebullient Hugh Copley strode into the Customs shed and rescued me from the officer who was deeply suspicious of the precious basket I was clutching (only the draft Nyasa Report!). I was supposed to stay with the Worthington family, now living in Nairobi where Barton was Scientific Secretary to the East African High Commission, but they were not yet back from Uganda. When they did arrive, it was splendid to see them again. The three daughters were all very independent characters, but his wife Stella seemed a little apprehensive of my new status as Barton's colleague.

The plan was for me to continue by train to Kisumu on Lake Victoria, where the Kenya Fishery Officer Stephen Deathe and his wife would look after me until Bobby Beauchamp arrived by car to take me to Jinja. The telegram that Bobby received from Barton read: 'Miss Lowe in hands of death stop up to you to make further arrangements'. So he did! It was raining hard in Kisumu and we were shown a dramatic run of small fishes (*Alestes*) migrating from the lake up a small stream to spawn. They were being fished hard by all the local men and women with hand baskets. This run continued for several days, which was of great interest as such runs became rare.

In Jinja the EAFRO laboratory was being laid out based on the plans for the Virus Research Laboratory in Entebbe, to save architects fees. The site originally chosen by Barton and others in 1944 had, however, been changed. When Bobby Beauchamp arrived he had found that the original site (on Nasu Point) was officially designated for 'offensive trades' in the belief that fish would smell! So the lab was built near the staff houses then under construction, looking out over the lake in the Napoleon Gulf, not far from the Ripon Falls, over which the Nile started its long journey northwards. Not long after this the river was harnessed for hydroelectric power at the Owen Falls a few miles downstream (as Winston Churchill had suggested in 1907 on his visit to Uganda). The dam at Owen Falls submerged the Ripon Falls in 1954.

Bobby and I both stayed at the nearby old Ibis Hotel, a friendly place inhabited by various government officers, such as the one enforcing the Sleeping Sickness Control regulations along the Busoga shore of the lake at that time. There was no local fishing here in those days, and big trouble when locals poached a hippo, so EAFRO would be studying a virgin fishery once fishing started. At dinner round the long communal table I was asked whether I would 'be returning to Jinja', a question overheard by Bobby from the far end of the table, who commented loudly 'I thought that was understood !' So after dinner he 'interviewed' me and I was surprised to find I was to be in charge of the fish side of EAFRO's research programme, although Bobby had needed to do battle with the Governor of Uganda who thought that any female on the staff should only be paid a secretary's wage.

To continue homewards I left Jinja on a small goods train (the only European passenger) heading northwards to Namasagali on the Nile south of Lake Kyoga. Then I went by ferry down the river and across the lake to Masindi Port and from there by car to Masinde Hotel. Here, I found to my great surprise, when fifty years later I consulted my diary, I shared a room with Elspeth Huxley, whose books about her early life in Kenya I later so much enjoyed.

The month-long journey down the Nile is really another story. I travelled by lake steamer from Butiaba on Lake Albert, then by a stern wheeler pushing many crowded barges down river. We had to stop to refuel with wood at various places (it was the last wood-burning trip as they were about to convert to oil). At stops we were greeted by tall Dinka and Shilluk men, balancing with their spear on one leg while minding their great herds of cattle. It took a week to wind our way through the vast Nile sudd, which was wonderful for bird watching (although muslim passengers praying on the top deck had difficulty deciding which way was Mecca). We had good cabins but could also sleep on camp beds in mosquito- netted 'bug hutches' on the top deck which was much cooler. The deserts, with their clear dry air, were crossed by train, visiting Khartoum en route. Here I dined with Julian Rzoska who was then teaching at the Gordon Memorial College. We also visited the old Aswan dam. Then on to Cairo by train – the guard threatened to throw my tin trunk into the desert 'as it was too heavy for a passenger train'. In Cairo we stayed on a houseboat on the Nile, went to see the pyramids by tram, and the wonderful treasures (including those from Tutankhamen's tomb) in the Cairo Museum. But I then discovered that Thomas Cook's Travel Agents had omitted to book the requested onward passage by sea to the UK. I had to go to Port Said to await events, eventually boarding a crowded troop ship returning to the UK from India. This was the worst part of the journey.

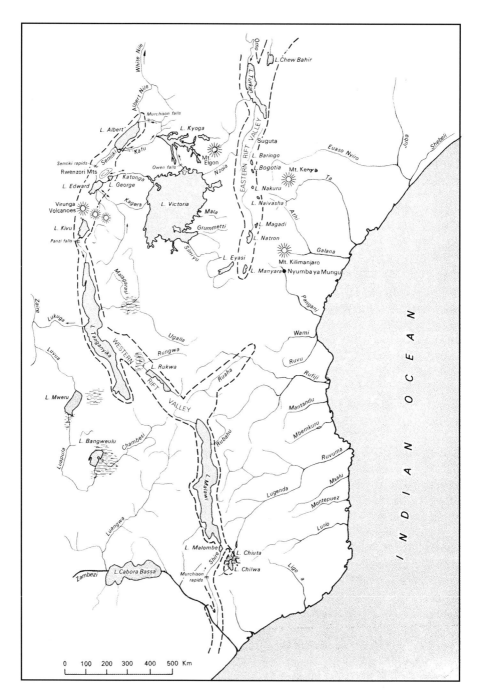

*Map of Eastern Africa showing the two Rift Valleys,
the lakes and major drainage basins.*

The EAFRO building with staff mending nets on the lawn about 1950.

The EAFRO research vessel setting gill nets out on Lake Victoria.

Jinja fish landing on the north shore of Lake Victoria, about 1967.

A group of women singing at the Busoga Women's Club,
about 1950.

Chapter 3
EAFRO and Lake Victoria

I spent a 'long leave' of several months in the UK, mainly in writing the report on Fish and Fisheries of Lake Nyasa, while based at the FBA on Lake Windermere and at the British Museum (Natural History) in London. I had a somewhat hilarious interview at the Colonial Office, then in Whitehall, to determine if I was worthy of permanent employment in the about-to-be created UK Overseas Research Service. Apparently I was and thus I returned to East Africa in November 1948.

This time, I flew up the Nile on the Sunderland flying boat, itself a memorable experience. From Southampton Water, after a late start due to fog, we flew first to Marseilles and then stayed overnight in Sicily. Next day, after stopping at Alexandria, we flew up the Nile to Luxor, where I had made such a magical visit to Karnak temple by the light of the full moon on the way home the previous year. Then upriver, over the Nile sudd which had taken me nearly a week to traverse by paddle steamer the previous year. Now I was perched on the stairs to the upper deck of the flying boat where a window looked down on the winding river channels. As the flying boat did not fly very high this gave excellent views of the country below. We landed on the Nile to refuel at Malakal and, some hours later, swooshed down on to Lake Victoria at Port Bell near Kampala in Uganda. Here we were sprayed vigorously with DDT, to slay any lurking mosquitoes, which unfortunately stimulated the passenger behind me in the queue to lose her breakfast. After three days en route, a tender landed us at Port Bell where I was welcomed by Bobby Beauchamp and driven to Jinja, which was to be my home for the next five years.

When I arrived the building of the East African Fisheries Research Organisation (EAFRO) laboratory and staff houses was almost complete and Stephen Deathe was already sampling the lake fishes. The laboratory was a long, low, white, red tiled, T-shaped building. Large airy rooms flanked the central library, meeting room and Director's office. Here Bobby Beauchamp, a hydrologist, who had been an initial member of the FBA staff on Windermere, presided over us. Two rooms became laboratories for the fish studies, one inhabited by me, the next by Humphry Greenwood when he arrived in 1950 to join the team. Another room, that of the hydrologist/algologist Geoffrey Fish, was packed with apparatus for water analyses and phytoplankton cultures. The entomologist W.W. (Bill) Macdonald had a room that was full of equipment for rearing the larvae of the aquatic insects which were found to be so important in the food of many fish species. Sadly, we had no zooplankton specialist (these studies had to await the HEST teams' work at the south end of the lake in the 1970s). Cai Cridland from Denmark, who was

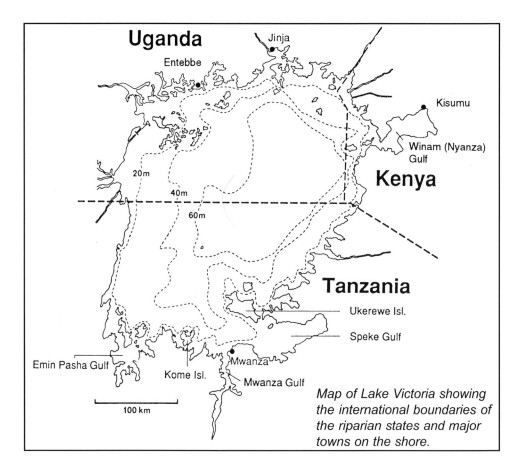

Map of Lake Victoria showing the international boundaries of the riparian states and major towns on the shore.

in charge of laboratory management, also undertook some tank experiments with freshwater snails and small fish. Near the side entrance, outside which our ridgeback dogs, Taffy and Swirrel, used to await us patiently by day, the night-watchman, a Nubian with a formidable bow and arrow, guarded the lab by night. Near the entrance was a room with a huge concrete sink for dissecting and preserving fish samples. The sink was large enough for Peggy Brown (later Varley), who spent a sabbatical at EAFRO from mid 1950–51, and I to do a post mortem on a baby elephant – all sorts of zoological jobs came to the laboratory. Here too was the large fridge, out of which a still-alive crocodile, parked there as dead by the visiting Hugh Cott, emerged to startle Yosiah, the chief laboratory assistant (who on another occasion was bewitched, necessitating being taken to the local hospital – another story).

The Annual Reports of EAFRO, compiled by Bobby Beauchamp until he retired in 1962, give excellent summaries of the aims and progress of the organization, and much has already been written about the work achieved at EAFRO which made it the 'most important such research station in Africa' (see box). So here I will just relive some memories of life on the EAFRO staff in 1948–54.

First impressions when I arrived back in Jinja in 1948 were tinged with a slight sadness at having to live in a township, compared with my house on the shores of Lake Nyasa and I missed Nyasa's clear waters through which one could watch the colourful fishes around the rocks. By comparison, Lake Victoria seemed a muddy puddle – albeit a huge one (68,800 km ^{2}, the size of Ireland). But my house was just alongside the laboratory and looked out over the Napoleon Gulf of the lake and I still had hippos coming into the garden at night. Awakened by sounds of heavy munching, by banging a handy dustpan and brush I could chase the hippo into Humphry Greenwood's garden to eat his sweet potatoes instead. One hippo unfortunately stepped on and broke the septic tank cover. In broad daylight another hippo used to stand under a very small tree on the laboratory lawn, oblivious of passing traffic. In the evenings we had delightful walks by the swampy edge of the lake, where pied kingfishers dived into the shallows, below the cliffs along the path to the Ripon Falls. Here a memorial plaque announced that Speke first saw the source of the Nile here on 28 July 1862. Around small islands in the river antique-looking black open bill storks (*Anastomus lamelligerus*) paddled around the rocks looking for the large aquatic snails on which they feed. Towards dusk, flights of white egrets and cormorants flew to their evening roosts. Otters played around the rocks while large *Barbus* fish jumped to gain access to the lake at the top of the Ripon Falls. They were fished for by local Africans

The EAFRO laboratory at Jinja on Coronation Day 1953.

Examples of sources of information about the work of EAFRO

The laboratory has been described, with photographs of many of the scientific staff, by Peter Jackson in his excellent account of *Freshwater fisheries research organizations in Central and Eastern Africa: A personal recollection'*. Peter first visited EAFRO in March 1952, when directing a sister institution, JFRO (Joint Fisheries Research Organization for Northern Rhodesia and Nyasaland) based at Fort Rosebery in Zambia. Later, in 1965, he returned to EAFFRO (by then FF for Freshwater Fisheries, to distinguish it from the EAMFRO, Marine laboratory in Zanzibar) as Director (until 1967). Later he became Project Manager of the FAO Lake Victoria Fisheries Project, housed in a new wing attached to the original EAFRO laboratory, until he retired from FAO in March 1972.

I have also written about early days at EAFRO in *The changing ecosystem of Lake Victoria* and in *EAFRO and after: a guide to key events affecting Fish Communities in Lake Victoria*, published in the festschrift for Humphry Greenwood after his untimely death in London in 1995; also in a joint paper with Barton Worthington on *African lakes reviewed: creation and destruction of Biodiversity.*

Another aspect of EAFRO was also described in an FBA Annual Report by Fryer & Talling 1986 *Africa: the FBA Connection.*

---

standing in the river using long rods, a peaceful scene against the turbulent backdrop of the rushing water.

Jinja township, on a low hill behind the lab, was home to the Provincial and District Administration offices (the Boma) surrounded by a green sward. The grass was kept down by prisoners slashing at it with metal hoops. The main street was lined with dukas, small shops mostly run by Indians, which supplied our needs – except for fruit which was brought in baskets to kitchen door by local African traders. Outside the dukas, on the pavements, Africans operating sewing machines were able to copy any cotton garment. There were two banks, a cinema (showing 'must see' films), and a garage run by two turbaned Sikh brothers, with a notice announcing 'penal beating' for the many bashed up trucks.

As my house was so near to the EAFRO laboratory I had visitors who worked there late into the night calling in for cups of tea. It was all very informal and friendly. In Jinja I also had many friends in different walks of life. There were exciting journeys accompanying Catherine Hastie when she was learning to drive her newly acquired car. She was engaged in developing women's clubs in Busoga and after visiting a club in the Gombolola, local government building, perched high on the top of a fertile hill near Jinja, we made a nerve-racking descent, weaving our way between the lush green banana trees, because Catherine was not yet sure which was the accelerator and which the brake. The route was lined with ullulating Basoga women in their colourful long cotton dresses. Together with good friends Henry Osmaston, Busoga's Forestry Officer, and his enterprising wife known as 'Mouse', we climbed Uganda's mountains, including helping to set up the first hut on Ruwenezori with the Uganda Mountain Club. This was a memorable weekend in 1949 (hilariously described by Mouse, in her book *Uganda before Amin*). We three returned to Ruwenzori to spend Christmas in the Emin-Gessi valley, sharing our Xmas pudding with a skull found in a cave up near the snowline. This was after leopards had visited our tents near the Bigo Bog at 13,000 feet, to the great excitement of the porters. Another holiday weekend we climbed Mount Elgon on the Kenya border.

Jinja had a fledgling sailing club (although as yet no club-house), and we swam in the lake from my sailing boat 'Lone Star'. There was also a golf course, famous for the local rule which allowed a player, without penalty, to pick the ball out of a hippo footprint, of which there were many. At night

grazing hippos were a hazard, and the golf 'greens' were of brown sand. Some people played tennis but 'Popsy' (mixed sex) hockey was all I ever played. This was agonising after a course of intravenous injections to cure bilharzia, when *Schistosoma mansoni* invaded me while working in Lake Albert's lagoons. Scots and English country dancing at the golf club was another form of exercise available but I preferred wandering around, watching the beautiful and melodious birds which frequented the

'Mouse' Osmaston (left), who became a life long friend, accompanying me out fishing on Lake Victoria.
(Photo Henry Osmaston.)

Examining a gill net catch, with Mormyrus, *in the fish room at EAFRO.*

gardens with their flowering shrubs and trees. There were nectar-gathering sunbirds, large touracos, including the go-away bird flopping around on branches of tall trees, palm swifts which nested under the huge fan-shaped leaves of the avenue of tall palms near the lake, weaver birds making their nests on reeds overhanging the swampy areas of the lake. There were also many kinds of kingfisher, herons around the lake and swamps, pelicans roosting at night on tops of tall trees and there were crowned cranes (*Balearica regulorum* – Uganda's national emblem) stalking in the grass.

Feeding a tame cormorant in the EAFRO grounds near my house, in the hope I could train it to catch fish for me.

An aerial view of Jinja taken about 1952.
The EAFRO building is in the middle distance.

Numerous kinds of dragonflies patrolled the swamps by day, and at night huge swarms of large Ephemeroptera lakeflies were attracted to the street lights (including *Povilla adusta*, the boring mayfly, so called because the larvae which live inside reeds also bore into wooden boats). In the houses geckoes ran up the walls seeking insects and the tinkling of many kinds of small frogs filled the warm night air.

The 1929 Colonial Office Report on the Fish and Fisheries of Lake Victoria, by Michael Graham (of the Lowestoft laboratory), had recommended the creation of an East African Fisheries Research Station and a Lake Victoria Fisheries Service. The idea was kept alive by Barton Worthington who, when on wartime duty in the Middle East, was asked by the British Colonial Office to prepare a suitable memorandum. For this he revisited East Africa several times, and in October 1944 met representatives of the three territories sharing the lake's waters to discuss the proposed plans. They all strongly supported the formation of both the Research laboratory and a Lake Victoria Fisheries Service. A black and white photograph of this historic meeting shows Barton Worthington with Hugh Copley, Fish Warden Kenya Colony, Colonel Charles Pitman, Game and Fish Warden, Uganda, with Stephen Deathe of the Kenya Fishery Department. Another photograph shows the sites chosen for the EAFRO laboratory, and for staff housing in Jinja, close to where the Nile leaves Lake Victoria. But, as already mentioned, when Bobby Beauchamp arrived to

Hugh Copley fishing for Barbus *in the Nile at Ripon Falls.*

build the laboratory in 1947 he discovered that the site allocated for this purpose had been put, by the city fathers, into an area designated for 'offensive trades'. So he arranged for the laboratory to be built on the site previously earmarked for the houses. Earlier, in 1945, shortly after the end of World War 2, the sum of £115,000 had been made available under a C.D. & W. (Colonial Development and Welfare) Scheme for the construction of the EAFRO laboratory and its running costs for the first five years. Building, which started in 1946, was completed in 1949 and the laboratory was formally opened by the Governor of Uganda in 1950, by which time eighteen months research had already laid a foundation of basic facts.

The general policy of EAFRO was to work as a scientific team, aiming to cover the sequence of events leading from the chemical and physical conditions of the water ultimately to the growth of the various populations of fish. It was very important to find out which factors control the *rate* of production in these tropical lakes, where conditions are very different from those in temperate lakes with their well-defined seasonal changes. For all the main commercial fishes we needed to determine their rates of growth and reproduction and what controlled their numbers. Also what prospects were there for developing other fisheries to take the pressure off the two endemic tilapia species?

It was great to work in a team again. On Lake Nyasa I had to set and maintain the experimental nets myself. At EAFRO Stephen Deathe (later replaced by Douglas Roberts) carried out all the fishing, using a small bottom trawl and fleets of gill nets of 2 to 5 inches stretched mesh, set in surface and bottom waters within 50 miles of Jinja. In the laboratory we then identified and measured all the fishes, recording their stomach contents to determine their feeding habits at different stages of their life history. It was also important to note the state of their gonads to determine whether they had definite breeding seasons, and if so, at what time of year in relation to hydrological events. The results were coordinated by Bobby Beauchamp in the Annual Reports of EAFRO and then incorporated into papers in scientific journals. The vast amount of data on the foods of the non-cichlid fishes caught in the routine gillnets had to await a masterly analysis, using Hollerith punch cards (this was in pre-computer days), by entomologist Philip Corbet who joined the staff to replace Bill Macdonald in 1954.

Although it is so large the equatorial Lake Victoria is less than 90 m deep. Much shallower and younger than the deep rift lakes, Tanganyika and Malawi, Victoria is probably only some 12,000 years old in its present form. Prior to this, westward flowing rivers crossed this area emptying into the western rift valley lakes. The present coastline of the lake is very irregular, with large

Stephen Deathe setting the standard gill net fleet.

gulfs and deeply indented with shallow, protected bays, islands and exposed sandy beaches. Occasional rocky outcrops and papyrus swamps fringe much of the lake. The turbid water has little annual variation in temperature (mean surface temperature about 24°C, that of the bottom only about a degree lower). Despite its equatorial position, the open waters of the lake were found to have an annual cycle of stratification with a thermocline at 40–60 m for much of the year but when the southeast tradewinds caused mixing in July–August oxygen was carried to the bottom waters. Geoff Fish discovered that an internal seiche slopped cooler bottom water into the shallow gulfs near Jinja causing localised stratification at different times of year from that in the main lake. The resulting deoxygenation in the bottom water affected nutrient release from the thick bottom deposits formed by the rain of dead plankton in the gulfs. The phosphates and nitrates were barely traceable in the open water as these nutrients were immediately taken up by the phytoplankton. There was also a shortage of the sulphates and silicates needed for diatom growth. The rate at which nutrients are released from the bottom mud is greatly affected by whether water above the mud is deoxygenated or not and the variations in density of the plankton affect the production of tilapia.

The Ripon Falls from the air in 1952
before the Owen Falls Dam was built and the Falls were drowned.

*Humphry and Marjorie Greenwood seeing me off
at my departure from EAFRO in 1954.*

This led to the realisation that 'Lake Victoria is many lakes within a lake'. The rain of dead plankton accumulated in the bottom ooze of the sheltered bays where tilapia feed. As the decomposition of vegetable material in these deposits is slower than that of the animal products excreted into the water column, Beauchamp hypothesised that in these shallow tropical lakes the rate of production (and so the fish yield) would be reduced by the removal of large numbers of herbivores (such as tilapia and hippos). Would our observations support this theory?

First, identifications had to be made of all the fish species (as far as then possible – many new ones were also discovered which it took time to describe). Some twenty species of tilapias were of commercial importance in various East African waters. How were they distributed? How much did they move about, where did they spawn and look after their young, was breeding seasonal? How fast did they reproduce and grow? We needed to know the quantity and quality of their foods, what predators they had – other fish species, crocodiles, birds, and fishermen. Many other aspects of their biology required investigation. Humphry Greenwood started what became his life-long work (continued at the BM(NH) in London) on the taxonomy of the very complex and previously little investigated flocks of the smaller haplochromine cichlids. These had radiated in the lake to use all types of foods available, and became of enormous international interest for studies of evolution.

EAFRO also sought other fish species which might be numerous enough to support fisheries and take the strain off the tilapia populations. About 50% of the weight of fish landed in the routine gillnetting experiments was tilapia, mainly *O. esculentus*. In the deeper water the elephant snout fish, *Mormyrus kannume*, was extremely abundant (13% of the catch). This endemic fish, growing to over 60 cm long, had electric organs in the tail, a useful device for avoiding predators when feeding on lake fly larvae in the bottom mud. Large piscivorous catfishes *Bagrus docmac* formed 4% of the catch and *Clarias* 3%. The lungfish *Protopterus* (3%) which ate bivalve molluscs as well as fish, were also caught, sometimes along with a few of the large insectivorous barbel *Barbus radcliffi* which leapt up the Ripon Falls. Some smaller *Schilbe* catfish also appeared in the surface nets. Occasionally the mud-feeding cyprinid *Labeo victorianus* were caught near inflowing rivers up which they migrated to spawn until over-fished by small-meshed gillnets set in the mouths of these rivers.

In January 1949 Bobby Beauchamp and I camped on Dagusi Island with Stephen Deathe to fish the deeper water of the open lake. *Mormyrus* were so plentiful in our catches that a small fishery for these was encouraged from Dagusi Island, financed by the Busoga Native Administration. News of this in a local newspaper frightened an overseas supplier to write to EAFRO to

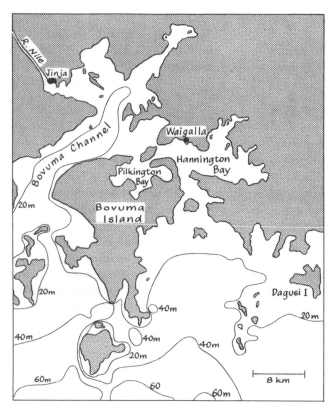

Map of the islands at the mouth of the River Nile showing the location of Jinja, Pilkington Bay, Hannington Bay and Dagusi Island.

enquire whether these catches would affect their exports of dried stock fish to East Africa? Sadly this venture was not a commercial success. Fishing was attempted from sailing dhows, but the local fishermen needed engine-power to fish in the deeper waters. Also it was discovered that Basoga women had a taboo against eating *Mormyrus*. Their local name 'kasulubana' meant 'throw out the baby', so it was evidently reputed to cause abortion.

The abundant *Mormyrus kannume*, had stomachs crammed with lake fly larvae (mainly chironomid and chaoborid Diptera) of which numerous species were discovered. These larvae also had a role in the release of nutrients from the bottom mud. So the entomologist Bill Macdonald concentrated on their life cycles. He first had to rear them in the laboratory, then adults were sent away to be identified, and new species described, by experts in museums overseas. Bill's work revealed that the main species had a two-month long life cycle in the mud and water column before they emerged as huge clouds of flies that looked like smoke over the lake.

The *Mormyrus* became very scarce following the introduction of Nile perch (*Lates*) from Lake Albert (where they fed on mormyrids) into Lake Victoria in the mid 1950s. This helps to explain the present huge abundance of chironomid midges, as so graphically shown in *The Lake of Flies* filmed in the 1990s for TV audiences worldwide. Other 'lakeflies' include the much larger Ephemeroptera (known as 'mayflies' in UK trout streams) which were later shown to have a lunar rhythm of emergence from the lake, vast numbers being attracted to lights in Jinja in the dark hours after full moon.

Trials with the small bottom trawl showed a huge mass of haplochromine cichlids of numerous species, many unidentified, living in Lake Victoria. These species flocks had radiated to use all the varied food sources available: plankton and plants, insect larvae, snails, prawns, small fishes – there were even paedophage species specialised to take eggs and larval young from the mouths of brooding female haplochromines. There was also a surprising number of piscivorous species feeding mainly on other cichlids (including juvenile tilapia). Humphry Greenwood did a great job recording these, with notes on their biology, material of the greatest interest for biologists world wide studying how new species evolve, and how so many can live sympatrically within one lake. But a whole suite of zooplankton-feeding pelagic species, and another of rock dwellers (comparable to those in Lake Malawi), were not discovered until the 1970s when a Dutch team from the University of Leiden (known as the Haplochromis Ecology Survey Team, HEST) spent some twenty years working out of Mwanza at the south end of the lake (as so vividly described in *Darwins Dreampond* by Thys Goldschmidt). Their research was stimulated by a commercial trawl fishery for haplochromines which had by then been developed from Mwanza (see Chapter 8 for more details).

EAFRO's launch on Lake Victoria.

EAFRO also had a policy of encouraging visiting scientists to add to our understanding of the lake, which had the additional advantage of keeping the staff in touch with research elsewhere. I particularly enjoyed working with Hugh Cott from Cambridge University who was studying the ecology of the then plentiful crocodiles. Humphry and I identified the fishes in their stomachs. George Carter, also from Cambridge, came at the same time (1951-2) to make pioneer studies of Uganda's many papyrus swamps. Another Cambridge visitor was J.T. ('Fanny') Saunders, whom we had long known as an FBA Councillor. After staying in Government House for high level consultations on education in Uganda, he visited EAFRO, full of enthusiasm, to enquire about mormyrid electric fishes for his Cambridge colleague Hans Lissmann. Hans was comparing the extraordinary convergences in ecology and behaviour of two quite unrelated groups of electric fishes, the mormyrids in Africa and the gymnotids in South America. I had the happy task of rowing J.T. Saunders round Jinja Bay while he trailed a device by which he could listen to any electric discharges from mormyrids below. With headphones covering his ears he was oblivious of the large hippopotamus snorting at us as it suddenly surfaced in front of our small rowing boat. With his back to the hippo he said 'row on, I can't hear a thing'. Luckily the hippo did not upset the boat. In the lab a *Mormyrus* in one tank would attack a wire leading from an adjacent tank containing another one. This was intriguing and we demonstrated these interactions at local agricultural shows for which EAFRO produced exhibits.

Another visitor was Jack Lester who came from London Zoo to collect snakes and birds. He arrived after an adventurous journey during which his plane had to ditch in the Mediterranean Sea en route. Luckily no one was drowned, as their SOS was spotted by an American air force plane which alerted a passing ship to collect them from their rubber dinghies and take them to Malta. There they were refused entry to the hotel dining room as 'improperly dressed'. Sadly they had to throw all their luggage, including the Zoo's cameras, and the plane's spare wheel (and their shoes) into the sea to lighten the plane before ditching. As Jack had been in the Royal Air Force during the war, he was called on to report on this incident. Later he accompanied me to Lake Bunyoni in southwest Uganda, where he informed local Africans that he was collecting for a zoo. The result was that on returning to the rest house one evening we were greeted with a merry clatter of wooden chairs being dragged around the concrete floor by numerous large toads firmly tied to each, a veritable Cinderella coach scene.

Bobby Beauchamp stressed that we should work as a team. With his seemingly very relaxed attitude he wove the strands of each new discovery into a coherent whole theory for testing. Re-reading the EAFRO Annual Reports collated by him I am deeply impressed by his masterly summaries assessing the significance of the many aspects of the work of his members of staff and of the many international visitors who came for short periods. While Acting Director for two periods when he was on long leave overseas I had a direct view of the many problems involved.

Research on the other East African lakes was done on an expeditionary basis, generally by motor vehicle, including the old grey lab. truck, or our own cars. Later we had a mobile laboratory on a lorry chassis, for which we all had to get a lorry driving licence. Collections and samples had to be brought back to Jinja for study. Research in the open waters of the vast Lake Victoria was restricted by lack of a seaworthy vessel capable of research in these often stormy waters, but cooperation with the Lake

Bobby Beauchamp, the first Director of EAFRO, was a very important influence on my life and work.

Victoria Fisheries Service, which had a motorised fishing vessel (MFV) in each of the three territories, enabled me to make safaris with the fishery officers to sample tilapia all around the lake, where the LVFS had a system of fish recorders on many beaches.

After I left the EAFRO staff at the end of 1953 I returned there in September 1954 for three months to complete analyses of LVFS catch records and write up papers collating data on the biology of the Lake Victoria endemic tilapia, and of the Nile tilapia *O. niloticus* and accompanying *O. leucostictus*. It was great to be back again, staying with the Beauchamps. Humphry Greenwood was completing a book on *The Fishes of Uganda.* Entomologist Philip Corbet, who had replaced Bill Macdonald, had taken over my house (complete with much-loved dog Swirrel) and was using the 'Hollerith' cards to sort out the immense amount of data on foods eaten by non-cichlid fishes from EAFRO catches over many years. Audfin Tjønnland, a visitor from Norway was investigating the lunar cycle of the ephemeropteran mayflies emerging in such huge numbers from the lake. With Geoff Fish I also sampled a number of lakes behind water supply dams stocked with various species of tilapia.

The Lake Victoria tilapia

My main project at EAFRO was to study the biology of the tilapias, the principal commercial species in most of the East African lakes, except Lake Tanganyika. What tilapia species were involved? How were different age groups distributed in each lake? How fast did the fish grow and reproduce and were they able to maintain viable fisheries? What controlled their

Geoff Fish sampling the water to investigate the algae.

The Owen Falls Dam which uses the power of the River Nile where it leaves Lake Victoria to generate electricity. The Ripon Falls, just upstream, disappeared when the dam was completed in 1954.

When I lived at Jinja and worked at EAFRO I owned a sailing boat and enjoyed events such as the Jinja regatta and the canoe races.

*The elephant snout fish (*Mormyrus*) eats lake fly larvae from the bottom mud and used to be very abundant in fish catches from Lake Victoria. It has become less abundant since the introduction of Nile perch.*

The shoebill, or whaleheaded stork, Balaeniceps rex *lives among dense papyrus in the swamps around Lake Victoria. Although the area of suitable habitat is now much reduced it is still occasionally possible to see these large, extraordinary birds.*

Bill Macdonald, the original entomologist at EAFRO, setting out on a sampling trip.

numbers? How much were numbers influenced by limitations in quantity and quality of food, competition between species for spawning or brooding grounds, predation by the many piscivorous fish species which cropped different size groups, and other piscivores, including crocodiles, otters and the innumerable fish-eating birds and, above all, man? The ever increasing human populations around the lakes, changes in fishing gear, introductions of exotic species and human activities in the drainage basins such as clearing land and pollution, were also found to be interacting, leading to dramatic changes within the lakes.

First I concentrated on the biology of the two tilapia species endemic to Lake Victoria, the 'ngege' (*O. esculentus* – first described by Michael Graham) and 'mbiru' (*O. variabilis*). Both were only found in Lakes Victoria and Kyoga until they were artificially spread around East Africa and introduced into many smaller lakes, dams and ponds. How did they share the lake's resources and interact with other species? How much did they move about and use different habitats at different stages of their life histories? What did they eat? Like all tilapias they were basically herbivores, feeding on algae and detritus, but what did they digest?

In addition to samples from routine fishing on the lake within 50 miles of EAFRO, I travelled with the officers of the local Fisheries Service. We lived on board their motorised fishing vessels, which had been specially built in Kisumu. The *MFV Heron* was based at Mwanza to cover Tanganyika Territory waters (which I visited with Desmond Kelsall in early May 1949); the *MFV*

George Cole (Chief Fisheries Officer LVFS) supervising the capture of exotic tilapia from Kisumu ponds in 1954, to stock Lake Victoria.

Pelican was based at Kisumu to cover Kenyan waters (visited with FO Gilbert in August 1949 and again with FO Curry in October 1949). The *MFV Darter* was based at Entebbe to cover Uganda waters, in which we worked in the Sesse Islands (with FO Gilbert in December 1950). On this Sesse Island tour we were accompanied by my old friend from FBA days Peggy Brown who was spending a sabbatical leave (mid 1950–1951) from the UK at EAFRO studying the growth of haplochromine cichlids. At EAFRO we also analysed the LVFS catch records from around the lake. After I left these analyses were continued by David Garrod, who looked at the population dynamics of the endemic tilapias.

Tanganyika Territory received the first Fishery Vessel to be commissioned so my first visit was to Mwanza, where Commander George Cole, head of the LVFS, was then stationed, as well as FO Desmond Kelsall. Travelling to Mwanza on the lake steamer, clockwise round the lake via Bukoba, we stopped at various ports to unload and load cargo and passengers. This gave an opportunity to see the western shores of the lake and the Kagera River inflow. Passengers included an American family on safari accompanied by a 'white hunter'. When we visited a small island on which many large crocodiles were basking he handed me his elephant gun. What a recoil! He then shot a large crocodile. Presented with its skull, I arrived in Mwanza to be met, with this skull in addition to all my fish collecting gear, by the genial George Cole. I was staying with the Coles who readily agreed to bury the head in an anthill in their garden for the ants to clean the skull while I was away on the *Heron*.

This was successful, but evidently Bad Magic! On returning to Mwanza I learned from his delightful wife, Jean, that the garden boy she had been training left at once 'without even collecting his wages'. Despite this, we continued to be good friends. In later years I visited them twice in Australia, where they finally retired to Magnetic Island after an adventurous trip in the trimaran they built in Kenya. They sailed it, plus Granny Cole aged 90, to New Zealand, as recounted in Jean's book *Trimaran against the Trades.*

With Desmond Kelsall and his wife Joan aboard the *Heron* we visited numerous fishing beaches. We penetrated to the very south end of Smith Sound, which seemed like the end of the world, where Desmond found very good duck shooting in the swamps. Then we sailed into Speke Gulf and to Ukerewe Island. This Tanzanian coast has huge rocks, unlike the swampy coast near Jinja, around which the Dutch HEST team much later discovered a new flock of rock-dwelling cichlids, comparable to the 'mbuna' in Lake Malawi.

The three visits I made to the Kavirondo Gulf (now called Nyanza or Winam Gulf) in Kenyan waters were mainly to see how many juvenile tilapia were caught in the small-meshed beach seine nets used here by local Africans to catch haplochromines and 'omena' (small cyprinids *Rastrineobola argentea,* called 'dagaa' in Tanganyika waters). I slept on the hatches on deck and one vivid memory is of sheep fat dripping from the larder cage, slung below the MFV`s awning, on to my waterproof sleeping bag. The residual smell of it, combined with that of fish, later lured a leopard into my tent when camped near Bigo Bog on Mount Ruwenzori.

On our trip around the Sesse Islands in December 1950 we were accompanied by Paul Musaala, a schoolboy from the islands. When we

Talking to Sesse Island fishers and (right) examining their catch of haplochromines on the drying racks.

collected Paul from Kisubi School near Entebbe, his headmaster turned out to be the Dutch Father Kuypers with whom I had shared chemistry classes at Liverpool University when he and his compatriot, Father Damien, 'needed an English degree' for their missionary work in Africa. Another charming memory is of an old lady, who wanted a passage with us to another island to visit relatives for Xmas. She first packed up gifts to take with her of dried mushrooms and other goodies extracted from small banana leaf parcels tied to the wooden beams of her grass-roofed hut. Peggy and I were also delighted to see sitatunga (*Tragelaphus spekei*) living on the islands, although their hooves were not as long as those of populations found in very swampy areas. Skins of this now very rare species were even being used as sheets on which to dry coffee beans.

On these trips we anchored each night and set experimental gillnets, and at each beach we examined the catches caught by local fishermen. We

---

Tilapia spawning, growth and age determination in Lake Victoria

O. esculentus from enclosed waters, such as the Kavirondo Gulf and Smith Sound matured at a smaller size than did those from the main lake. *O. variabilis* in the Jinja region matured at 22cm TL (225 gm), in contrast with *O. esculentus* at 25–26 cm (300–350 gm). All over the lake fewest *O. esculentus* spawned between June and August, when the open waters were mixed, carrying oxygen deep into the lake, with peaks in September and February to May in northern waters, and November to January in southern waters. These breeding peaks coincided with the months of most rain.

The catches per net of *O. esculentus* were low between July and August, and it was suggested that these fish moved out into more open waters during the months of mixing. While *O. esculentus* were away from the beaches, the catches of *O. variabilis* increased in the seine catches. Regardless of time of year, breeding males and females contained little food; when not breeding they were packed with algaceous food. The larger ones had fat ribbons along the gut, all year round.

The production of young throughout the year made determinations of the age and growth rate of Lake Victoria tilapia very difficult, using progression of length frequency modes. But at the south end of the lake *O. esculentus* appeared to grow to about 15 cm TL (60 gm) in the first year, to 22 cm (190gm) in the second year, and 27 cm (400gm) in the third year. Growth slowed down very much once the tilapia started to breed. In both these species males and females grew at the same rate and matured at the same size, probably in their third year.

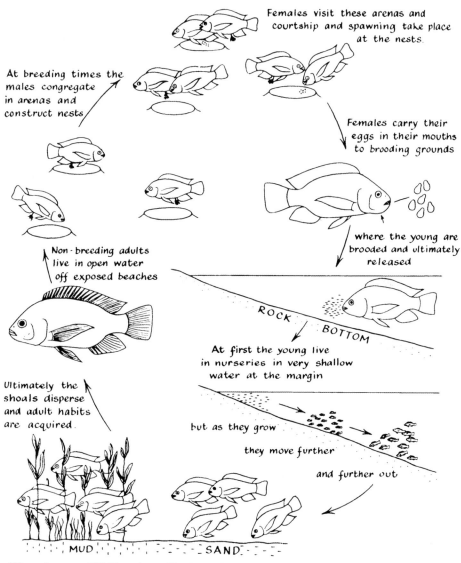

The life cycle of Tilapia variabilis *in Lake Victoria. (from Fryer and Iles, 1972.)*

examined stomach contents to determine what the different species were eating and their gonads to see which fish were in breeding condition. The seasonal distribution of *T. esculenta* catches, from LVFS records of catches by fishermen at selected beaches around the whole lake, shows the kind of picture we were building up of the movements of the two endemic tilapia species in relation to seasonal rainfall patterns.

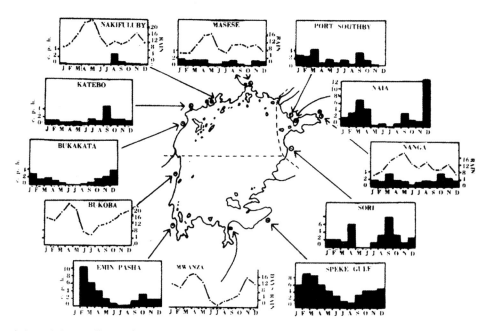

A hand-drawn figure (pre-computer days) of the seasonal variation in numbers of
Tilapia esculenta *caught by local fishermen around Lake Victoria in 1950. The*
seasonal distribution of rainfall is also shown for various locations around the lake.

Both the native species lived in different zones of the lake according to
their size and sexual condition. As I had found among the Lake Malawi tilapia,
juveniles left by brooding females in cover, in swampy areas or turbid water,
later inhabited more open shores. They disappeared offshore as they grew,
where they were caught in surface-set, small-mesh gillnets. They become more
benthic in habit when adult, and were then caught in bottom-set gillnets (of 4
and 5 inch diagonal mesh). *Oreochromis variabilis* did not grow as large as *O.
esculentus. Oreochromis variabilis* had two colour forms; in the Jinja area 32 %
of the female fish but only about 5% of the males showed the aberrant piebald
and orange colour form. Concentrations of ripe males of this species in the
gillnet catches indicated spawning areas, whereas brooding females, detectable
by the mouth pouch even after they had spat out most of their larval young
when caught, indicated brooding areas.

As some ripe females would be found at any time of year it proved difficult
to assess maturation ages from length frequencies. There were, however, peaks
in numbers of tilapia spawning during the main rains. Such is the immensity
of Lake Victoria, these were equinoxial (i.e. two rains per year) at the north
end of the lake, but more unimodal (October-December) at the southern end.
Female gonads contained ova of about three sizes, indicating that three batches
of young might be produced in fairly quick succession within a breeding
period. A female was occasionally caught with ova already ripening in her

ovaries while she still had eggs or yolked young in her mouth. The scales of females were found to show spawning rings, but it was not known whether most individuals spawned at both peak times (ie having two breeding periods per year, each leaving spawning rings). It was important to know this for estimations of ages and mortality rates from scale rings (as later calculated by David Garrod).

This was the state of information on these endemic Lake Victoria tilapia in 1954 when I left EAFRO. But all that was to change. *O. esculentus*, so called for its particularly delicious flavour, has now completely vanished from the lake.

Early catch records of Tilapia from Lake Victoria

Catches in 5 inch mesh gillnets in Kenya and Uganda waters comprised 50% *O. esculentus*, 10% *O. variabilis* and 40% other species, mainly non-cichlids. In Tanganyika waters the catch per unit effort of *O. esculentus* in the 5 inch net was higher.

Catches were about thirty per net in the virgin waters around Jinja when first fished by EAFRO, but declined fairly rapidly in Pilkington Bay during the long-term experimental fishing there, continued until 1955 by David Garrod. In the Kavirondo/ Winam Gulf catches had fallen from over 25 per 5 inch gillnet prior to 1920 to about 6 per net in 1928 and to 1.6 per net in 1955.

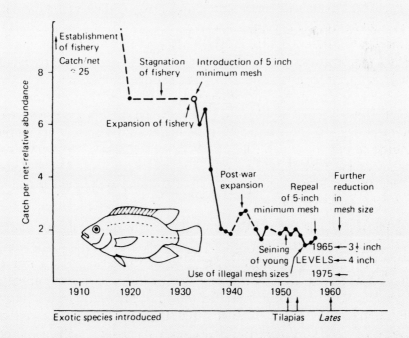

The decline in catches of tilapia in gill nets from the Kenya waters of Lake Victoria.

How did this come about? In 1954, in an attempt to boost tilapia catches, *Tilapia zillii,* a macrophyte-feeder present in Lake Albert, was introduced to Lake Victoria. As an inshore dweller it was thought this would not interfere with the endemic tilapias and would help to clear swamps. With it came *O. leucostictus,* and more important for future events, the Nile tilapia *O. niloticus.*

Robin Welcomme, who arrived to join the staff in January 1963, analysed how these introduced tilapias took over from the endemic species, events preceded by a dramatic rise in lake level in 1961 following exceptionally heavy rains which flooded the lakeside swamps. This rise, which extended the brooding grounds in these swamps, at first boosted *O. esculentus* catches but the introduced *O. niloticus* eventually replaced this species (it now seems with some hybridisation). *O. niloticus* has proved to be a very adaptable hardy species, able to exploit more varied food sources (including some insect larvae) than the phytophagous *O. esculentus.* It also produced more eggs and its large females were able to brood larger numbers of young. Furthermore, when Nile perch (also introduced into Lake Victoria from Lake Albert about 1954) multiplied and consumed so many indigenous fishes, *O. niloticus,* which had coexisted with *Lates* for aeons in Lake Albert, survived its introduction into Lake Victoria better than did the indigenous tilapias.

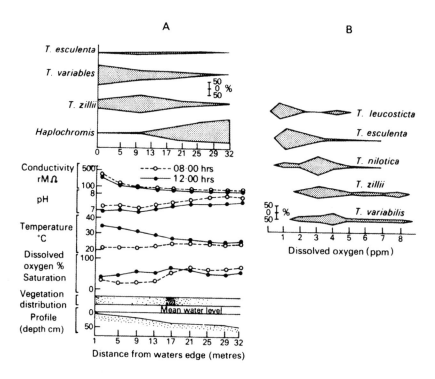

The relative distributions of juvenile tilapia off Lake Victoria beaches.
(From Welcomme 1964).

*In John Balirwa's laboratory (office) at Jinja
during my visit in 2001.*

*With Robin Welcomme looking back at the visitors book on our
return to EAFFRO for a conference, in 2001.*

*Looking across Lake George from the western shore.
The horizon is marked by the escarpment of the Rift Valley*

*The water of Lake George looks like
pea soup due to the dense population
of blue-green algae (known as
Cyanobacteria these days) which float
to the surface when the water is calm
but are redistributed throughout the
water column when the wind mixes
the water of this very shallow (2.5 m)
lake, as it does most afternoons.
The floating Nile cabbage (Pistia
stratiotes), seen below, used to be
very abundant on the surface of Lake
George but has declined markedly in
recent years probably due to an
episode of copper pollution.*

These introductions changed the whole ecology of the lake, as studied by the Dutch Team (HEST) from Lieden University (see Chapter 9). In 1972 HEST set up a research station near Mwanza in Tanzania. From there they have continued to monitor the lake's many changes. Although the lake lost an estimated *c* 200 haplochromine species as a result of the Nile perch's depredations, the total number of haplochromine species now known to have evolved in the lake is very much greater than believed by Humphry Greenwood, from his studies at the north end of the lake, because of the many new species that HEST has later discovered in the south. This is all the more surprising as evidence from cores of bottom mud now suggests that Lake Victoria almost dried up a mere 14,000 years ago. How could so many species have evolved in such a short time?

Although *O. esculentus* is now thought to be 'extinct' from the main Lake Victoria, it is still found in small satellite lakes that are free of *O. niloticus* and Nile perch (eg. in Lake Kanabola in the Kenyan swamps). *O. variabilis* is now rare in Lake Victoria`s catches. But these clever tilapias, aided by man, have now appeared elsewhere, in particular in Tanzania's largest man-made lake Nyumba-ya-Mungu in the Pangani River system and now in Lake Rukwa (see Chapter 5).

In Lake Victoria *T. zillii* first appeared in gillnet catches in 1956. It spread rapidly at the north end of the lake and was abundant by 1964. It became the dominant species in former *O. variabilis* areas, living in shallow marginal waters all round the lake. Its fry and juveniles inhabited shelving rocky shores in sheltered places, situations favoured as *O. variabilis* nurseries. *O. niloticus* and O. *leucostictus*, which appeared in the commercial records in 1960, became much more abundant after 1964. *O. leucostictus* became the dominant species in lagoons around the lake, and near the papyrus in shallow muddy bays, while *O. niloticus* became dominant on the former *O. esculentus* grounds. Introgression between *O. esculentus* and *O. niloticus* was later found to be rampant. Factors affecting the relative distributions of juvenile tilapia were studied by Robin Welcomme.

There appeared to be little competition for food between the adults, *T. zillii* taking higher plant material, *O. esculentus* planktonic diatoms. *O. niloticus* and *O. variabilis* had more flexible diets, feeding either on the bottom or on epiphytic or planktonic diatoms, depending on the habitat. *O. leucostictus* fed exclusively on bottom material. Spatial segregation also helped to reduce competition, *O. leucostictus* being confined to shallow lagoons near and often behind the papyrus fringe (in water 30 cm to 5 m deep), while *T. zillii* and *O. variabilis* spread into harder bottomed areas and more exposed water. The larger *O. esculentus* lived in mud-bottomed bays (c 5–10m deep), *O. niloticus* was found in most habitats. All the introduced species grew to a large size and were in good condition (with a high weight for length ratio).

Competition for breeding grounds was more apparent than for food, and the lack of suitable places for spawning and nursery grounds appeared to be a factor limiting population expansion. This view was supported by the dramatic increase in *O. esculentus* in catches during 1964–65 following the unprecedented increase in lake level (1.4 m above the previous highest recorded level) in 1961–3. Flooded areas behind the papyrus fringe were used as *O. esculentus* nurseries. *O. esculentus* evidently spawned where they could find firm enough bottom in the sheltered gulfs, but their juveniles lived in lagoons at the lake's edge. Clean, firmer substrates were needed by the substratum-spawning *T. zillii* (which is not a mouth brooder). The ousting of *O. variabilis* by *T. zillii* appeared to be due to competition between them for breeding and nursery grounds. *O. leucostictus* spawned in shallow (c 30 cm deep) water in mud-bottomed areas at the edge of lagoons. *O. niloticus* appeared more catholic in its taste and was found in association with the other species.

The staff of EAFRO gathered to see me off when I finally left in 1954.
At the back from the left: Geoff Fish, Cai Cridland, (Pat Daly)
and Bobby Beauchamp. In front, Marjorie Greenwood and daughter Pamela, Phillip
Corbet, Swirrel, Kay Burford, Humphry Greenwood and, standing, Douglas Roberts.

Chapter 4
The Nile tilapia at home

Sandwiched between the Lake Victoria studies, the tilapia trail led me on safaris to other lakes in all three East African territories, covering an immense area, to unravel the biology of their indigenous tilapia species. I loved these trips with the wide open views on so many long drives and meeting the African fishermen on the various lakes. I took every chance to see as much as possible and my log books bring back the sights, sounds and smells of the African bush. These projects were greatly helped by the resident Fisheries Officers in each territory, attached to the Game & Fisheries Departments in Uganda and Kenya, under Captain Pitman based in Entebbe and Hugh Copley in Nairobi, both of whom had helped to set up EAFRO, and with the Department of Agriculture and Fisheries in Tanganyika Territory.

The ecological studies of the Nile tilapia (*O. niloticus*), which is indigenous to the East African lakes, described in this chapter, came to be of particular interest because of the major importance of this species later, both in Lake Victoria (when stocked there in the mid 1950s) and for fish culture throughout the warm waters of the world. Worthington had already discovered that this species was important in the fisheries of many East African lakes, and that it coexisted with the large piscivorous Nile perch (*Lates*) in Lakes Albert and Rudolf (Turkana) (and indeed also in West Africa). It was also the main catch

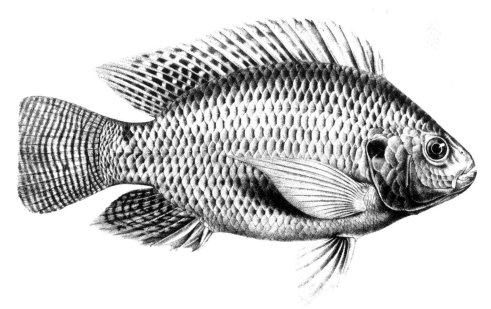

The Nile tilapia
(Tilapia nilotica, *now* Oreochromis niloticus). (Boulenger 1907.)

in Lake George, Lake Edward and other Uganda lakes where *Lates* was absent. How did its ecology differ in these two types of lake?

From EAFRO we first studied *O. niloticus* in Lakes George and Edward and then in Lake Albert in the Western Rift Valley in Uganda, and in Lake Rudolf (now Lake Turkana) in Kenya, as well as in many smaller lakes and dams. The water from Lake George flows down the broad Kazinga Channel into Lake Edward and together they form a 'cichlid lake' with over sixty cichlid species (92% of them endemic) in contrast to Lake Albert which has only eleven cichlid species (36% of them endemic). On the shore of Lake George the newly created Uganda Fish Marketing Corporation (TUFMAC) was developing a commercial fishery, due to start in late 1950.

The Koki lakes

However, Captain Pitman's first request for assistance from EAFRO was for us to visit small lakes and dams in West Uganda to see what had become of the 'bluegill sunfish'. These were *Lepomis macrochirus*, a North American centrarchid, kindly(?) donated by the Americans during the war, to stock Ugandan waters in order to augment local food supplies. These sunfish had been parked in the Kabaka's lake, a small lake of ritual significance near Kampala, from where the Fishery Department Fish Guards took small fish to stock lakes and dams throughout western and northern Uganda, which are especially numerous in Ankole and Teso. Because it is very difficult to identify small fishes, especially cichlids, many species of which had not then been described, it is necessary to understand modern man's role in introducing non-native species to different drainage systems in order to work out the original zoogeographical relationships of East African fishes.

Did any of these alien bluegill sunfishes still survive? To answer this, I set off in March 1949 on my first EAFRO safari, on the dusty red roads of Uganda, in the rattling grey EAFRO truck ('puncture', 'puncture' read the log book). I was accompanied by laboratory assistant Yosiah, and Kalimenti (who looked after me) and the truck was piled high with experimental fishing gear and collecting equipment. En route we lunched with Captain Pitman in Entebbe to make arrangements to visit the Koki lakes with Fishery Officer Gardett. But after crossing the Equator (sign posted on the Masaka road), we first visited Lake Nabugabo. This small lake is cut off from the northwest shore of Lake Victoria by a sand bar dated at 4000 years old. Here we examined catches of *O. esculentus* and other fishes. It was in this lake that Humphry Greenwood later found several haplochromine species which were distinct from related species in the main lake, and had evidently developed in Nabugabo, at what was then considered a record rate of evolution.

The next day Gardett took us to the Koki lakes (Kijanebalola, Chanagwora and Kachira) which lie in an ancient drainage system between Lakes Victoria and Edward. From Annual Reports of the Uganda Fisheries Department I found that lakes Kijanebalola and Kachira had been stocked in 1936 with Lake Edward O. *niloticus* via Lake Bunyoni, and again in 1939 from Lake Saka. In the opaque waters of Kijanebalola a fishery had been opened in 1942, six years after the lake was first stocked. The fishery was expanded in 1945 and in the same year O. *esculentus* from the Kabaka's lake in Kampala was introduced. The fishery was at the height of its prosperity in 1947 but in 1948 there was a net shortage, and in 1949 and 1952 bad droughts reduced the lake area and hundreds of tilapia died.

It was reported that tilapia never grew very large in Lake Kijanebalola and when we visited the lake in March 1949 they were said to be smaller than formerly and TUFMAC had ceased to buy them for this reason. A sample we examined from commercial gill nets all appeared to be O. *niloticus* (modal size 19 cm). Feeding on phytoplankton in this very opaque lake they were in poor condition and nearly all mature at 17 cm long. Next day we cycled on rough tracks to the adjacent and interconnected Lake Chanagwora. Here the O. *niloticus* sampled were starting to breed at 23 cm long but were in very poor condition, feeding on phytoplankton in this similarly opaque lake. We next visited Lake Kachira, which although connected to Chanagwora by swamps had clear water with stands of aquatic plants. Here the O. *niloticus* grew larger, and were said to have averaged 550 gm in 1947, with a fishery opened in 1948. In these three interconnected lakes all the tilapia we examined were O. *niloticus;* no O. *esculentus* or bluegill sunfish were seen.

We later heard (1952) that Kijanebalola had dried up since our 1949 visit, and was being restocked from Lake Bunyoni. Fry from Lake Bunyoni had also been taken to three other lakes in Kigezi (Mutanda, Mulehe and Mogisha) and to Lake Saka, a crater lake in Toro, in 1935. So tilapia, and doubtless other small cichlids with them, have evidently been moved around these Ugandan lakes frequently and for a long time.

Nile tilapia in some of Uganda's smaller lakes c1950				
			O. niloticus	
	pH	conduct-ivity	Maximum length	Length at maturity
Lake Kijanebalola	9.4	850 µS	33 cm	17 cm
Lake Chanagwora	8.2	450 µS	32 cm	23 cm
Lake Nkugute	8.7	c89 µS	30 cm	24 cm
Lake Niungu	9.6	400 µS		18 cm
Lake Katinda	9.4	600 µS	29 cm	27 cm

In 1931 Barton Worthington, who was interested in the fish fauna of this ancient drainage connection between Lakes Victoria and Edward/George, spent over a week sampling these Koki Lakes, including the larger (c 25 km², 3.5 m deep) Lake Nakivali lying further west in this drainage system, which we did not visit. Here he found only *Clarias* catfish, hooked by some twenty five fishermen who also trapped small haplochromines. As he could find no tilapia, Worthington recommended they be introduced, and in 1939 some 18,000 fry from the Kazinga Channel were stocked into Nakivali, an introduction which proved a tremendous success. In 1942 a gillnet fishery was established which expanded rapidly. The Fisheries Department reported that by 1953 the licenced fishermen, settled in new houses there, earned more than £20,000. They were using plank-built boats to supply the whole of the surrounding district with fish and were exporting a surplus 150 tons to the Congo. Dr Hickling who later visited Nakivali, cited this as a 'success story of what can be done by transplantation of fish to a new site, the new village a far cry from the ruffians reported here by Pitman in 1926 and the fishery for mudfish in 1931'.

On the way back to Jinja, when I left the car to climb an inviting roadside hill that seemed to want to be visited, a passing African commented 'that is a sacred hill, and any prayers from the top will be answered'. And, yes, my prayer to remain in Africa was answered. In Kampala we called in at Makerere University to discuss these Koki lakes with Leonard Beadle, Professor of Zoology, and his colleague the botanist Robert Milburn, who later became a great support to the IBP team working on Lake George. Here I also met Professor Baker, Makerere`s new Professor of Geography, another old friend from Liverpool University.

Lakes George and Edward

The second safari of 1949 was primarily to Lake George. This had first been explored by Barton Worthington in 1932 but was closed to any fishery for many years under Sleeping Sickness Control regulations. It was here that TUFMAC under its Project Manager, the 'Dundas of Dundas' (a Scots title), was setting up a gillnet fishery to supply dried tilapia by road to mines and other centres. What were the prospects for this fishery? The equatorial Lake George (250 km² in area, less than 3 m deep) is connected via the Kazinga Channel with the much larger and deeper Lake Edward. This in turn drains northwards via the Semliki River, flowing west of the Ruwenzori Mountains of the Moon, into Lake Albert and thence to the Nile. As it was important to study the tilapia of these lakes at different times of year, further visits to Lake George were made in February and October 1950 and June 1952 (and again in 1967).

On that first visit to Lakes George and Edward (10–27 June 1949) we were accompanied by Alan Brook, an algologist from Khartoum University who was on honeymoon in Uganda with his geographer wife. The nearly 500 km journey from Jinja ended at Kichwamba Hotel perched high on the eastern escarpment of the Rift Valley. We arrived before sunset in time to see the vast panorama across the Rift Valley to the foothills of the 15,000+ feet high Ruwenzori mountains on the opposite side of the Kazinga Channel, their snow-capped peaks out-lined against the evening sky. What a view! Kichwamba was indeed what a long-lost book had called 'Halfway to Paradise'. Away to the north gleamed Lake George while

The retired E.A. Temple-Perkins at his home on the escarpment at Kichwamba in about 1968. He is talking to Dr Michael Lock, a botanist working in the Queen Elizabeth National Park.

far below us the Kazinga Channel flowed across the valley floor to Lake Edward which stretched away to the distant south. We were very fortunate to have this clear view. H.M. Stanley, when seeking the source of the River Nile in 1870, travelled around the cloud-covered Ruwenzoris for three months

Weighing fish at Katunguru on the Kazinga Channel en route to Lake George.

An aerial view of Lake George from above the eastern escarpment, in about 1969. The Kazinga Channel can be seen in the distance winding its way to the north end of Lake Edward. The TUFMAC factory was on the west shore opposite the gap between the islands.

The western (Congo) shore of Lake Edward provides a complete contrast between this large rift lake and Lake George. The eastern shore of Lake Edward slopes gently into the water but the depth increases greatly towards the western shore where the escarpment plunges straight down into the lake. (From S. & E.B. Worthington, 1933.)

without seeing their white peaks. The local Africans attributed these equatorial snows to salt, well known to them because they collected salt from the small crater Lake Katwe (near Lake Edward). Next morning on the grassy slopes far below the hotel, herds of elephants, thirty or forty at a time, wandered among the scattered acacia trees. No wonder a number of old Uganda residents, including the ex-Provincial Commissioner, E.A. Temple-Perkins (who had helped Barton Worthington prepare the *Development Plan for Uganda*) were building their retirement homes here. The Uganda Game and Fisheries Department also had a Game Ranger (Bill Pridham) and a Fishery Officer (van Ingen) living nearby, who helped us to sample tilapias in the local lakes.

It was always fun working with the Game Rangers as game was so abundant in this area. Later this became the Queen Elizabeth National Park (Uganda's first national park) with its headquarters on the Mweya peninsula raised between the Kazinga Channel and Lake Edward. One memorable incident was coming upon a group of giant forest hogs (*Hylochoerus meinertzhageni*), at that time uncommon in this area, noisily trying to ease an injured one out of a wallow. When they charged us Bill threw his hat on the ground which distracted them. Elephants and buffalos emerged from the thickets while hippos were very abundant in the Kazinga Channel and in Lake George. But there were no crocodiles; they had evidently been deterred from moving up the Semliki River by the Semliki Rapids alongside which the

The catch of a 5 inch gill net, mostly tilapia, from Lake George.
(From Worthington, 1932.)

river banks were clothed in thick forest. Many years later, after this forest had been cleared crocodiles appeared in Lake Edward and the Kazinga Channel.

On his pioneer explorations to this area in 1932 Worthington had suggested that tilapia might migrate from Lake Edward to swamps at the north end of Lake George to breed. TUFMAC wanted to know whether the Lake George populations were distinct from those of Lake Edward. Where did they all breed?

In February 1950 when I visited the TUFMAC base at Kasenyi on Lake George, I had to camp in my Ford V8 car parked near the lake shore, because Dundas did not allow women to stay in the TUFMAC quarters, although his staff kindly invited me to dinner. On a later visit, when sleeping in a tent by the lake, there was an earthquake at midnight with its epicentre nearby. The numerous hippos which were grazing around the tent, galumphed noisily back to the lake and the boys who were sleeping on the fisheries launch, reported the 'water boiled' as gases from the mud bubbled up around the boat.

We used experimental gillnets in both lakes and the Channel, and looked at lots of catches by local fishermen from traps and small seines. While setting our gillnets we slept on the Fisheries launch, in a local guesthouse, or crammed into a hut on a longer trip to Lake Edward. While I was guarding gillnets set overnight my wrist watch was swept overboard with the nets I was setting in Lake George.

Our samples showed that some tilapia were ripe at all times of year (peak spawning times varying from year to year) and were breeding in all three areas – no need for any migrations from Edward to George. We also found the tilapia populations in Lake George, as yet little exploited, included much larger fish than those in the fished areas of the Channel and Lake Edward. So it seemed that TUFMAC could consider the Lake George population as a separate entity.

On a later (1952) visit to Lake George with the Fisheries Department we tagged some tilapias. Again there was no evidence of movement from one lake to the other, and juvenile tilapia less than 12 cm long lived along the shore in Lake George as well as in the Channel and Lake Edward. Adults were more evenly distributed in the shallow open waters of Lake George, which were generally opaque with dense populations of algae.

The TUFMAC fishery

In pre-war years following a sleeping sickness epidemic, Lake George had been officially closed to fishing, although it was admitted that poaching occurred on an immense scale. In 1949 the Uganda Government decided to open the lake to commercial fishing as a controlled monopoly run by The Uganda Fish Marketing Corporation (TUFMAC). A depot was established at Kasenyi on the western shore of the lake, and fishermen were concentrated

Outside and inside the TUFMAC factory in 1951.
Clearly still under construction as can be seen from the left hand picture.

in five lakeside villages (Kasenyi, Kahendero (near Mohokya), Hamakunga, Kashaka and Muhyoro on the east coast) each to have ten Sesse canoes and dugouts with an issue of three five-inch mesh gillnets per canoe. Baganda fishermen were brought into the area to show the local people how to use gill nets. The aim was to land five tons of fresh fish, equivalent to about 5000 fish a day (mostly tilapia) to be processed into dried salted fish, which sold well in the Congo. The quantity of firewood that would be necessary prevented expansion of smoked fish production. In 1954, when the development of the nearby Kilembe copper mines brought aircraft to Kasese, frozen fillets were flown to Entebbe every week. In 1955 a fish meal plant was set up to convert fish scrap into cattle food.

An aerial view of the TUFMAC factory in 1972. (Photo JPEC Darlington.)

What became of this TUFMAC fishery? In the first year some three million tilapias averaging nearly 1 kg in weight were sold to TUFMAC, and many more fish were landed illegally. As the fishermen earned so much money they were in no hurry to earn more, so the total fishing effort never exceeded 70% of what was possible. Replacement of flax gillnets by nylon ones boosted catches, but the average size of tilapia declined. From 1959 the fishermen no longer had to sell through TUFMAC, and its management was transferred to a private company. Local fisheries also continued to remove large numbers from the Kazinga Channel and Lake Edward and many were undoubtedly poached from Lake George. How long would Lake George be able to maintain this fishing pressure? The 1950–59 Annual Reports of the Uganda Game & Fisheries Department showed an average catch of over 3 million tilapia a year (representing some 135 kg per hectare per year), together with 740,000 *Protopterus*, 420,000 *Bagrus,* and 200,000 *Clarias*. So Lake George was producing one of the highest yields per unit area recorded for any natural water body (estimates ranged from 9–14.7 tonnes per km^2 per year with tilapia catches fluctuating around 2,700 tonnes a year). At this time there was no decline in total catches but the size of the individual tilapia landed decreased considerably, from nearly 2lb (1.9 kg) in 1950 to 1.34 lb (0.35 kg) in 1957. The proportion of tilapia in the catch also decreased from 90% to about 30%. After fishing had reduced the population of the larger-sized tilapia, gillnets smaller than the legal 5-inch (127 mm) stretched mesh came into general use. In the 1970s there were transport difficulties which, together with the increased poaching, exacerbated the decline of this once very profitable fishery.

While teaching at Makerere University in 1967, I revisited Lake George to see the UK/Uganda International Biological Programme (IBP) team who were on a five year project to investigate production at all trophic levels in this equatorial lake. They found that the *O. niloticus* maturation and final sizes had been diminished by intensive fishing. In 1950, when the commercial fishing by TUFMAC started, 50% of the *O. niloticus* females were mature at 27 cm TL. By 1960 this had fallen to 24 cm and in 1972 it was 20 cm. Smaller females produce fewer eggs and can only mouth-brood small numbers of young, so no wonder the fishery declined after such heavy cropping. It was estimated that more than seven million *O. niloticus* had been removed from Lake George between February 1950 and June 1952. The accompanying tilapia species *(O. leucostictus)* also showed a decline in maturation size (to 14 cm TL) nine years after the fishery started, although, as a smaller species, it had not been as heavily fished as had the larger *O. niloticus.* The hippo population had also been much reduced (by culling and disease). This decline in catches added support to Bobby Beauchamp's warning that the removal of many large herbivores from the system would inevitably lead to a decline in the rate of production in such a tropical lake, although some other factors may have also been involved, such as availability of lake bottom areas suitable for tilapia breeding.

Estimates of production in different trophic levels in Lake George 1967–72		
Trophic level	kJ m⁻²y⁻¹	%
Net primary production	23200	100
Secondary production	650	3
Tertiary production	150	0.65
Yield	50	0.21
(From Burgis and Dunn 1978.)		

The IBP team working on Lake George from 1967–1972 found that 95% of the biomass in the lake water was composed of planktonic algae, mainly the blue-green (cyanobacterium) *Microcystis*. Contrary to earlier beliefs that the fish could not digest these algae, members of the team (Dave and Chris Moriarty) showed that they were digested, but in the intestines of the tilapia rather than in the stomach which was previously the only part of the gut examined. They also showed that the digestion occurred in a diurnal physiological cycle, after the tilapia stomach had changed pH in the late morning. Furthermore, the tilapia obtained most of their nourishment from

Lesley McGowan and Ian Dunn in the IBP lab during my visit in 1967.

Corrected units: $kJ\ m^{-2}y^{-1}$

these blue-green algae. This was an important discovery for fish culture, as our earlier stomach samples, generally using fish from gillnets set overnight, had given the misleading impression that tilapia were unable to utilise the blue-green algae found in their stomachs.

The IBP team found that in Lake George this algal production was cropped by three herbivorous species: *O. niloticus*, *Haplochromis nigripinnis* and the zooplankton crustacean *Thermocyclops hyalinus*. The piscivorous fishes comprised *Bagrus docmac*, *Clarias lazera*, *Polypterus senegalus* and *Haplochromis squamipinnis* (which took juvenile fish). The two herbivorous fish species formed over 60% of the total biomass in the open lake, the piscivorous fishes only about 20%. It was suggested that in Lake George tilapia numbers were limited by a shortage of suitable spawning places in this soft-bottomed lake. Did the numerous hippos have a role in creating suitable places by clearing away the bottom debris?

EAFRO had thought that in Lake George the very abundant hippos probably had a major role in the lake's apparently high productivity, scattering immense amounts of dung after their nightly forays to feed on grassy slopes. In this shallow lake hippos would keep the bottom deposits well stirred, releasing nutrients which were taken up rapidly by the blue-green algae. In September 1957 there was a very heavy mortality of fish in Lake George following a violent storm which was attributed to the stirring up of deoxygenated bottom deposits because it was followed by a heavy bloom of blue-green algae a day or two after the storm. In fact, the IBP team later showed that the contribution of hippos to the nutrients in the lake was relatively minor and the algal populations were maintained by internal recycling rather than hippo shit.

Nile tilapia in Uganda's smaller lakes

Crater lakes in Ankole and Toro were sampled when I had an inflatable rubber dingy from which to set gillnets. The nets brought a lot of very hungry leeches into the dingy, plus Nile tilapia but no bluegill sunfishes. The lakes fished included Lake Nkugute, with very clear water in which *O. niloticus* were in very poor condition. Their condition was also poor In Lake Niungu but the tilapia in Lake Katinda were in better condition (see data earlier in this chapter).

Nile tilapia were also examined from many other lakes and dams which had been stocked by the Uganda Fisheries Department over many years. In Lake Bunyoni these tilapia were atypical, suggesting hybridisation had occurred with other tilapia species introduced into the same lake. Lake Bunyoni had received *O. niloticus* from Lake Edward (in 1927, 1928, 1929) and '*T. nigra*' (= *O. niger*) from Lake Naivasha in Kenya (in 1932). Both species became established. In 1934 Captain Pitman noted that *O. niger* were generally caught in the central waters of Lake Bunyoni, *O. niloticus* round the edge. These species seem to have hybridised. The pure *niger* disappeared from Lake Bunyoni, and in 1944 *O. esculentus* from the Kabaka's lake in Kampala was introduced. In 1952 when I examined large numbers of tilapia from this lake no *O. niger* or *O. esculentus* were found; the tilapias here all resembled *O. niloticus*.

The distribution of *O. niloticus* within these lakes depended on the ecological conditions. In lakes turbid with blue-green algae, such as Kijanebalola, Chanagwora and Nakivali, the *O. niloticus* appeared to be fairly evenly distributed (as in Lake George). In the clear water lakes and dams with stands of aquatic plants, such as Kachira and Bunyoni, shoals of *O. niloticus* could be seen among the plants.

Lake Bunyoni fish were used to stock other waters. They were taken to Lake Saka in Toro in 1935, Kijanebalola, one of the Koki lakes, received fry from Lake Bunyoni in 1936 and a further stocking from Lake Saka in 1939. Fry from Bunyoni were also used to stock other lakes in Kigezi and from thence were taken to lakes and dams in Ruanda-Urundi (now Rwanda and Burundi). Hence many of the '*nilotica*' introduced into other waters were probably not pure *O. niloticus*. I also found suspected hybrids in Lake Nkugute, a crater lake in Ankole, where in February 1944 *O. esculentus* from the Kabaka's lake had been introduced. Some of the *O. niloticus* stocked into Lake Victoria in the mid 1950s, which grew very large and became the main tilapia in that lake's commercial fisheries, may also have hybridised with *esculentus*, which then disappeared from the commercial catches in this lake. *O. niloticus* is a tough species, able to coexist with predators such as Nile perch, with which it has evolved, and to thrive on varied diets (in Victoria eating many invertebrates). In Madagascar it took over from *O. niger* in lakes where they were both introduced, and it is now found in fish ponds throughout the tropics, in pure or hybridised form (see chapter 10).

The *Lates* lakes: Nile tilapia cohabiting with large piscivores

Visits were made to Lake Albert in November 1949, March 1950, and June 1952. There, in addition to *Oreochromis niloticus* we also found the smaller tilapia *O. leucostictus*, previously only known from Lake Edward, and another two nilotic tilapia species, *Sarotherodon galilaeus* and *Tilapia zillii*.

The tilapias found in Lake Albert, into which Lake Edward drains via the Semliki River, and also in Lake Rudolf in Kenya, were particularly interesting for two reasons. First, in these two lakes the tilapias occurred alongside large piscivores, Nile perch (*Lates*) and tiger fish (*Hydrocynus*), which are absent from the other lakes. How did the tilapia manage to coexist with these predators? This problem became of even greater interest after both Nile perch and Nile tilapia (*O. niloticus*) were introduced into Lakes Victoria and Kyoga in the mid 1950s, events followed by radical changes to the other fauna in

*A typical Nile perch (*Lates niloticus*) weighing 31 kg from Lake Albert in 1928. The record for this species exceeds 100 kg. The fisherman in the white hat, Pangrasio, later initiated the first commercial fishery on Lake Turkana in 1934. (Photo from Worthington 1929.)*

these lakes. Secondly, in both lakes Albert and Rudolf, Worthington had discovered populations of dwarf *niloticus* living in confined areas, in lagoons alongside Lake Albert and in the crater lakes of Central Island in Lake Rudolf. Would these fish grow large under different conditions? This aspect was very important as 'dwarfing' in tilapias was a problem of great concern to fish culturists growing tilapia in ponds in many parts of the tropics. We needed to know what 'switched' tilapia from growth to reproduction.

Lake Albert

The 100 mile long Lake Albert, its waters shared with the then Belgian Congo, receives the Semliki River at its southern end and the Victoria Nile in the northeast, very near to its northern outflow into the Albert Nile. The western, Congo shore is mostly very steep, but most of the eastern, Uganda side is flat land, on which Uganda kobs (*Kobus kob*) sparred on their lekking arenas. This coast of the lake had prominent sand spits behind which lay shallow lagoons (at Kaiso, Buhuku and Tonya), which were well described and figured in Worthingon's 1929 report.

After the turbid waters of Lake Victoria with its numerous very similar and difficult-to-identify haplochromine species, it was a delight to come to a lake with clearer waters, long sandy beaches and quite different fish. This fish fauna was dominated by large nilotic species which had failed to gain

The Kazinga Channel (above) flows about 30 km from Lake George to Lake Edward (out to the right). Both photographs were taken from the Mweya Peninsula which separates the mouth of the Channel from Lake Edward which can just be seen to the left in the right-hand photograph.

The north end of Lake Edward near Katwe in 1970: the lower part of the Mweya Peninsula is in the middle distance with the Congo escarpment on the horizon.

In 1962 the docks at Butiaba, on the East shore of
Lake Albert were flooded by very high lake levels.

Above: the River Nile just below Murchison
Falls, on its way down to the North end of Lake
Albert. Left: hauling in the nets out on Lake
Albert. All the photographs on this page were
taken by Jim Green in September 1962.

Tonya, a village about half way along the eastern shore of Lake Albert with the
escarpment towering behind but quite a shallow shoreline at this point.

access to lakes Kyoga and Victoria above the Murchison Falls on the Victoria Nile, or to lakes Edward and George above the Semliki rapids. These included the large piscivorous Nile perch, tiger fish, and cyprinids *Labeo*, large moon-shaped *Citharinus* ('mpoi'), *Distichodus* and large species of *Alestes* and other characoid fishes. Large distinctive catfishes such as *Auchenoglanis* were also present along with a number of mormyrids and many other species with a wide distribution from the Niger to the Nile, but which were not found in the other East African lakes except Lake Rudolf. Only a few exceptions, all air-breathers (such as the ancient fish *Polypterus senegalensis*), had gained access to Lakes Victoria, George and Edward.

In Lake Albert most fishes were caught in shore seines fished from the sandy beaches. We did some experimental gillnetting in lagoons and inshore waters where the tilapia were mostly living, as well using a small mesh seine, but crocodile damage was too great for gillnets to be used as a commercial way of fishing. The large piscivores, Nile perch and tigerfish, both good 'sport fish', were caught on hooks.

At the top of Murchison Falls where the Victoria Nile surges through a channel so narrow that a good (but foolhardy!) athlete could almost jump across it. The Falls were discovered by Baker and his wife in 1889 when they were searching for the origins of the Nile. A few kilometers further downstream the river enters the north-east corner of Lake Albert before heading north down the Albert Nile to Sudan.

*A group of elephants on the shore of Lake Albert at a point
where the Rift escarpment descends steeply into the lake, about 1950.*

*Looking down from the escarpment to Kaiso Spit on the east shore of Lake Albert.
Here a narrow sand bar has been built up by wind and waves to form a lagoon
separated from the main lake. The steep west shore is only faintly visible under the
clouds. (Photo E.B. Worthington 1931.)*

My first visit to Lake Albert (7–11 November 1949) followed a trip by launch with the Osmastons, and other friends from Jinja, to see the magnificent Murchison Falls. Below the falls, ringed with rainbows in the spray, huge numbers of crocodiles lie on the sandy banks of the river. This was a great place to see many varieties of game – rhino, buffalo, herds of elephants, water buck, numerous hippos and crocodiles and it is now within the Murchison Falls National Park. Sleeping on the open deck of the launch in the light of a full moon made it a magical trip. Just after our visit the railway launch was hired for the making of the famous Humphrey Bogart and Katherine Hepburn film 'The African Queen' (supposedly taking place in the Congo), but the stand-in actors making this part of the film all got dysentery and probably considered the place less magical that I had done.

On this first visit to Lake Albert the principal aims were to compare breeding sizes of *O. niloticus* in the main lake with those in the lagoons visited by Worthington on his 1932 expedition. The intent was also to find out as much as possible about the habits of the three tilapia species in this lake: namely the other nilotic species *Sarotherodon galilaeus* and *Tilapia zillii*, but also *O. leucostictus*, previously only known from Lake Edward. How did they share habitats? I also had to collect fish peculiar to Lake Albert for the EAFRO reference collection, learning the local names for a whole new fish fauna. The lake was noted for violent storms; was this the trip when my tent in Butiaba blew away in a sudden wind, so strong that my Ford V8 was just missed by an empty 60 gallon oil drum flying across the road, and my clothes were scattered among nearby trees?

Stephenson ('Stevie') who had been on both the Graham survey of Lake Victoria and with Barton Worthington on the 1929 Lake Albert survey, and was then stationed at the Butiaba Marine, took me sailing on the lake. With the Uganda Fishery Officer 'Bart', C.F. Bartholomew, we seined small fishes from Butiaba harbour and lagoon and used a fleet of experimental gillnets around Butiaba. With a local resident one evening we landed a five foot long 95 lb Nile perch ('mputa'), 40 inches in girth with luminescent red gold eyes, from Butiaba`s sandy spit. Bart hooked another 40 inch 24.5 lb 'mputa' just off the reeds. They reported that all the big ones were female and mputa young were seen from January to March. In the shallows swam shoals of small tilapia, their sizes varying according to depth, and these shallows boiled with activity as small tigerfish chased them in the light of the full moon. In the lagoon our small seine caught numerous 10-16 cm juvenile tilapia of three species, *niloticus*, *galilaeus* and *leucostictus*, also one *Haplochromis* and a small 12 cm *Lates* already with luminous red-gold eyes. The *O. leucostictus* were said to spawn in the reeds. *Sarotherodon galilaeus* were said to nest in the shallows and a ripening female we caught had green eggs in the ovary, and also carried parasitic *Argulus* fish lice. The *T. zillii* we caught also had green eggs (distinguishing them from

T. rendalli, much used in Congo ponds which has yellow eggs). We returned to Jinja with many samples and specimens on 12 November 1949.

In March 1950 (immediately after a Lake George safari) I returned to Lake Albert for a longer visit with 'Bart'. He was a delightful character, son of the creator of Bartholomew`s World Atlas who had introduced contour colouring on to maps. With his brother he had continued working with the atlas until they agreed that one brother was enough in the firm, so he applied to be a Fisheries Officer in Uganda. The much younger Don Rhodes, who had come to train as a Fisheries Officer, was also with us. Together we visited the lagoons along the east coast, camping on the long hooked sand spits near the Tonya and Buhuku lagoons, which had both been visited by Barton Worthington on his 1929 survey. At Bukuku we shared the spit with a nesting large leather-backed `turtle`, really the water-tortoise (*Trionix nilotica*). This is another nilotic species not found in Lake Victoria, although *Trionix* fossils were common in the paleolake Kurungu which preceeded Lake Victoria. There was also a crocodile nest, from which the twelve inch long young crocs squeaked as they hatched out by our tents. Meanwhile an adult crocodile was making noises nearby, but we did not then know the mother's habit of assisting the young by carrying them from nest to water in her mouth.

Returning to Butiaba we then travelled north along the east coast of the lake to Dadami Point where a rich African had a fishery using large seine nets, and had lots of local information about the habits of the fishes. In the main lake the tilapias (mostly *O. niloticus*, but with some *O. galilaeus* and *T. zillii*) frequented inshore waters until large enough to avoid predation by Nile perch and tiger fish (as Worthington had suggested). On this March visit the lake level was low and the lagoons were very shallow with extremely alkaline water. At Buhuku lagoon (ph 9.2, conductivity 7,200 µS) the shore was strewn with dead dwarf *O. niloticus*. The small seine look over 700 semi-moribund ones, many of their eyes opaque. The females had degenerate ovaries, though the larger (14 cm TL) males showed characteristic *O. niloticus* breeding colours. Tonya lagoon was also very alkaline, but there was a small channel connecting it to the main lake through which dwarf tilapia were leaving, and fishermen were catching them in thousands in small seine nets at the lagoon entrance. The *O. niloticus* in these lagoons, though small, were mature (females considerably smaller than the males and containing large but few ova). In the main lake *O. niloticus* up to 45 cm TL were speared at night by local fishermen.

In Lake Albert (and in Lake Rudolf) the *O. niloticus* had much stouter spines than those in Lake Edward, which lacked the piscivorous fishes, probably reflecting greater predation pressure. But Trewavas still considered the Albert and Edward *O. niloticus* belonged to the same subspecies, called *O. n. eduardianus,* whereas the Rudolf one she named subspecies *O. n. vulcani,* after

Tilapia nilotica *from the main Lake Albert (top) and from one of the lagoons (bottom) showing the huge difference in body size at maturation.*

Largest total lengths and maturation sizes of T. nilotica (now O. niloticus) in Lake Albert in 1950

	Largest TL	Mature length
main lake	>40 cm	28 cm
lagoons	26 cm	12 cm Males
		14 cm Females

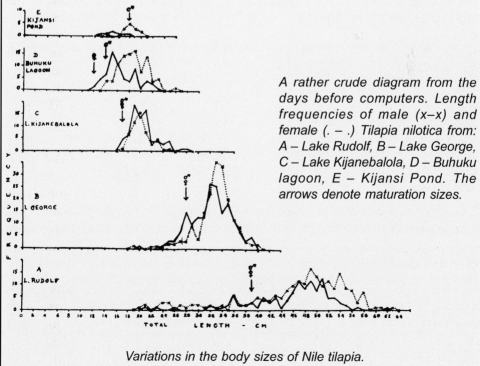

A rather crude diagram from the days before computers. Length frequencies of male (x–x) and female (. – .) Tilapia nilotica from: A – Lake Rudolf, B – Lake George, C – Lake Kijanebalola, D – Buhuku lagoon, E – Kijansi Pond. The arrows denote maturation sizes.

Variations in the body sizes of Nile tilapia.

the small '*Tilapia vulcani*' which Worthington had collected from the crater lakes on Rudolf`'s Central Island, but which were later considered to be 'hunger forms' of those in the main lake.

Lake Albert was visited again in June 1952, but on this occasion with Roy Wyndham. The purpose was to visit the Semliki delta at the south end of the lake, where a fishery for the large characid *Citharinus* ('mpoi') appeared to be in decline. We called in at Tonya and Buhuku lagoons en route and, as the lake was much higher, the lagoons were flooded. We had stayed with the Wyndhams en route to Lake Albert to prepare for the safari but as Roy's departure was unexpectedly delayed, we went ahead to camp on the remote Semliki delta. When Roy arrived he was horrified to be greeted by an ornate silver fruit dish – a treasured family heirloom – in which his cook, instructed to 'pack everything on the table', had brought three oranges. ('My wife will have contacted the police'). So we camped in style!

From here we visited the Belgian fishery officer at Kisenyi, as the Belgians fished the western half of the Semliki delta. Discussions were held on the possibility of making two reserves here, or whether to have a closed season for fishing because the *Citharinus* ('mpoi') were becoming scarce. These fish were said to have a defined breeding season, reputedly in October–November at the north end of the lake, Here, according to Fishery Officer Gardett, huge catches of *Citharinus* were once caught in large seine nets near Butiaba, operated by two Greek fishermen on contract to TUFMAC, but now the stock was apparently fished out.

On this trip we were also accompanied by Hugh Cott from Cambridge University who was visiting EAFRO to study the numerous crocodiles and fish eating birds. He had found that the diet of crocodiles changed as they grew. Those less than a metre long consumed mainly insects and spiders, with molluscs and amphibians. Vertebrates then become increasingly important, beginning with fishes. Those crocodiles longer than 4–5 m contained more reptiles and mammals. Crocodile stomachs always contained stones which he showed seemed to be eaten deliberately as ballast, not as an aid to digestion.

Dr Cott also collected data on the food of the more important fish-eating birds, particularly cormorants and darters which were numerous and widely distributed. The larger cormorant (*Phalacocorax carbo*) tended to fish in more open waters with well developed diurnal flight-lines. This species was rare on Lake Albert and the Semliki River in June but very abundant on Lake Victoria. The smaller *P. africanus* and the darter *Anhinga rufa* fed close inshore, mostly on different *Haplochromis* species. In Lake George the two species of pelican (the rosy pelican *P. rufescens* and large white *P. onocrotalus*) both fed largely on tilapia. Among the several species of heron only the goliath heron (*Ardea goliath*) and purple heron (*A. purpurea*) appeared to feed exclusively on fish, including tilapia.

Hugh Cott measuring a young crocodile.

Pied kingfishers were very common, diving into the shallows of Lake Victoria, where they took many small pelagic cyprinids (*Rastrineobola*).

What fish did the predatory *Lates* eat? Mike Gee who joined EAFFRO later collated information on differences in their diet in lakes Albert and Rudolf, compared with those from Lakes Victoria and Kyoga where Nile perch had been introduced in the mid 1950s. In Albert mormyrids were important prey but juvenile *Lates* ate a wide range of species including prawns (*Caridina*) and Odonata nymphs. Very large ones ate more of the smaller fish rather than choosing large fish. Prey fish, including tilapia, lived inshore near cover until large enough to avoid being eaten by the *Lates*, when they were found offshore.

O. niloticus populations were also examined from many other Uganda lakes and dams where they had been introduced in the 1940/1950s. In some of these the fish grew very large while populations were small but then multiplied rapidly and became dwarfed. In other lakes *O. niloticus* apparently never grew large, which may have been related to a paucity of good quality food. In 1973 Iles took the view that 'stunting' is best summarised as 'the population stunted and the pond became overcrowded' rather than the prevailing view that 'the pond became overcrowded and the population then stunted'. The data we collected on *O. niloticus* from these lakes brought out great variation in maturation and final sizes. *O. niloticus* from large lakes matured at, and attained, a much larger size than those from the lagoons, the largest being from Lake Rudolf, whereas in L. Albert, although they grew to over 40 cm in the main lake, in the lagoons they only grew to 26 cm. In the lakes the males and females did not differ much in maturation or final size, but in smaller water bodies, where fish were dwarfed, males were much larger, and more numerous, than females. In a series of lakes, *O. niloticus* in poor condition (low weight for length) matured at a smaller size than did those in good condition. The growth and maturation rates were not known, but in some newly stocked waters *O. niloticus* grew to 35 gm (equivalent to c 26cm TL) and started to breed when seven or eight months old. In equatorial waters *O. niloticus* could be found in breeding condition at any time of the year, but peak spawning coincided with the rainy season. At higher latitudes this species breeds mainly in the rainy season. Dwarf *O. niloticus* from the lagoons were heavily parasitized.

Many other species of tilapia also show this variable growth rate. Tilapias probably evolved in lagoons alongside rivers. These shrink very much in the dry season and are then heavily fished by birds and other predators. This dwarfing strategy means that tilapia can repopulate a lake very rapidly and grow large when floods come (as was shown in the case of Lake Chilwa in Malawi). The Sagana fish pond experiments in Kenya with *O. niger* (see Chapter 5) also showed that 'dwarf fish' continued to grow to a large size if moved into a pond with more space. Later analyses of the plasticity in size and age at which *O. niloticus* matured, in eight man-made lakes in the Ivory Coast, indicated that the range of variation in age at maturity between populations was greater than that of size at maturity. Faster growing fish matured earlier. Stunted tilapia are precocious breeders, they can mature in three months compared with 2–4 years in lake populations. How do they do this?

In 1984 Pauly took the view that there is no sudden 'switch', pointing out that diminishing oxygen supply per unit of body weight serves in growing fish as a master factor in inducing the transition from juvenile to adult. Any stress factors (such as high temperatures, crowding, osmotic costs) which raise the maintenance metabolism would then result in a reduced final size of the fish. The Lake Albert lagoon fish were certainly very stressed; in the main lake where *O. niloticus* grew to 42 cm TL, maturing at 28 cm, the fish were in very good condition. By contrast, in the four alkaline lagoons they were certainly in very poor condition (low weight for length, heavily parasitized, some blinded and moribund) and the females were maturing at 12 cm, males at 14 cm.

Lake Rudolf (Turkana)

Lake Rudolf, now called Lake Turkana, is an inland drainage basin, with no outlet, which was formerly connected to the Nile system. It has a relict nilotic fish fauna, sharing with Lake Albert the tilapias *O. niloticus*, *S. galilaeus* and *T. zillii* (but not *O. leucostictus*) and many of the large fish species, including the piscivorous *Lates* and *Hydrocynus*. Would tilapia here live in the same way as they did in Lake Albert?

A Turkana fisherman waits with his spear and trap on the shore of Lake Rudolf (above) in 1953. Others use beach seine nets as on the right.

Turkana men rowing us on Lake Rudolf to do our sampling – 1953.

Further afield – to Kenya and Tanzania.

*The snow capped summit of Mount Kilimanjaro towers above the
surrounding savannah to a height of 19740 feet above sea level
– the highest mountain in Africa.*

*The Kenya coast at Jardini. The line of surf in the distance marks the reef.
After climbing Kilimanjaro Peggy and I went to the coast for a holiday before
going on to visit the fish pond projects on the Pangani River system.*

I did not get to Lake Rudolf, which is in northern Kenya, until January 1953, after spending Christmas with the Worthington family at their home near Nairobi. On New Years Day I drove, with Paulo (as factotum) and Bob Ross, algologist from the British Museum (Natural History), to Kitale en route to Lake Rudolf. The Mau Mau emergency was in full swing, but it was a beautiful drive, passing zebras by Lake Naivasha and giraffe by Eldoret. We lunched at Mau Summit at the old house, with its lovely garden belonging to Bob and Eva Veasey, pioneers who had lived there since the early 1920s. We then moved on to stay overnight with Bob's old friends the Jacksons who lived on a coffee plantation near Kitale, on the slopes of Mount Elgon. In Kitale we had to get a permit from the DC and the Police to enter the Northwest Frontier District (where the Jomo Kenyatta trial was in progress at Lodwa), and Bob had to have a tooth out.

At that time the Northern Frontier District of Kenya (NFD) was still being raided from the north and visiting women were not encouraged. I was only permitted to enter the district because the ex-District Officer Lodwa, Denis McKay, now managing a fishery on the west shore of Lake Rudolf, had his wife Susan living there. The drive to Lodwa was rough (a notice on the escarpment read 'private burial ground for careless motorists') but we had splendid wide views of the huge mountain mass of Debasien, with other blue, knife-edged hills, groups of camels and Grants gazelles. One dry sand river we crossed had a rope tied to a tree which we later heard was there to mark where a government lorry had been washed down and buried in a flash flood. The District Officer said he had been instructed to 'put a guard on it', but only the end of the rope was visible!

It was dark when we reached Lodwa resthouse, where we dined with the District Officer Lowdell. Morning revealed black lava hills, sand, and groups of guarded mau mau prisoners. Here we had to await an escort lorry which was having its main spring replaced. The drive was across the Turkana desert, with its red gravel hills and blue sky. There were a few sand rivers with doum palms, and near the lake we were greeted by a soda smell and water birds. Finally, reaching Ferguson's Gulf we camped with Susan and Denis McKay who had set up the fishery here. We slept on the beach and next day we met Pangrasio, who had been a fisheries assistant on both the 1927–28 Fishery Survey of Lake Victoria, led by Graham, and the 1929 survey of Lake Albert led by Worthington. He was now stationed on Lake Rudolf supervising a tilapia seine fishery in Ferguson's Gulf for the Kenya Fishery Department. It was very hot and we were glad to bathe in the lake.

Crocodiles were much in evidence. Hugh Cott had shown me how the juveniles lie with their head on a sandy beach at dusk to catch insects and spiders so I found it easy to demonstrate this by picking up a small one. But when Denis poked it, its sharp little teeth caught his finger. It would not let go, and in my efforts to free his finger I too was trapped. This most romantic situation, with two of us pinned together by one crocodile was only solved by his wife Susan prising open its small jaws with a large carving knife.

The local method of fishing was to put a large basket over each of the many large tilapia (*O. niloticus*) 'nests' or spawning plaques that could be seen in the sand through the shallow water. The guarding male fish was then removed through a hole in the top of the basket. We spent six days here fishing and exploring the main lake by motor launch. The *O. niloticus* were the largest we had seen from any lake. The seine regularly brought in over a hundred, each more than 4.5 kg in weight, whereas in Lake Albert only a few up to 2 kg had been seen, and in Lakes George and Edward none larger than 1.5 kg. In Rudolf they were feeding on diatoms and here in the Gulf they were also digesting blue-green algae and were in very good condition.

In Lake Rudolf the tilapias appeared to be most abundant in shallow waters near the western shore, especially in the sheltered Ferguson's Gulf, and near the calmer eastern shore of this very windy lake. An inshore distribution was thought by Worthington to be due to the abundance of large predatory fish offshore. We were not able to visit Central Island where Worthington had found dwarf *Tilapia nilotica* in the crater lakes, and numerous nesting crocodiles.

When we left the lake we followed Mackay's truck to Lodwa through a mirage, and went on to stay at Moroto Resthouse. The Karamajong villages of thatched mud huts were very picturesque. The tall men were naked except for a dramatic head dress, while the ostrich denuded of its feathers to make them stalked the village. When we scrambled up an exfoliated granite hill by the roadside we found a small rain pool full of lively crustaceans (*Chirocephalus*) making the most of their short lives in order to produce drought-resistant resting eggs before the pool dried up. On the way to Mbale resthouse, where we stayed on our way back to Jinja, while aboard the Lake Salisbury ferry in the swamps, we met a whale-headed stork (*Balaeniceps rex*) the first I had ever seen, an exciting encounter.

Some years later (1972–75) when a team of biologists from the UK, directed by Tony Hopson, studied the biology of Lake Rudolf's fishes, it became clear that Ferguson's Gulf was like a fishpond within the lake, producing phenomenal catches of tilapia from this small area in certain years, depending on the lake level. When we were there in January 1953 the lake was fairly high, with cattle grazing on rushes growing in the lake as there was so little to eat in the surrounding desert country. These cattle fertilised the gulf water. A Lake Rudolf fishery was developed but failed, as explained when Jeppe Kolding from the University of Bergen made a special study of 'Lake Turkana, an ever-changing mixed environment'. It seems that fish production here is governed by water levels in this lake which has riverine traits but no outflow from the system.

A Turkana fisherman with his traditional trap which he held over tilapia nests on the shore of Lake Rudolf in order to lift out the male tilapia.

In 1953 we had found large tilapia from the main lake reaching 39 cm TL before becoming sexually mature but Hopson later found some maturing at a smaller size, and Jeppe Kolding found that the median size at maturity had decreased by 13 cm over 30 years (to 26 cm in 1982). In the crater lakes they matured at 10–12 cm, and brooding females less than 93 mm SL were taken from hot springs near the lake.

The Hopson survey distinguished four main fish communities, all much affected seasonally by the August to October inflow of the Omo River from the north, bringing in nutrients, and by long-term fluctuations in lake level. Most of the large characoid and catfish species migrated north to the Omo delta to spawn in the flood season. Both *Lates* species spawned offshore in the open lake. The littoral zone (0–4 m deep) was dominated by tilapias which spawned there, with *O. niloticus* on sandy, *O. galilaeus* on softer and *T. zillii* on harder bottoms. *Clarias*, *Lates* and *Raiamas* (*syn Barilius*) were the dominant piscivores. An inshore demersal zone (4–15 m deep) was inhabited by soft deposit feeders, *Labeo*, *Citharinus*, *Distichodus*, with the piscivorous *Bagrus docmac*. In the offshore demersal zone (8–20 m deep according to season) lived *Barbus turkanae* and *Bagrus bayad*. The epipelagic zone had small zooplanktivorous species pursued by *Hydrocynus forskalii*, *Lates longispinus* and *Schilbe uranoscopus*. But at night the communities were not so distinct as some species moved inshore and towards the surface.

The tilapias played an important role in Lake Turkana's ecosystem and were apparently the main prey of crocodiles, pelicans and *Lates niloticus*. Ferguson's Gulf had large flocks of pelicans and consumption rates of 0.3 to 3 tonnes of fish a year per pelican have been estimated from other lakes. Consumption by *Lates niloticus* in Turkana was estimated as 10,000–14,000 tonnes of tilapia per year.

The abundance of *O. niloticus* followed the fluctuations in lake level. In certain years they were able to proliferate enormously in shallow sheltered areas. For example in 1976 Ferguson's Gulf yielded a staggering 16,000 tonnes from an area about 10 km^2 (Kolding 1993). Smaller 'booms' occurred in 1963, 1970 and 1982, but in years of low lake level Ferguson's Gulf dried out. On re-flooding, as the lake level rose, dried dung from cattle feeding on the lake shores added nutrients to those from the large bird populations, and the Gulf produced large blooms of nitrogen-fixing cyanobacteria (*Microcystis*) not found in the open lake. Chlorophyll concentration was then three orders of magnitude higher in the Gulf than in the main lake.

There was no evidence of breeding seasonality in *O. niloticus* but in the Gulf numbers rose to a peak during the flood season (August to November) when inundated grassy areas on the lake margins provided food and shelter for the fish fry. Seasonal variations in the fry survival rate appeared to be the main factor affecting tilapia numbers. As food production did not appear to limit the Gulf population Kolding thought that predation pressures on the early stages probably did. He pointed out that predator pressures differed in the Gulf from those in the main lake. In the Gulf intense predation by pelicans, crocodiles and man took mostly large specimens, but there were few fish predators as their access was restricted by the oxygen conditions. As the lake level fell, progressively more adverse conditions in the shallows forced the tilapia into the deeper main lake where waiting predatory fish cropped the smallest individuals most heavily, so selection then favoured the large sizes. Maturation sizes of *O. niloticus* were smaller in the Gulf (though food was plentiful), which Kolding suggested was a direct effect of reduced or fluctuating oxygen conditions. He concluded that the observed phenotypic plasticity of *O. niloticus* in Lake Turkana was closely related to the fluctuating environment and changes in mortality pressures, which resembles conditions in floodplains where this species probably evolved.

Chapter 5
Further afield

After visiting the Sesse Islands with the Lake Victoria Fisheries Service, on Christmas Eve 1950 Peggy Brown and I embarked on a long 'local leave' cum working visit to Kenya and the Pangani River system.

The 300 mile drive from Jinja to Nairobi was a dramatic start during which the radiator of my old Ford V8 boiled all the way, throwing hot water over the windscreen (and Peggy). We were saved by the 14 gallon milk churn, that we had with us for Pangani fish specimens, which we were able to fill up with water when we crossed the Nzoia River and then replenish the radiator at twenty minute intervals. These long car journeys, on very corrugated roads that smothered everything with lateritic red dust, were always rather precarious. Was it on this Nairobi journey (or a previous one?) that a nun had suddenly emerged from behind a hedge and asked us for a 'short lift'? We could not refuse, but then she produced a second nun to the detriment of my car's special pump-up shock absorbers. While I was lying in the road under the car to fix them, an inquisitive hen which came pecking around was squashed by a passing car, its air-filled bones popping alongside my ear. It might have been my head that popped! Quite a shattering experience. Peggy remembers that our only puncture on this trip was on the one bit of tarmac – near Nairobi. We were in disgrace for arriving too late for Stella Worthington's carol concert at their home in Kikuyu. But next day we attended Xmas service as part of the crowded congregation in Nairobi cathedral.

Then we drove on to visit the well-known Kenya pioneer Colonel Ewart S. Grogan at his home in Taveta, where we stayed from 27–29th December, to see tilapia in Lake Jipe and his fish ponds. We were invited to visit him again

Peggy with our good friend Swirrel and our car – my Ford V8.

Filling cans in the Nzoia River to top up the car radiator on the way to Nairobi.

in January to see Lake Chala and to measure all the fishes from one of his ponds, but first we spent New Year (1951) climbing to the top of Mount Kilimanjaro and then went down to the Kenya coast.

Climbing Kilimanjaro

To climb Kilimanjaro, the highest mountain in Africa, Peggy and I drove to the Marungu Hotel in Moshi where we were joined by two friends from Uganda: David Gillett, a medical entomologist from the Virus Research Laboratory in Entebbe, and Charles Kindersley a consulting engineer helping to build the Owen Falls hydroelectric dam across the Nile at Jinja. Next day (30 December) with a local African guide (Kamatari) and porters to accompany us we set off up the mountain. First we climbed up through banana gardens to the sound of cow bells on the native cattle and with African totos running alongside us, one with a catapult. In the distance gleamed Lake Jipe. We crossed several streams and met women, each with a short sickle, coming down the mountain loaded with bundles of grass. Outside their square huts, thatched with banana leaves, other women were hulling coffee beans, red juices oozing from the hulls. Then the lovely smell of pine forest, and further up we met tree heathers and giant St John's Wort (but unlike Mount Elgon, Kilimanjaro has no well defined bamboo zone), and many other wild flowers including African violets, red hot pokers, ground orchids and everlasting flowers, *Helichrysum*.

It took us five hours to reach Bismark hut around late afternoon, where we stayed the first night. At 9,500 feet this hut was backed by forest trees coated in lichens, mosses and ferns, though the country was very much drier than on Ruwenzori where I had climbed the previous year. There were no streams (or perhaps they were hidden in the undergrowth?) and we were accompanied by the clack clack of tree-heather branches. To the bewilderment and amusement of the porters, we distinguished ourselves, at the behest of entomologist David, by going into the forest at dusk, climbing up a large tree and sitting there with glass tubes to catch whatever species of mosquito would be biting the resident monkeys. The brave men were first to ascend the tree. Peggy and I followed, but this meant we had to be the first to climb down, when it was by then pitch dark. The world below awaited us with its weird animal noises (of bush babies?) and whatever lurked beneath us in this elephant-frequented forest.

Next day we climbed on to stay at Peters Hut (12,500 feet), first through forest then suddenly open grassland with golden everlasting flowers, their grey woolly leaves a protection against the cold nights and dry winds. We had good views of Mwenzi, Kilimanjaro's smaller peak, and glimpses of our objective, Kibo the highest peak. Purple and yellow flowers predominated, with broom-like bushes, proteas and, near the hut, a giant groundsel. A small stream flowed through a carpet of blue lobelias in the wet patches, and veronica-like bush heather. We did need a botanist with us! But we also met lizards and a chameleon, and two Walt Disney character grasshoppers, and were visited by a white-collared raven. Turning over stones in the stream (a limnologist's must) revealed small black planarian worms, mayfly nymphs, and other larvae. It was a starry night, the peaks clear.

We left Peters Hut around 9.15 am and took nearly three hours to reach the top of the saddle. Kibo was in cloud most of the day, although the end of the Razel glacier was visible. Vegetation faded out; the eland reported to live

Ro sitting at Gilman's Point on Kilimanjaro.

here were nowhere to be seen and on the increasingly bare lava plain the dust was blown into ripples like sea sand. Around 3 pm we reached Kibo Hut near the bottom of the cone scree at 16,000 feet, where all water and fuel needed to be brought up from below by the porters. We left there at 0215, to toil up the 3000 feet of scree (a two steps forward, one slip back climb) to reach Gilman's Point at 0845. There was no sign of the dead leopard, embalmed by cold, reported near here by previous expeditions. Around ten o'clock we left for the summit (19,740 feet asl) which we reached at midday by walking round the rim of the volcano, on snow and with a wall of ice on the outer slopes. It was clear on top with sun gleaming on marvellous far views of the plains below. On the way down I found I had become slightly snow blind but we managed the descent, back to Gilman's Point by 1400, then downhill via Kibo to Bismark hut by 15.15, from where we arrived back at the Marungu Hotel as darkness fell.

Forty years later Peggy and I, when flying to Madagascar, passed over Kilimanjaro's summit. We two old ladies were leaping about in the plane to the surprise of fellow passengers, saying excitedly 'look where we stood forty years ago, on the very top !' From the aircraft we had a good view of how much the snow had retreated and the glacier had shrunk (as has happened on Ruwenzori too), and now, in 2006, the snow and ice have almost vanished from much of Kilimanjaro's crown.

After climbing Kilimanjaro we descended to sea level and the next day drove to the Indian Ocean coast of Kenya, wondering why we could not keep awake. We were going to stay with the Worthington family again, this time at Diani Beach where they shared a beach house. From there we would go to the Kenya Government Fishery Department house at Shimoni, where we were introduced to the delights of goggling to see coral reef fishes. This introduction to coral, first in the lagoon and on the outer reef at Diani beach and then further south down the coast, was eye-opening to a freshwater biologist. There was a marked tide, and our Ugandan house boy Kalimenti, who had never seen the sea before, was very alarmed that if the sea came so far up the beach one day, why not much further the next time and drown us all? We were warned of other dangers, including the many spectacular poisonous lion fish (*Pterois*) which lurked under reef overhangs in the lagoon, also the very abundant long-spined *Diadema* sea urchins which frequent these East African reefs. To this day I bear a coral scar on my leg, in response to what I did when instructed by the children who said firmly when producing a small bottle of fluid 'Mummy says we must always put this on a coral cut'. Ever obedient, I did so before they added 'Oh dear, that's a decomposing starfish!' But the colours of fish and sea, the palm shadowed beaches, sights, sounds, and smells, were so unbelievably marvellous that in later life whenever I could I escaped to snorkel on coral reefs in many parts of the world.

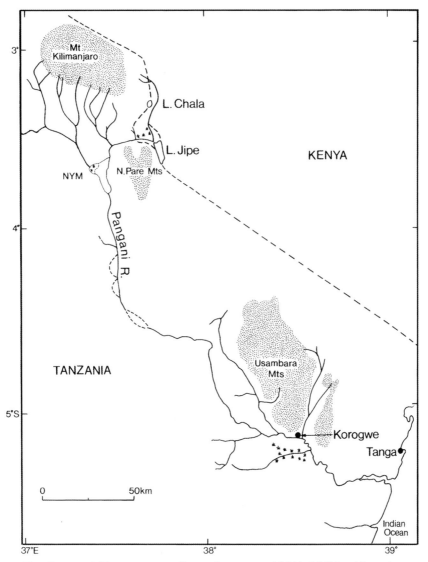

The Pangani River system (from Trewavas 1983). NYM = Nyumba ya Mungu, Tanzania's largest man-made lake, formed in 1964. The border between Kenya and Tanzania loops north of Kilimanjaro because Queen Victoria promised the Kaiser the highest mountain in East Africa!

South to the Pangani River System

Once called the Ruvu, the Pangani River flowed through Tanganyika Territory in a south-easterly direction to the Indian Ocean, from Lake Jipe which lies just southeast of Mount Kilimanjaro.

Both before and after our visits to Kilimanjaro and the coast we went to see the fish ponds made by Colonel Ewart Grogan ('Grogs') near Lake Jipe.

Colonel Grogan landing a
tilapia from one of his ponds.

This was a great experience. Edward Paice in his very readable biography *'Lost Lion of Empire; the life of 'Cape-to-Cairo Grogan'* describes Grogan, dubbed in the blurb as 'the boldest and the baddest of a bold bad gang of pioneering settlers in Kenya', as 'gifted far beyond the ordinary; possessed of disarmingly good looks, magnetic charm, a formidable intellect and a near boundless ego, he was famed throughout the British Empire as one of the most brilliant – and controversial – figures of African colonial history'. Now rather elderly and graced with a pointed white beard, after a phase of growing grapefruits Grogan had suddenly taken to creating fish ponds near Lake Jipe. What tilapia would we find there? Our stay with him in his newly built 'Grogan`s castle' on top of Girigan Hill was a fascinating experience as he 'first came to Africa about the time your mothers would be being born'. Tales of his early life included descriptions of his walk from the Cape to Cairo through the Nile sudd, which was only possible because it was an exceptionally dry year. So he was able to burn his way ahead, accompanied by convicts released from prison for this arduous trip. All this was in order to earn his wife.

His many splendid tales of early life in Africa included the coming of the railway to Nairobi (in *'Man-eaters of Tsavo'* days). When asked where to buy land near what grew to be Nairobi, his response had been to examine where most tracks – of humans and animals – crossed the area. That would be the best place. A good choice, as this was outside what became Nairobi's main mosque, where more people passed by than anywhere else in the growing town.

On our first visit (27–29 December) we fished in nearby Lake Jipe and he angled for tilapia in his ponds. On the second visit (15–17 January) we had an expedition to Lake Chala, and next day he emptied one of his fish ponds so that we could examine all the tilapia (700+ of them!).

Lake Jipe contained one or possibly two as yet undescribed species of tilapia related to *O. mossambicus* (and we had just discovered another two in the Pangani system at Korogwe). Lake Chala, a small crater lake on the slopes of Mount Kilimanjaro nineteen kilometres north of Lake Jipe, had yet another tilapia species *Oreochromis hunteri*. This is of special significance for tilapia studies since this endemic species happens to be the 'type species' of the genus *Oreochromis* (meaning 'mountain chromis'), the generic name that Trewavas had, by the Rules of International Zoological Nomenclature, to use for all the species of female mouth-brooding tilapias in her later revision of the tilapias (1983).

Lake Jipe was connected with the Pangani River in wet seasons through a series of swamps. In 1951 the lake was about twelve miles long by one and a half miles wide but said to be silting up and spreading. It was only a few feet deep over much of its area, with large patches of water plants, *Potamogeton* and *Najas*, rising to the surface, and frequented by numerous herons and other water birds. The two tilapiine species found in Lake Jipe and grown in Grogan's ponds both turned out to be new to science. I later described them as *Oreochromis jipe* (mostly easy to identify with four anal spines) and *O. girigan* (with three such spines). Each of these species resembled *O. mossambicus,* found in rivers flowing to Africa's east coast further south, in which the adult males developed elongated jaws and a concave profile. The larger tilapia from Lake

Grogan's fish ponds 1951.

Trapping fish as one of Colonel Grogan's ponds is drained down.

Lake Chala.

Jipe, amongst which *O. girigan* were found to predominate, were caught by beating the water around gillnets set by day among the patches of water weed. Tilapia fry, 2–10 cm long, used for stocking the ponds were caught by pulling a sack cloth to the shore through a clearing in the reeds bordering the lake, and seemed to be mostly *O. jipe*. All the angled ones from the pond and the majority from the emptied pond were certainly the four spined *O. jipe* (216 males, 17– 27 cm long, to 36 females, 15–17 cm long), whereas in the gillnets set in the lake *O. girigan* predominated (41 males of 16–32 cm, maturation size 21 cm, to 26 females 16–32 cm maturing at 17 cm).

There was no apparent inflow or outflow to the deep, clear Lake Chala, whose shores were rocky and shelved steeply into deep water. Shoals of small immature tilapia, *O. hunteri*, fed on algae and bottom debris between the rocks and shore, with large numbers of crabs and prawns. Our Chala expedition

Examining the catch after Colonel Grogan had emptied one of his ponds for us.

Sir Harry Johnston's sketch of Lake Jipe.
From The Kilima-njaro Expedition (1886).

Lake Jipe tilapia from Colonel Grogan's pond.

(15 January) started with 'Grogs' shooting a water buck to provide guts for bait to attract the tilapia which, perhaps surprisingly, it did. We caught twenty five *O. hunteri*, but none larger than 12.5 cm total length and these appeared to be 'hunger forms'. Two apparently brooding females only 11 cm long were

The Pangani species

After examination of the Pangani species at the BM(NH) in London, Trewavas (1966) concluded that *Oreochromis hunteri*, *O. jipe*, *O. girigan*, and *O. pangani* were a group of interrelated species standing apart from other eastern tilapias (distinguished especially by their high vertebrae and scale numbers). As Lake Jipe is seasonally connected with the Pangani river the two species found in this lake were derivable from *O. pangani*, and distinguished by the respective coarsening (in *O. girigan*) and refining (in *O. jipe*) of their pharyngeal dentition, teeth which fitted their respective diets of coarse bottom debris and fine plankton.

Since Lake Chala is a crater lake with no outlet it is conceivable that *O. hunteri* got there by man's agency, but it was already there in 1889 and there is no record of its introduction. As the *O. girigan* and *O. jipe* introduced into ponds at Korogwe had been widely distributed to other parts of the Pangani system, it was impossible to say whether they were originally confined to Lake Jipe.

Lake Chala and Colonel Grogan (with beard).

among the catch, and abundant juveniles were scoop netted from shoals around the rocks. There appeared to be little shallow sandy space between the rocks where they could spawn. Lake Chala, like many other such lakes, had a legend of a drowned village.

The pond that Colonel Grogan emptied for us on our January visit, had been stocked with a thousand fingerlings on 18 October 1949, but produced only 424 large tilapia. Where had they all gone? There were crocodiles here and numerous fish-eating birds that must have accounted for at least some of them. Many different treatments, including feeding the tilapia with maize meal, and the addition of ducks and geese, had been tried on some of the stocked ponds to explore various commercial possibilities. Dried tilapia were sold to nearby sisal estates but it was concluded that the ponds would not be a paying proposition (unless, possibly if they could be stocked and fished every three months). *O. esculentus*, the Lake Victoria species, and *T. rendalli* turned up in

The Ruzizi River flows south from Lake Kivu to Lake Tanganyika.
It enters the north end of the lake near Bujumbura, the capital of Burundi shown
below. This photograph was taken in 1989.

Fishing boats on the east shore of Lake Tanganyika In 1975.
The metal frames hold lights to attract the pelagic clupeids.

In the 1970s motorised vessels towed groups of canoes
out into the open water, set them in a circle around a
large ring net. The swarms of Tanganyika sardines
attracted to the lights were scooped up and later dried
and smoked before being packed in plastic packets.

The beach at Ujiji on Lake Tanganyika. The crowd is loading sacks of dried
Ndagala on to the boats to take their catch across to Congo in 1953.

Lake Jipe in 1976, and 1985 respectively). In Lake Chala, in addition to the endemic *O. hunteri*, *O. pangani* and *Tilapia rendalli* were also found in 1985, almost certainly introduced by man (Dadzie, Haller & Trewavas 1988).

After we left the coast and before our return visit to Colonel Grogan we drove to Korogwe via Amani in Tanganyika Territory to visit one of Peggy's former students at Cambridge, Belinda Kemp. She was studying termites at the former German Agricultural Station in its beautiful gardens atop a very steep hill. From here, after a perilous descent as the car brakes failed, we continued to Tanganyika's Experimental Fish Culture Station at Korogwe on the lower Pangani. Here Major R.E. Gould, Fish Culturist to the Tanganyika Government, had established experimental fish ponds from which he stocked many other dams and ponds. He was investigating growth among many tilapia species, including the two endemics from Lake Jipe and another two unnamed species from the Pangani (later described by me as *O. pangani* and *O. korogwe*). The Kenyan Fish Warden (Hugh Copley) was rightly very angry with Major Gould for taking tilapia species over the Tanganyika/Kenya border (as a gift) without getting permission or recording such transfers.

These Korogwe ponds also gave us useful information about growth and multiplication rates of the Lake Victoria *O. esculentus* and *O. variabilis*, which had been stocked here as fry collected from the mouths of parent fish at Mwanza by the LVFS Fishery Officer. After a three day rail journey, they had been introduced into the Korogwe ponds on 16 June 1950. When we examined them seven and half months later (21 January 1950), the *O. esculentus* had grown to 16–19 cm long and had produced young which were already 7 cm long. In Lake Victoria *O. esculentus* were normally about 25 cm long when they matured. The pond yielded nine males and seven females and had numerous 'nests' (spawning plaques each about a foot in diameter) in the

Talking to Major Gould while touring his experimental fish ponds at Korogwe.

The small pond (40x20 ft) at Korogwe used for growing on tilapia fry for stocking the larger ponds.

Major Gould showing us the spawning plaques of a Pangani tilapia species (above) and of T. esculentus *which resemble those of* T. nilotica *(seen in close up to the left) at the edge of one of his ponds at Korogwe.*

bottom mud. Analysis of their gut contents showed they had eaten very little nutritious food. The *T. variabilis* were only 13–19 cm long, twelve males and thirteen females, but only one nest was seen. In both species males and females had grown to the same size, in contrast with the Pangani species in which the males had grown considerably larger (23-30 cm) than the females and there were many more males than females. Scales from females showed 'spawning marks', confirming that these rings may be of use in determining the number of times a tilapia has spawned. When the ponds were drained, the species of tilapia present was often given away by their characteristic 'nest' forms in the bottom mud. These nest shapes, together with different male spawning colours, may have been of evolutionary significance in keeping sympatric species distinct.

Much later (1964) a man-made lake, the 180 km² reservoir Nyumba ya Mungu – 'House of God' – formed behind a new hydroelectric barrage across the upper Pangani river. This lake was found to contain *O. esculentus* living on phytoplankton in the open waters, with the two local species *O. p. pangani* and *O. jipe*, together with *T. rendalli* feeding on periphyton. These *O. esculentus* must have come from escapes into the Pangani River of the fry introduced to Korogwe ponds from Mwanza in June 1950. As Roland Bailey later discovered these *O. esculentus* became important in the local fish market. Many of these tilapia were also widely stocked in dams and ponds, and their relative growth rates were later tested at Baobab Farm near Mombasa, run by Rene Haller, in old cement workings on the Kenya coast. I visited there in February 1981 with Ethelwynn Trewavas (see chapter 10).

The *O. karogwe* collected at Korogwe I had taken to be a subspecies of *O. mossambicus* (*O.m. karogwe*). Like *O. spilurus* this species was said by Gould to have a high salt tolerance. The other east-flowing African rivers contained different tilapia species. *O. spilurus* was present in the lower Athi (here called the Galana River), which further upstream (called the Athi above the Lugard Falls) had a subspecies *O. spilurus niger*, which was used for pond trials at the Nyeri fish culture station near Mount Kenya that we visited later on this safari. There it was known as *Tilapia nigra*. On our 1981 trip Ethelwynn and I sought *O. s. niger*, but by then no pure stock could be found, as all of them appeared to have been contaminated by hybridization with other stocked or escaped species.

Another east coast river species which became famous was the 'Zanzibar tilapia' *Tilapia hornorum*. Originally from the Wami river system in Tanganyika, this species was probably introduced into Zanzibar about 1918 and was taken to the Malacca Tropical Fish Culture Research Institute in Malaya where it was studied by C.F. Hickling. *O. hornorum* was later considered by Trewavas to be subspecies of *O. urolepis*.

Oreochromis mossambicus, so much used in fish culture in the Far East, originated in rivers further south. Its home was the Lower Zambesi and coastal rivers and lagoons south to Algoa Bay in South Africa. It lived in both fresh and brackish water so this proved to be a very useful species to stock in slightly saline and/or cooler water in many parts of the world, especially in the Philippines. It also hybridises with many other tilapias, but does not grow as fast or as large as *O. niloticus* and its various hybrids.

Back in Nairobi after all this travelling the car had to be fixed, and while there we visited the famous Coryndon Natural History Museum. With Barton Worthington we had a session with the Colonial Development Organisation representative (Baron Gowstowski) to discuss their plans for a commercial tilapia fishery to be developed on land adjacent to Colonel Grogan's ponds.

Peggy and I (this time accompanied by Barton's daughter Griselda Worthington) then set out northwards for the second part of this safari, to visit Kenya's RR & DC (River Research and Development Centre) trout hatchery at Nyeri on the slopes of Mount Kenya. As an authority on trout, Peggy had much to do here and was interested in the programme that was stocking Mount Kenya's streams with brown (*Salmo trutta*) and rainbow trout (*S. gairdneri*). We stayed with the Director Vernon van Someren (who took over as Director of EAFFRO when Bobby Beauchamp retired). From here we also visited the tilapia culture experiments in progress at the Kenya Government Experimental Fish Farm at nearby Sagana. At the weekend Hugh and Gwen Copley arrived to discuss the five year plan for these tilapia experiments.

The RRDC and Sagana fish ponds

The Kenya Game and Fish Department (under Hugh Copley) had already developed a good trout fishery in the high altitude streams that were almost devoid of indigenous fishes, except for a few small catfishes (*Amphilius*) and eels (*Anguilla*). At Nyeri, the laboratory included a trout hatchery and an insect house where the many insect larvae, which were the main trout food, together with other invertebrates, were hatched out to determine the species involved. Once again, our drive there was not without incident. My trusty Ford vaporised at altitude and we could only restart the engine by pushing the car towards a large white board, emblazoned with a black skull, which indicated the precipitous edge of the rift escarpment alongside the narrow road. Always imperturbable, Peggy kept calm by consuming chocolate truffles.

But we did make it up to Nyeri, a very pleasant wooden laboratory, with a good library, in the forest which reverberated with the loud noise of tree hyraxes. Griselda was a very good angler but her main desire was to walk in the forest at night hoping to see rhino by a salt lick. We thought we should accompany her, but never met a rhino. Years later Griselda, now an eminent Australian poet crystallized these adventures by including these lines in her poem *Sagana River Fishing Party 1951*:

'Let her come with us, give you a break',
Driving the Austin north from Nairobi
Sulky woman child in back seat.
Juddering the corrugations, singing:
'We`re going to Sagana, hakuna matata'
'We're gong to Sagana, hakuna matata'

Peggy stands under a fever tree grinning
Eating dust and chocolate truffles
While Ro wraps wet handkerchiefs round the carburettor'

And after a graphic description of catching a large trout at dusk the poem continues –

'Dragging fishtail along the dead dark path
a stick cracks ahead
three buffalo cross the track
Heavy horn heads low
moonlight on dripping nostrils.
'Where the dickens have you been
at this time of night down the river?
Don't you know what the Mau Mau do
to girls like you?'
Peggy sitting in the only comfortable chair
holding out truffles
'You gotta show me where that pool is manyana,
that's the biggest trout ever come from the Sagana'

During our time at Nyeri, when Hugh and Gwen Copley came for a weekend visit, they took us to see 'Lizzie's Lodge', the beautiful well-appointed house in the woods which the people of Kenya gave to Princess Elizabeth as a wedding gift, and for which the Copleys had a key. This was not far from 'Treetops', the game-watching lodge built in the trees above a salt lick visited nightly by elephants, buffalo and many other forest animals. Treetops became world-famous as Princess Elizabeth was staying there the night her father, King George VI, died in London and Elizabeth descended from the tree house to become Queen of the United Kingdom and Commonwealth.

At Nyeri we learned a great deal about management of trout in African streams. The eyed ova of rainbow and brown trout, and later some charr (*Salvelinus*), had originally been flown out to Kenya from the UK for trials. Now in the Kenya hatchery the hen rainbows matured in 18 months and spawned in June to August, the time of overcast skies and floods. Spawning here evidently ties up with light and floods, but is not at the time of lowest water temperatures, irrespective of spawning season in their home countries. Traps across the river recorded the upstream and downstream movements

On the terrace of Lizzie's Lodge.

of the fish. Samples were also taken of their bottom food. This comprised mainly larval insects, which were hatched out in the insect house and then had to be sent away to experts for identification. There were no peak emergences of insects here (as happens with many insects in Lake Victoria), just 'fewer in floods because of nymph destruction'. The standing crop of this fish food appeared to be about 4.5 g/m^2 on a gravel bottom. Crabs were not included but there were plenty of planarian flat worms and insects such as *Baetis*, *Afroneurus*, *Caenis* and many others. *Baetis* and *Simulium* predominated but with considerable differences according to the altitude. Chironomid larvae were commonest near the hatchery, larvae of the stonefly *Neoperla* were found only on the Lower Sagana.

Peggy and I were initiated into electro-fishing experiments to estimate trout populations in the river, using a very primitive device. This was used in the 12–13 yard wide river averaging up to one foot deep, with 250 paces between stop nets. A 6 volt battery with a vibrator unit (as used in battery wireless sets turning DC current into AC of higher voltage) producing 115 volts which were then transformed into 220 volts. The floating electrode, 10 foot x 18 inches, was of 1/2in chicken-wire mesh on a large wooden frame. The downstream bottom electrode was a roll of similar wire netting, approximately 15 ft wide unrolled across the stream bottom, with about 18 paces (40ft) of cable. An operator in waterproof rubber boots controlled the switch. Two assistants pulled the floating electrode slowly upstream from side to side of the river, followed by African lab boys with square wood-handled landing nets to catch the fish. Peggy and I were warned (very seriously) against touching the water, but we wondered how the old man at the back would fare, in his leaky Wellington boots and trailing a metal bucket. (He survived.) The trout were then marked with jaw tags and returned to the river. The process was repeated next day and recaptures used to estimate the trout population. Peggy and I were interested in the different reactions of individual trout to this device.

The Kenya Government Fish Farm at Sagana, at 4000 feet altitude, on the slopes of Mount Kenya, had 200 acres of ponds and a planned five-year programme. Here they first concentrated on trying to find how to develop a 'males only' monoculture of *T. nigra* (*O. niger*), and on the growth of *T. melanopleura,* which elsewhere had been used to control growth of aquatic vegetation. P.J.P. (Peter) Whitehead (who later became a leading marine fish scientist at the British Museum (Natural History) and at FAO in Rome) produced a series of useful papers on the best conditions for rearing these monocultures of male *T. nigra*. Young Martindale, whom we knew as a lad on the FBA staff on Lake Windermere, was now an assistant at Nyeri and

The primitive electric fish shocker in action.

*Young Martindale and Vernon
van Someren (wearing a hat)
fin clipping trout at the RRDC.*

Sagana. This arrangement was probably made when Winifred Frost (WEF) of the FBA staff visited Nyeri trout research station in the early 1950s to study the eels which migrate up these Kenya streams from the Indian Ocean. On that visit she had found that of the three species of eel in the east-flowing rivers of Kenya, *Anguilla nebulosa* was the most abundant above 3000 feet, *A. mossambica* was rare and *A. bicolor* apparently restricted to the lower reaches of the rivers. Our 1951 visit there was just at the start of the Mau-Mau rebellion and later Martindale was drafted into the army and very sadly died as a result. In 1953, Mau-Mau operations in this area led to the closure of both the RRDC Laboratory and the Fish Culture unit. Tilapia experiments continued when the latter was reopened in 1955, but the River Research laboratory then became just a trout hatchery.

Collecting the specimens and data is only the first step in describing new species. When we arrived back in Jinja, the car was fully loaded with field notebooks of data, and the 14 gallon milk churn was full of tilapia fixed in neutralised formalin, each with an identifying station number (often in its mouth). These specimens all had to be transferred to alcohol as soon as possible (formalin made them very brittle) for scale and fin spines counts and other measurements to be made in order to compare them with known species. This study was started in Jinja and continued at the museum in London where they had to be compared with the 'type species' of related fishes before they could be described and named as new species.

The field notebooks were also full of fascinating comments on the country through which we passed – the wide skies with wonderful sunsets, the long views, the vegetation, the bird life, and numerous types of insects encountered,

The electric catfish Malapterurus electricus *which is widely distributed in tropical Africa, including the Nile and Congo basins, also occurs in Lake Tanganyika.*

Left, Lamprologus leleupi, *a cichlid from Lake Tanganyika in an aquarium display.*

Tilapia malagarasi *from the Malagarasi Swamp.*

The Virunga Volcanoes lie across the floor of the Rift Valley between Lakes Edward and Kivu. Their emergence interrupted the northward flow of water to Lake Edward and the Nile catchment. From the south side of the volcanoes water now flows south to Lake Kivu and then to Lake Tanganyika via the Ruzizi River.

Fishing canoes on Lake Kivu responding to the detonation of explosives used by researchers for detecting tilapia shoals (see text).

many of which were also collected for later identification at the BM(NH). Other mementoes of the trip included lots of black and white photographs and Kodachrome slides of our Kilimanjaro climb, even the crown of everlasting flowers (fragrant *Helichrysum*) woven for us by the porters in recognition that we had reached the summit. There were also records of our first encounters with coral fishes. The first colour photographs I ever took of these included clown fishes (*Amphiprion*) which live in large sea anemones. These photos had to be taken through a calm sea at very low tide as no underwater cameras were then available. We caught mud skippers (*Periophthalmus*) off the rocks and among the mangroves, and beach-combed exquisite shells thrown up on the sandy shores patrolled by rapidly running ocypodid ghost crabs, their eyes on long stalks. We also found little hermit crabs looking for new shell homes, ... endless marvels. Now, more than 50 years later, I am exploring the tin trunk in my Sussex study full of these notebooks, logs and photographs, but I do miss the smells of smokey Africa, and sounds like the bird calls, frog and insect choruses at dusk, which accompanied these field notes.

The next weekend, homeward bound for Jinja, we visited a childhood friend (Elizabeth Logie, sister of Charlotte Kipling the FBAs statistician) at Thompsons Falls. Her husband was the Kenya Government Forestry Officer. He took us high into the Aberdare Mountains, where his department was cutting fire-fighting trails to help combat the growing Mau-Mau resistance in this area. Soon after this the Logie family were transferred to New Guinea, to her mother's relief as she thought New Guinea would be 'much less dangerous than Kenya'. We arrived back in Jinja on January 28th 1951.

'Crowns everlasting'. Back at the hut after we had reached the summit of Kilimanjaro our porters presented us with sweet-smelling Helichrysum everlasting flowers for our hats, as souvenirs of our achievement.

The advent of tilapia culture in East Africa

Over 4000 years ago several Egyptian tomb paintings depicted Nile tilapia (clearly *O. niloticus* from the striped tail fin) in garden ponds. In the 1920s numerous cattle-watering dams created in the drier areas of East Africa had also been stocked with fish, most often tilapia from any available source, but pond culture of tilapia only took off in the 1940s–1960s. During World War II, when Belgians living in the Congo and Ruwanda relied on pond tilapia for food, information was needed on the best species to stock under the varied climatic and soil conditions in this huge country. So an experimental Fish Culture Research Station was set up in Katanga at Elizabethville (now Lubumbashi). In 1949 this station was visited by East African Fisheries and EAFRO staff during the first *Conference Piscicole Anglo-Belge*. The event was organised in Elizabethville by the Scientific Council for Africa South of the Sahara, of which Barton Worthington had become Secretary General. This greatly stimulated interest in tilapia pond culture in the East African territories. The Belgians were experimenting mainly with *T. melanopleura*, a plant-eater which cleared weeds from dams and fed on vegetable waste from farms. They were also interested in the microphagous *T. nilotica* and *T. macrochir*. The latter is an Upper Zambezi species important in fisheries in Lake Bangweulu and some other lakes, as recounted by Huet (1957) and in papers by De Bont. Stocked in numerous dams, escaping tilapia could gain access to rivers. These included the Kagera draining into Lake Victoria, as evidenced by a male *T. nilotica* caught in the Kagera delta before any deliberate introductions of this species were made into Victoria in the mid-1950s.

A follow-up *Symposium on African Hydrology and Inland Fisheries* was held in Entebbe, Uganda in 1952. This deprecated the transport of fishes and aquatic plants from one drainage basin to another and stressed the importance of first testing local species of tilapias and catfishes (*Labeo* and *Clarias*) in ponds before carrying out trials of species which had proved useful in other regions. This was despite the presence of Dr Zwilling who was visiting Uganda to promote the use of carp (*Cyprinus carpio*) from Israel in African ponds, which were later tried out at Uganda's Fish Farm near Entebbe. The meeting had another interesting repercussion for me, as the geologist sitting at another table in the hotel dining room, observing with amusement our animated discussions, was Richard McConnell (see Chapter 7).

Uganda's fish landings in 1951, recorded by Fish Scouts of the Game Department and listed in their Annual Reports, came mainly from Lakes Victoria and Kyoga (10,000 and 2500 tons respectively), Lakes George and Edward (5600 tons), and the Nakivali complex (1200 tons). However, the 700+ dams in the southwest and drier northeast, together with fish from over 7000 ponds, produced an additional 500 tons, mainly tilapia, as well as unrecorded catches for local use. EAFRO and LVFS had many requests to identify tilapia from East African dams, so an annotated key for their identification was published in the *East African Agricultural Journal* in 1955. The species then in use included *T. zillii* and *T. rendalli*, two plant-eating fish useful in controlling aquatic vegetation (readily distinguishable by body colour and the green ovaries in ripe *T. zillii* compared with orange ones in *T. rendalli*).

Of the Lake Victoria species, *T. esculenta*, a phytoplankton-feeder did not grow well in dams or ponds, nor did *Sarotherodon galilaeus* from Lake Albert which is adapted to feed on very fine particles. *T. variabilis* thrived much better as did the Nile tilapia *T. nilotica*, which is readily recognisable by the vertical black stripes on the tail fin, and the smaller, white-flecked, darker green *T. leucostictus*.

In Kenya the Athi river species *T. nigra* was stocked in cooler ponds at higher altitudes, and in Tanganyika *T. macrochir* was among those distributed from the Karogwe Fish Farm. Studies of their relative fecundities showed that substrate-spawning *T. zillii* produced more eggs than did the mouth-brooders; in all of these species egg numbers increased with female body size. A comprehensive study of the Congo tilapia species was produced in 1964 by Thys van der Audenaerde working with Max Poll at Tervuren Museum, in Belgium, together with an annotated bibliography of the already numerous tilapia papers. Aquarium observations on *T. leucosticta* at EAFRO indicated that the eggs hatch about six days after fertilization and the fry first emerge from the mother's mouth five days after hatching. They are then brooded during the daytime when danger threatens and at night for about two weeks, then only at night for about a further week. In aquaria *T. mossambica* females ejected brooded young 10–12 days after spawning, then brooded them again if disturbed during the first five days of their free-swimming life.

In the early 1950s fish farms were set up by the Fishery Departments in all three East African territories to distribute small tilapia and explore the best conditions for culture in pond complexes. As previously described, in 1951 Peggy Brown and I visited those in Kenya at Sagana on the Upper Tana, Colonel Grogan's commercial pond trials near Lake Jipe and the Korogwe fish farm in Tanganyika. In 1953 Uganda created a large experimental fish farm at Kajansi near Entebbe, from where Nile perch might have escaped into the nearby Lake Victoria in the exceptionally high floods of 1962.

The main problem shown by all these tilapia was their propensity to mature at a very early age and small size, then ceasing to grow but breeding prolifically in the ponds. How could one make them grow into a commercially acceptable larger size? This was attempted with *T. nigra* (a species in which, like *T. mossambicus*, juvenile males grow faster and larger than females), at the Sagana station in Kenya. A breakthrough for this problem came from the production of fast-growing hybrids of *T. mossambica* with a related species *T. hornorum*.

In an attempt to produce 'hybrid vigour' in tilapia growth, quite unexpectedly male *T. hornorum* from Zanzibar, when crossed with female T. *mossambica* brought from Malacca, produced 100% male offspring, which were splendid for stocking ponds. The reciprocal cross produced a different result, and this discovery started a whole series of experimental tilapia crosses in many parts of the world, including Asia, Israel, USA, as well as in other African countries.

This work on tilapia culture developed in Asia using fish endemic to Africa rather than in Africa itself because Dr Hickling on his worldwide travels had been very impressed by the long tradition of fish culture in ponds in Asia, especially of Indian and Chinese carps. By contrast, in Africa, where fishes were generally available from natural waters without having to feed them, no such traditions had developed. Moreover, in Africa abandoned fish ponds, in which malaria-carrying mosquitoes bred, were not at all popular with the medical authorities.

Lake Tanganyika

Bobby Beauchamp, a pioneer of hydrological studies on Lake Tanganyika, had always looked forward to the establishment of a substation of EAFRO based on Lake Tanganyika. So he arranged for me and Humphry Greenwood to visit the lake in August-September 1952. This was in response to an invitation from Jock Lockley, the Tanganyika Inland Fisheries Officer based at Kigoma, containing interesting information about the as yet unexplored Malagarasi river swamps that drained into Lake Tanganyika south of Kigoma.

To get there, with over 500lbs of collecting gear, we travelled on Lake Victoria's steamer from Kisumu via Musoma on the eastern shore, and on overnight to Mwanza. Here LVFS Fishery Officer Gilbert met us and put us on the overnight train to Tabora. Next day we explored locally, visiting the German boma and the explorer David Livingstone's old house. Tabora's stores, run mainly by Arabs, were hung with the colourful kanga cotton cloths worn by all the women, and the market had piles of fruits and tilapia fished from the swamps. In the evening we boarded a goods train, travelling on bunks in the caboose (staff cabin), while the train ran along the very fertile Luichi river valley, which marked out the old slave route, with its oil palms and mango trees and gardens of cassava, beans, maize, bananas, small hills and beehives in the trees. We crossed the swamps, including two miles of track shared by road and rail, and next morning arrived in Kigoma where we were met by Jock and Debora Lockley. They proved to be excellent hosts in this very cheerful, informal community. One of their friends who helped us was 'Kammy', a khaki-clad relic of the Austro-Hungarian Empire who had emigrated to Abyssinia in the 1920s, where he and his brother had helped to build the Emperor's palace. Some undisclosed incident had given him a glass eye, which he clinked cheerfully with his whiskey glass – to the surprise of uninitiated guests.

It was delightful to be back close to mountains and on a deep rift valley lake again, with clear water through which we could watch the numerous brightly coloured fishes that lived along the rocky shores and long sandy beaches. In shape and limnology Lake Tanganyika is very much like Lake Malawi, but these two lakes have very different fish faunas. Lake Tanganyika drains westwards, via the Lukuga river to the Congo system, from where it obtained most of its ancestral fishes, whereas Malawi is part of the Zambezi River drainage system. So, on Lake Tanganyika we had to learn a whole new fish fauna. Lying 3° to 9° South of the Equator and 420 miles long, Tanganyika is the second deepest lake in the world (1470m) after Lake Baikal. Like Lake Malawi, it is permanently stratified with an anoxic hypolimnion (below about 240 m) uninhabited by fishes.

Dating back an estimated twenty million years, Lake Tanganyika is the oldest of the African Great Lakes. Its oldest faunal relationships are with the Congo basin which in late Pliocene times was an internal drainage basin containing a large lake (or lakes), in which the open water biota could have become adapted to lacustrine conditions. The three sub-basins were at one time isolated lakes. The Ruzizi River now enters the north end of Lake Tanganyika. The reversal of its flow when the Virunga volcanoes pushed up from the floor of the Rift Valley introduced a few nilotic elements, including the tilapia *O. niloticus*, to Lake Tanganyika. The present lake was colonised by about six distinct lines of cichlids; and has many examples of intra-lacustrine endemism, particularly among its littoral cichlids. The role of cover among rocks appears to have been of vital importance for cichlid evolution here as the lake has many piscivorous fishes, including four endemic *Lates* species

The western escarpment of the Rift Valley rises steeply across Lake Tanganyika as cattle plod their way up from the beach on the east shore.

'Tanganyika sardines' - the clupeids Limnothrissa miodon *and* Stolothrissa tanganikae – *drying in the sun on racks on the beach.*

and two of tiger fish (*Hydrocynus*). The Malagarasi River, which drains the country east of the lake, has some endemic fishes which (as we found) are related to those in the Congo system, but are not found in the lake.

Tanganyika has 24 fish families, more than any other lake. Eighteen occur in tributaries and marshes around the lake, 12 in the littoral and sub-littoral zones, but only seven in the benthic and four in the pelagic zone. The lake now has nearly 300 fish species (80% of them endemic). Although this is fewer species than in Lakes Malawi and Victoria, the cichlids have differentiated further than in these other lakes, reflecting the greater age of Tanganyika. Max Poll recognized 12 distinct tribes. Of the 115 non-cichlid species 46% are endemic, more than in any other African lake. These include two clupeid (sardine) species and four of centropomid predators, making an open water community that supports the main commercial fisheries. There are also species flocks of bagrid and mochokid catfishes and of mastacembelid spiny eels. There are also lots of endemic crabs and very thick-shelled snails, two species of otters, two of aquatic snakes, and plentiful crocodiles.

Despite being the rail terminus and a steamer port (base for the famous old German steamer the *SS Liemba*), Kigoma was then still remarkably undeveloped. A small town, it looked out over the clear blue waters of the lake at the edge of which there was a swimming pool, supposedly fenced off from crocodiles. Here we were introduced to a whole new fish fauna, and Humphry and I met one of the two venomous aquatic snakes. Lake Tanganyika had numerous species unknown to us from the other African lakes, including numerous very colourful cichlids, some convergent with 'mbuna' in Lake Malawi and others that were substratum spawners. Years later these were discovered by the Japanese/African scuba teams to have very diverse breeding habits. But, in contrast with the other lakes, the main commercial catch here was not of cichlids but the two endemic species of small pelagic sardines (*Limnothrissa* and *Stolothrissa*) known as 'ndagala'. These were attracted into scoop nets on dark nights by fires held in metal baskets on the prows of the canoes. As dusk fell the lake was dotted with twinkling lights from the numerous canoes setting out with hand-held scoop nets to catch 'ndagala'. On calm nights a distinctive sound rang out as the fishermen banged their paddles on the sides of their canoes, which they said helped to attract the fish. This was before the introduction of pressure lamps, so the prow of each canoe was fitted with a metal basket in which a special type of firewood was burnt to provide the light. A local industry supplied suitable firewood. When we visited nearby Ujiji, scene of the famous 'Dr Livingstone I presume' encounter when H.M. Stanley finally found the great explorer living there, Arab dhows were loading up sacks of sun dried 'ndagala' to take them across the lake to the Congo.

In the Fisheries launch we visited beaches around Kigoma to examine seine net catches made by the local fishermen. These included some of the endemic tilapia *Oreochromis* (*Neotilapia*) *tanganicae* which lives mainly inshore and behind sandy spits. However, we did not find any *O. niloticus*, which was said to live inshore in fluviatile areas and local swamps. In these swamps our experimental fyke nets caught large electric catfish (*Malapterurus electricus*), from one of which I got a terrific electric shock through my arm, when I misguidedly poked it with scissors while standing in rubber boots. Near the

Humphry Greenwood and Jock Lockley examining the fire baskets attached to the prows of canoes on the shore of Lake Tanganyika near Kigoma in 1953.

Malagarasi delta was a village where many of the inhabitants had an extra toe (or was it a finger?). With our plankton nets we collected a Tanganyika speciality, small jellyfishes (*Limnocnida tanganyikae*) which were temporarily parked in a tumbler of water on the launch. But when Jock inadvertently drank them we had to start again.

The Malagarasi Swamps

The tilapia trail then led on very successfully into the Malagarasi swamps, which drain country between Lakes Victoria and Tanganyika. Humphry and I made a base at Katare, several miles up from the lake. Arriving there by train from Kigoma at 2 am we were met by our amiable host Bill Done, a bachelor who was pleased to have company for nine days. Living such an isolated life one of his main joys was shooting the bats flying round the living room from the dinner table. As he originally came from Liverpool (like me), we developed a good rapport.

At Katare the Malagarasi swamps, which extend over about seven hundred square miles, were covered by blue water lilies (*Nymphea stellata*), with dense masses of *Ceratophyllum*, *Utricularia* and *Chara*. The crystal clear water at that time of year was less than ten feet deep, over bottom deposits of finely divided vegetable debris which contained a rich fauna of protozoa and rotifers, and also semi-digested faeces from the dense populations of fishes. These included species of *Alestes*, *Distichodus*, *Citharinus*, many mormyrids, the catfishes

Fishermen preparing their nets on the edge of the Malagarasi swamps.

Colourful breeding males of Tilapia karomo *from the Malagarasi swamps, showing their long genital tassels.*

Bagrus, Clarias, Heterobranchus, Schilbe and *Synodontis*, and the cyprinids *Labeo* and *Barbus*. The cichlids included two species of tilapia, haplochromines and *Serrranochromis*. All the fish we examined were in very good condition.

The two species of tilapia here, *O. karomo* and '*O.* cf *niloticus*' formed the basis of a local fishing industry. All of the tilapia living here with *O. karomo* had quiescent gonads at that time of year. When later examined at the BM(NH) by the tilapia doyenne Ethelwynn Trewavas, she decided that these so called 'cf *niloticus*' were a new species, named by her *O. malagarasi*. Interestingly, these appear to be most closely related to *O. (Nyasalapia) upembae* found in the Lualaba River (Upper Congo) with which they probably shared a common ancestor when the Malagarasi was part of the Congo system, and before the creation of Lake Tanganyika in its present form. The ancestor of *O. variabilis,* endemic to Lake Victoria, appears to be a close relative. Humphry Greenwood also found that among the haplochromine cichlids he collected here, one called *Haplochromis malagariensis,* turned out to be a new genus that he named *Orthochromis.* This also showed the greatest affinity with an upper Congo species and may have been ancestral to the endemic *Telmatochromis* in Lake Tanganyika.

Using bark canoes the fishermen caught the fish by bashing the water with a special club to drive them into gillnets set among the water lilies. No other species of tilapia were seen here, although '*T. melanopleura*' (= *T. rendalli*) and

A photograph taken through the clear waters of the Malagarasi swamps where a male T. karomo *is plainly visible guarding its circular 'nest' on the bottom.*

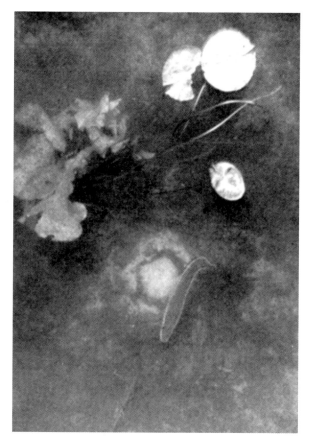

O. tanganicae were caught lower down the river. Both the *O. karomo* and *O. malagarasi* were in excellent condition, full of fat and packed with food. Both species were feeding on the soft flocculent deposits which carpet the swamp. The characteristic elongated jaws and series of teeth in *O. karomo* also seemed ideal for rasping epiphytic algae off the water plants.

The extraordinary productivity of these Malagarasi water-lily swamps (in marked contrast to those of Lake Kyoga) appeared to be mainly due to the presence of *Alestes macrophthalmus* and *Distichodus* species, both of which were found to be feeding on and partially digesting the leaves, buds and seeds of the water-lilies. Higher plant material, if eaten by other species of fish, usually remains undigested by them. It seems that here the partially digested remains of the water lilies, after passing through the guts of *Alestes* and *Distichodus,* formed a digestible food for several other fish, including both tilapia species and two *Haplochromis* species. These may utilise this food as it is, or derive their nourishment from the associated fauna of protozoans and rotifers. Some of the smaller species of fish, which fed on the soft bottom deposits provided food for the various predatory fish. The almost complete absence of either phyto- or zooplankton in these swamps was remarkable, as was the paucity

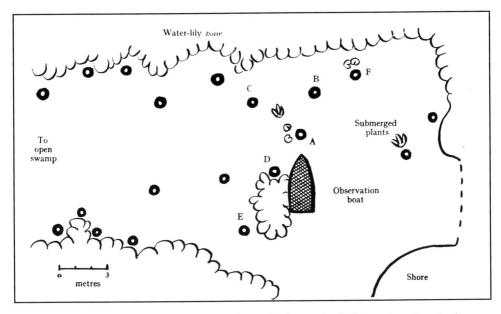

The distribution of Tilapia karomo *'nests' (plaques) at Katare Landing in the Malagarasi swamps.*

Three males swimming out from their respective plaques to entice a passing female to their plaque to lay her eggs. She then picks them up in her mouth.

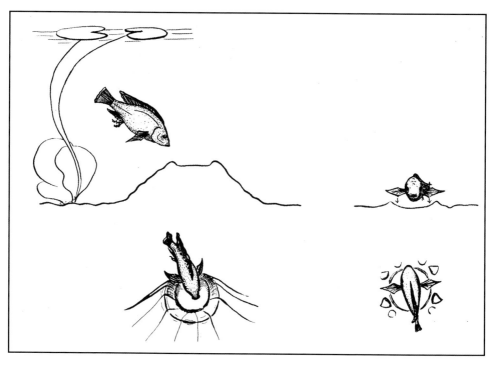

T. karomo *(left) makes a 'nest' on top of a mound in the substrate whereas*
T. variabilis *make their flat, circular nests surrounded by pits in the substrate.*

of both insects and molluscs. This was reflected in the feeding habits of the catfish (*Schilbe mystus*) which was eating insects in the open Malagarasi river, but in the swamps fed mainly on small *Haplochromis*.

At Katare jetty fish landing the water was so clear that it was possible to make a detailed study of the spawning behaviour of *O. karomo*. In these pre-scuba days, this presented a rare opportunity to study tilapia behaviour in the wild. A comparative study of *O. karomo* behaviour here with that of *O. variabilis* in the Kyoga swamps was later published in '*Behaviour*' with the kind help of the editor Gerhard Baerends. None of the *O. malagarasi* were in breeding condition at this time (September). The male *O. karomo*, which develops a highly coloured breeding dress with an elaborate long genital tassel, established a territory in the spawning area. Here he made a circular sand scrape, spawning plaque (once called a 'nest'), and cleared patches in the bottom debris which shone out like beacons.

Individual *O. karomo* males stayed in their territories, generally near the bottom, day and night, for days on end. They shot away only temporarily if seriously disturbed, as they were by the antics of swimming Muscovy ducks, or fishermen's canoes passing overhead. During this time the males ate very little. The ripe females wandered over the spawning grounds singly or three or four together, generally rather high in the water. As they swam over each territory the occupying male swam up and tried to lead the female to his clearly visible plaque. When he succeeded, eggs were laid and milt extruded. Eggs and milt were then picked up in the female's mouth and carried away by the female, all within two or three minutes. Some females visited four or five nests in succession before spawning, others went straight to a particular nest. Females carrying eggs and young left the spawning areas, so when considering measures to protect tilapia it is essential to differentiate between spawning and brooding grounds.

Lake Kivu

South of Lake Edward in the western rift valley lies Lake Kivu, a 400m deep 2370 km² stretch of water, shared by Rwanda and the Congo. Kivu used to drain northwards to Lake Edward and the Nile before the Virungu Volcanoes blocked its passage about 12,500 years ago. This reversed the drainage and the lake then spilled into Lake Tanganyika via the Ruzizi River. Kivu is populated by a subspecies of *Oreochromis niloticus* (*O. n. eduardianus*), in which Trewavas included *'Tilapia regani'*. This was the name formerly used for Lake Kivu's *O. niloticus*, which also occurs in the Ruzizi River and along the coasts of Lake Tanganyika.

My chance to see *O. niloticus* in Kivu came in November 1953 when, on 'local leave' with my visiting parents and a childhood friend, we went in Richard McConnell's large car to visit the Worthington family. Barton had

Lake Kivu.

recently moved to the CSA (Council for Africa South of the Sahara) headquarters in Bukavu on Lake Kivu. This proved a jolly trip with lots of adventures, meeting elephants at close quarters and other hazards. The old road, which followed the Ruzizi River from Lake Kivu to Uvira on Lake Tanganyika, had the most spectacular view east across the Rift Valley. Alongside Lake Kivu the road was so steep and narrow that cars and lorries could only travel south on Mondays, Wednesdays, Fridays, and north on the alternate days; Sundays were free for all, but no lorries. In one section, a signal was hoisted high on a pole, and drums were beaten, to warn that a car was on its way. Richard, ever a true geologist, stopped to examine rock formations, and left his precious magnifying lens by one of them. To retrieve it meant turning the car round on the very narrow road and travelling the wrong way back to the outcrop. We not only found the lens but the car squashed it flat. We then had to turn again on the narrow ledge to proceed in the right direction.

The previous September, when Barton had been appointed Scientific Director of the CSA, the Worthingtons had had a most dramatic move with all their household goods, including horses and a grand piano (on the same lorry) from their Nairobi home to Bukavu in Rwanda. They had stayed with me in Jinja en route. The first intimation I had was the arrival of a shooting brake, driven by Edna Lind of Makerere University, accompanied by Professor Pearsall from the University of London (an FBA Councillor), and five laying hens, two ducks, and many household goods. With much merriment they warned me of what was to follow with the lorry and rest of the entourage. The problem of not letting water from the horses into the grand piano was a minor one. The plank shelter rigged to shield the horses from the sun needed to be dismantled to allow the lorry to cross the Nzoia river bridge. The horses could only travel

Richard geologising on the lava that flowed into Lake Kivu near Goma, with regenerating ferns already established.

through the tsetse fly zone after dark, and they had to reach the Kivu road on the day they could travel south. In Jinja it was discovered that photo-graphs were needed for passes for the servants travelling with them.

At Goma on Lake Kivu in November 1953 we had a rendezvous with the team of Belgian hydrobiologists directed by Dr Andre Capart. They were a jolly crew who were studying these African lakes from the Congo side. Barton Worthington arrived from Bukavu and Bobby Beauchamp drove across from Jinja bringing with him Humphry Greenwood and Geoff Fish. On the lake we had a splendid demonstration of the first use of an echo-sounder to detect tilapia shoals. These gave a characteristic inverted V shaped echo trace in mid-water in the daytime, but the shoals dispersed at dusk and reformed at dawn. Shoals were found over a rocky bottom off the lava shores. Fish from two such shoals were examined. One shoal, in 10 m of water, contained tilapia of a similar size (29–36 cm TL) and included both sexes; 22 of the 45 males were ripe and among the 10 females some had young in the mouth. Gonad states indicated that about half the shoal was of actively breeding fish. Another day, 21 males and 3 females were caught together. It was surprising to find breeding and non-breeding fish together in one shoal.

We knew the echo-sounder traces were caused by tilapia from the slightly alarming process of using 'la dynamite', a stick of which, when lighted from a cigarette and thrown overboard, brought tilapias floating to the surface. The loud explosion alerted local fishermen to speed out from the shore in their canoes to collect this fish bonanza. In this deep lake, the bottom waters were rich in methane, and therefore out of bounds for the fish. The *niloticus* living in the mid-water shoals were feeding mainly on a spirochaete bacterium, superficially like the blue-green alga *Spirulina* but with much finer filaments. They also ate other small bacterial organisms and nanoplankton. The very fine pharyngeal teeth of the Kivu *niloticus* fitted them for this diet of very small organisms.

Humphry and I were also introduced to scuba diving for the first time. Dr Capart, who was a large man, had a rather experimental apparatus with three huge tanks, under the weight of which I could hardly stand up when on the deck ('but I do not think you will need any weights round your waist' he said). My cherished memory of this first scuba dive to the sunlit bottom of a shallow bay, was of this distinguished scientist in the briefest of bathing trunks presenting me with stones to keep me submerged.

We also visited the very splendid buildings of the Congo laboratory at Luvira, set up by Dr Luis van de Berge, and stayed in their rest house. I stayed there again nearly forty years later, on my way to see the lowland gorillas. By then the excellent library and collections had been removed to other institutions in what is now Democratic Republic of Congo, and some Japanese primatologists seemed to be the only scientists around.

*The official wedding photograph with me in the
outfit borrowed from Kitty Beauchamp.*

The wedding party at EAFRO.

Richard on the road to Lobatsi in the Bechuanaland Protectorate – now Botswana – in 1955.

Climbing out of a pan in the Kalahari Desert in our faithful 'caboose' camping wagon.

The Okavango River at Maun in 1956.

The dry season – the Tati River in 1956.

San Bushmen making fire in the Kalahari Desert.

Chapter 6

The 'marriage bar' and a new life

Marriage was not part of my life plan. I was very happy being a biologist in East Africa and had even turned down the offer of becoming Director of JFRO in Central Africa. As it was quite a thing for such a post to be offered to a woman in those days, had I been more 'women's lib' I suppose I would have accepted it. Then one day, when walking by the source of the Nile with Richard McConnell, hearing about his early adventures, the idea of joining forces with him on his next venture seemed rather attractive. He had been, as a budding geologist, with his father in the Canadian Rocky Mountains, then done a geological doctorate in the Alps, and driven alone across Africa in his old car 'Susan' from Tanganyika to Nigeria. He had a nice sense of humour, was very much his own man – and probably the first to be mad enough to have taken skis to Uganda with which he skied on the Ruwenzori's equatorial snowfield. So I 'threw my bonnet over the windmill' and on 31 December 1953 I borrowed a suit from Kitty Beauchamp and we were married by the District Commissioner in Jinja before leaving for Europe on vacation, and then moving to Bechuanaland Protectorate ('BP'). This left my surprised parents in Africa where they had come to visit their 'unmarried' daughter.

The UK's Overseas Research Service still had an antediluvian marriage bar (for women). This meant that I automatically had to resign from EAFRO,

My father and mother (talking to Kitty Beauchamp) at the wedding party.

in spite of the fact that, for the UK Home Civil Service, a formidable council of women, of which Ethelwynn Trewavas was the Honorary Secretary, had at long last won the battle for married women to remain in their posts - and receive 'equal pay for equal work'. Since Richard had just been appointed Director of the Bechuanaland Protectorate Geological Survey we were off to live in the Kalahari in southern Africa, so I could not battle to stay on at EAFRO. Kitty Beauchamp's comment was 'however could you have been so sensible as to marry Richard McConnell?' Looking back I can see that this decision led not just to a new life with very wide horizons, but to at least three new lives'. There were the Kalahari Days, at our first married home in Bechuanaland. Then 'across the pond' in North America, where I met Richard's relatives and visited many Museums, Universities and Fisheries laboratories in Canada and USA. This was followed by five glorious years when he was directing the geological survey in British Guiana (BG), the start of a whole new life studying the ecology of South American fishes and the delights and opportunities of comparing this new fauna and flora with those of the African tropics.

Before going to Bechuanaland after our marriage, we first visited England and then Richard's old skiing haunts and friends in Switzerland, where we travelled through deep snow on icy roads in 'Susan' his old car (now resident with friends in the UK). Then we went by sea to Cape Town en route to our new home in Lobatsi in 'BP' (now Botswana).

Kalahari Days (1954–1957)

From England we had sailed to Cape Town, where we were deposited from the 'cape roller' seas in stormy weather. We collected a new car and drove north across the karoo to Mafeking, then the Bechuanaland Protectorate HQ, en route to the Geological Survey Base in Lobatsi. Here we settled into a house below a cliff where baboons retired to sleep in safety. It had a well-stocked garden full of fruit trees – citrus, peaches, figs and many others, frequented by many colourful birds. In the next two years we had exciting trips exploring the Kalahari Desert and camping near pans frequented by numerous game animals. Among interesting visitors to Lobatsi was Laurens van der Post, with a team making a film on the lives of the San people, some of whom we occasionally met on our trips into the desert.

In September that year I flew back to Jinja for three months at EAFRO to complete various tilapia papers. The return journey from Uganda to BP involved an epic 3500 mile drive in my cloth-topped Landrover (the 'Flying bedstead') through Kenya, Tanganyika, Northern and Southern Rhodesia to Bechuanaland, an adventurous trip as the December rains had made a quagmire of many of the roads. Passing through Dodoma (in Tanganyika), where I stayed at the Geological HQ, I picked up Richard`s old cook Ramazani who came to look after us in BP, having been reassured by Paulo, my Jinja

*Ready to leave EAFRO and drive to Bechuanaland in my landrover,
known as the "flying bedstead", with my house in the background.*

houseboy, that I was a 'very good memsahib who never went into the kitchen'. So Ramazani and I were quite good friends by the time we arrived in Lobatsi.

Later, Richard and I crossed the Kalahari (in a 'caboose' camping vehicle) to the Okavango Delta, where the river meets the desert sands. While staying in Maun with the District Commissioner, we met another tilapia species (*Oreochromis macrochir*), being landed by African fishermen from gillnets set amongst the water lilies in these very beautiful riverine swamps. This Upper Zambezi tilapia species came from Lake Ngami and its type specimen was first described from there. However, it had already been stocked in many fish ponds in the Belgian Congo, from where it could escape into other river systems, so it came to be much more widely distributed (as mentioned earlier). Specimens from Rwanda ponds have even been found in the Kagera River flowing into Lake Victoria.

Lake Ngami was a large lake when visited by David Livingstone about 1859. In many years it dries up, but was once again a shallow lake with numerous water birds when we visited it. Yet when I flew back to EAFRO in 1954, we could see, far below us, the Makgadikgadi depression which was then such a vast stretch of water that a puzzled passenger asked me 'Is this Lake Victoria?'. We did not then know that this great saltpan north of the

Ramazani at the top of Victoria Falls, a stop-off on our journey to Bechuanaland.

Our home in Lobatsi, HQ of the Geological Survey of Bechuanaland Protectorate.

Kalahari Desert was once the huge paleo-Makgadikgadi lake which, in Pleistocene times, had hosted a rapidly evolving radiation of cichlid fishes, comparable in morphological diversity to that in the extant African Great Lakes. Splendid detective work published in 2005 by a team of eight scientists – fish systematists, paleogeologists and geographers – showed that when this lake dried up, *c*2000 years ago, it had seeded all the major river systems of southern Africa with ecologically diverse serranochromine cichlids, thus revealing 'how local evolutionary processes operating during a short window of ecological opportunity can have a major and lasting effect on biodiversity on a continental scale' (Joyce *et al*, 2005).

Our stay in BP (1954–56/7) included a period of unusually heavy rains which stirred many creatures into life – toads which had been aestivating in rock crevices, delicate aquatic insects which suddenly appeared in isolated pools, including a flight of dytiscid water beetles which emerged dramatically one evening to fly west into the sunset. In the Kalahari Desert seasonal rivers cut into their steep banks revealing bands of damp sand from previous rainy seasons. Water had been retained in the very fine, windblown sand deposits into which roots of the riverside *Acacia* trees penetrated to a great depth and this residual moisture in the sands enabled these trees to dot much of the landscape. BP's eastern boundary was Rudyard Kipling's 'great grey-green greasy Limpopo all set about with fever trees' which flooded magnificently, swirling debris before it, before the water disappeared into the sand leaving only occasional pools.

After two years exploring the Kalahari and Okavango from our Lobatsi base, Richard was asked to participate in the International Geological Congress in Mexico. This provided the opportunity to meet relatives and colleagues in

On safari in the wet season. Testing the depth before crossing the Molopo River.

Flood water rushing through Lobatsi in the wet season of January 1955.

North America, but on our way back to Africa via the UK, the Overseas Geological Survey suddenly decided to move Richard to British Guiana in South America (from 'BP to BG'). So we never returned to Africa and had to arrange for all our possessions in BP to be packed and shipped to BG – which took ages. I was very sad to leave Africa, but the move to a whole new continent in 1957 proved immensely stimulating, as I have already described in my book *Land of Waters*.

Widening Horizons: 'Across the pond'

En route to the Geological Congress we visited Richard's relatives in Canada, travelling by sea from Cape Town to New York on a small cargo ship of the Robin Line. Fortunately this vessel called in at Walvis Bay (in what is now Namibia) to collect special sheep skins and mineral ore, so several days there provided an opportunity to see the Namib desert. This was the 'Sheltering Desert' where Henno Martin, who became their Director of Geology, had hidden away during the war years, so he had a huge knowledge of the desert animals. From Cape Town it proved an interesting voyage as we followed an unusual route dictated by sea temperatures, to keep the cargo cool, crossing the usual shipping lanes and gaining time on the voyage to New York by using the sea currents to best advantage.

On arrival in New York, the US customs were very suspicious of a lump of rock from Lobatsi, which we had brought with us for age determination at NY University. We then travelled by train to Montreal. Richard's antecedents had lived in Canada for three generations. His father, Richard G. McConnell ('RG'), was one of the founders of the Canadian Geological Survey, and was famed for his explorations of the Canadian Northwest and for his studies on the geological structure of the Rocky Mountains. In 1886 he had collected the Burgess Shale in the Canadian Rockies, from what Stephen J. Gould later described as 'the most precious and unique of all fossil localities' a 'Crucible of Creation', with its Ediacaran Late Precambrian fossils, over 500 million year old. This was followed by RG's epic 4000 mile journey in 1887 and 1888 exploring the Yukon and MacKenzie River basins in northern British Columbia, over-wintering in the Arctic circle.

Before and after the International Geological Congress in Mexico I was taken to meet Richard's Canadian relatives and to McGill University. I also visited many fisheries people and ecologists, including those in the Fish Section of the American Museum of Natural History in New York, the Smithsonian Institution in Washington, ecologists in Professor W.C. Allee's department at Chicago University (whose *Principles of Animal Ecology*, by Allee, Emerson, Park, Park & Schmidt had been one of my guiding lights). We also enjoyed the splendid aquaria in New York and Chicago, and visited ichthyologists Bob and Fran Miller at Ann Arbor. Then I stayed with Carl Hubbs at the Scripps Institute in California and visited the Los Angeles Museum. Kind people taught me many new things in this huge continent.

Geological field trips in Mexico took us to Yucatan and Palenque, and we made visits to many other ancient sites and caves, where Richard's hat was used to catch small blind cave fishes. After the Congress, while Richard went on a hush hush visit connected with uranium deposits, I travelled widely by Greyhound bus, and camped with students at the bottom of the Grand Canyon. Richard and I met again in Denver – 'mile high city' (but lower than Nairobi) – to climb the Rocky Mountains, before crossing Canada on the Canadian Pacific Railway to visit his old home in Ottawa. This had a magnificent view over the Ottawa River, where huge logs were being rafted downstream. Finally, from Montreal we steamed down the St Lawrence Seaway, below a shimmering display of northern lights, before setting out on a rough sea crossing to England. There we learned that instead of returning to Bechuanaland, Richard was to direct the Geological Survey in British Guiana (now Guyana) in South America.

So after a short stay, we travelled from London, as two of the six passengers on a cargo ship bound for Barbados, from where we flew, with magnificent views of the Orinoco delta, to Georgetown, our home base for the next six years.

South America, a new life: the Land of Waters (1957–1962)

The move to a new continent with a new flora and fauna to investigate proved immensely stimulating, and was especially intriguing for me because South America was connected with Africa as part of Gondwanaland until the Atlantic Ocean opened up about 100 million year ago. So I would find some of the same fish families, including the cichlids (though not tilapia), descendents of groups present in Gondwanaland before the separation. But I also found remarkable convergences between quite unrelated groups of fish responding to comparable habitats and ways of life in the two continents. The Neotropical gymnotoids are a good example. Thought to be offshoots of characoid stock, they closely resemble the mormyroids with comparable habitats in African waters, both relying on their electric organs to help them live nocturnal lives, by emitting electric signals for location, and for social communication.

South America has few basic groups of freshwater fishes compared with Africa, but now has the largest number of species (probably over 5000) of any zoogeographical region. Unlike Africa, where we had been studying lacustrine fish faunas dominated by cichlids, here the emphasis was on riverine faunas dominated by radiations of characoids (and no cyprinids at all). Catfish families are also very diverse in South America and some are quite bizarre. The cichlids are not such important members of the fish communities as in Africa, but they include many well-known colourful aquarium fishes, such as the Angel fish *Pterophyllum*, the Oscar *Astronotus*, Discus *Symphysodon*, many *Cichlasoma*, species, and dwarf cichlids. These are exported in huge numbers from South America together with very colourful small characins, such as the neon tetras, and armoured catfishes. Perhaps you have seen some of these in an aquarium in your doctor's waiting room?

In sheer enjoyment of six years spent in this beautiful and varied part of South America, with its vast forests and savannas intersected by many large interconnecting rivers, I later recorded what I learned of its natural history in a book called *Land of Waters*, in addition to scientific papers on the fishes and birds. Looking back, I can see that my future thoughts on fish communities in tropical waters were coloured by these years of watching the interactions between the fishes in these vast natural aquaria. How did they signal to one another, to school and find mates? How did they avoid predators? How did they react to the constantly changing physical and chemical conditions as the waters rose and fell seasonally and from year to year?

The present very diverse South American fish fauna is the product of extensive radiations initiated during the long isolation of the continent during the Tertiary. Numerically, both in numbers of species and individuals, the fish fauna is dominated by characoids and siluroids (catfishes). The former include the most conservative living forms and some of the most specialised, with teeth and body form greatly modified according to the fish's diet and

British Guiana: Victoria regia lilies in a Botanic Garden canal in Georgetown.

Left: Richard observing cichlid breeding behaviour in a sugar estate irrigation canal.
Below Richard at a Rupununi airstrip with Sobraham Singh (in topi) who later became Director of the Geological Survey, and Stan Brock (in large hat), manager of the government cattle ranch.

Seine netting a pool on the Rupununi savannah at the end of the wet season. In the distance are the Kanaku Mountains.

Below: aboard the Cape St Mary during a trawl survey of the Guyana Shelf.

Above: The McTurk family outside their home at Karanambo. From the left, Diane, Tiny and Connie.
Below: Collecting bait for fishing on the coastal savanna.

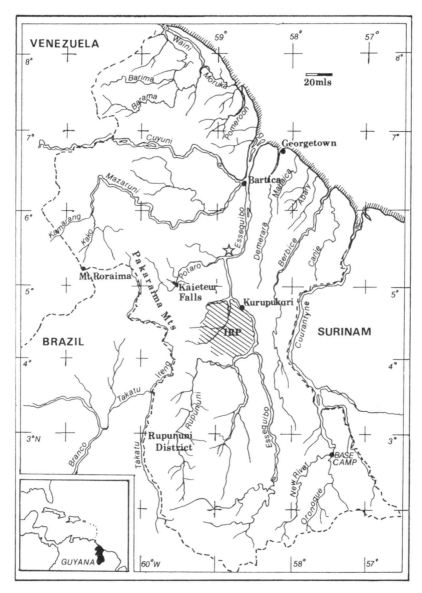

Map of Guyana showing the location of the Rupununi area which drains both to the Amazon, via the Rio Branco, and to the Essequibo. (The hatched area denotes the Iwokrama Rainforest Project and the star marks the location of Omai gold mine as described in 'Land of Waters'.)

way of life. Morphologically the characoid fishes with their marvellous adaptations to fill all kinds of ecological niches rival those of cichlids in the African Great lakes. The many families of catfishes (siluroids) also provide splendid examples of radiation, ranging in size from the giant *Brachyplatystoma* species, reputedly growing to three metres long, to minute trichomycterids which live in the gill cavities of other fishes (and are widely feared as they are reputed to be attracted by urine to enter the orifices of unwary bathers). Bottom dwelling catfishes of several families are armoured with scutes, including the very numerous and colourful Loricariidae.

Present-day South America is low lying, dominated by vast rivers such as the Amazon and Paranã but when we were there many of the river systems were relatively unexplored compared with Africa. South America lacks large lakes, but the rivers flood into the forest and over the savannas seasonally. The cichlids occur in a great range of habitats, from warm pools open to the sun to shaded forested waters. They are found in brackish estuaries and clear nutrient-poor rivers, where they have to compete with non-cichlids in feeding on exogenous foods, such as insects and fruits dropping into the streams. The South American cichlids are all basically substratum-spawners, although some such as *Geophagus* move their young by mouth to better oxygenated water. Most live in pairs in streams or swampy lakes, although there are a few rheophilic species. The predatory *Cichla ocellaris*, a noted 'sport fish' (stocked in Panama, see Chapter 9), is one of the world`s largest cichlid species, growing to over a metre long. Many of the cichlids are very hardy, able to withstand considerable changes in temperature, poorly oxygenated waters and varied chemical conditions. South America has no indigenous tilapia, but several species (including *O. mossambicus*, *O. niloticus*, *T. rendalli*, *T. zillii*) have been widely introduced into dams, especially in the drier areas like North-east Brazil.

The lives of the riverine fishes are governed by seasonal changes in water level which affect the physicochemical and biotic conditions. Most riverine fishes are very mobile, the large species of characoids and catfishes migrating long distances up or down river between spawning and feeding grounds. Cichlid movements are more local in scope, on and off the floodplains, in and out of lateral lakes. Cichlid breeding is less seasonal, but the fish communities in which they live are continually changing as other members of the fish fauna come and go. At night, catfishes and most other predators are active while the sight-orientated, diurnally active cichlids hide away motionless alongside banks, among forest litter or in shallows. Piscivorous fishes are abundant, such as the widely distributed characoid *Hoplias malabaricus*, serrasalmine pirana, and many others which prey on larval and juvenile cichlids. Numerous aquatic birds, reptiles and mammals, amongst other predators, take a heavy toll, especially when water bodies are shrinking in the dry seasons. Many river systems are still unexplored and cichlid information is scattered, often in aquarium literature and in reports of collections made over a wide area. In British Guiana the American Carl Eigenmann laid a good foundation for ecological studies by providing keys to the numerous species that he collected in 1912 when visiting BG to investigate the effect on the fish of the Kaieteur Falls (244 m high).

Early records of explorations of South American inland waters

Charles Warterton, an eccentric Englishman whose family owned sugar estates in British Guiana, in 1826 wrote his delightful *Wanderings in South America* about his time there in 1812–24. The Germans Richard and Robert Schomburgk published *Travels in British Guiana in 1840–1844,* translated into English in 1922 by Walter Roth (Director of the Georgetown Museum while we were there). In 1877 the geologist Charles Barrington-Brown described in his book '*Canoe and camp life in British Guiana*' his discovery of the Kaieteur waterfall, one of the highest and most beautiful in the world, when travelling down the Cuyuni river. The great naturalist William Beebe established a field station for the New York Zoological Society at Bartica near the junction of the Essequibo and Cuyuni River systems, about which he wrote many books (including *Our search for a Wilderness* 1910, followed by *Tropical Wildlife in British Guiana* in 1917 describing discoveries made from this station.

The freshwater fish fauna had been explored and the ecological groups described by Carl H. Eigenmann (1917) in the *Memoirs of the Carnegie Museum* after he had visited Guyana to compare fish faunas above and below the Kaieteur Falls (a volume which provided keys for identification of the fishes, invaluable for our later studies). An Oxford University Expedition, in which Owain and Paul Richards and Max Nicholson were among the participants, was described by Hingston in 1932 in his book *In the Guiana Forest*. George Carter from Cambridge University (UK) studied respiratory adaptations to low oxygen in the black acid rain-forest waters and published his results in the *Zoological Journal of the Linnean Society* in 1934.

Collecting animals for zoos and television was also about to reveal these biological riches to a wider public, with Gerald Durrell's *Three Singles to Adventure* published in 1954, and David Attenborough's *Zoo Quest to Guiana* in 1956.

A week after we arrived in BG, Dr Hickling, Fisheries Advisor to the UK Colonial Office, happened to visit Georgetown on his rounds and the Fisheries Officer Bertie Allsopp very kindly invited me to accompany them on a fish-collecting trip to the Rupununi savannas on the Brazilian border. We stayed with those kind and hospitable people Tiny and Connie McTurk, who had a lifelong experience of BG's natural history, at their cattle ranch at Karanambu. To get there we flew in an ancient Dakota with its wartime metal seats, over the cauliflower tops of tall trees emerging from the seemingly endless rain

*South American freshwater fishes I: **A** Stingray Potamotrygon (30 cm);*
***B** Lungfish Lepidosiren (50 cm); **C** Foureyes Anableps (15 cm); **D** Osteoglossum (50 cm);*
***E** Electric eel Electrophorus (60 cm); **F** Puffer Colomesus (5 cm); **G** Cichlasoma (10 cm);*
***H** Cichla (40 cm); **I** Crenicichla (25 cm); **J** Hoplosternum (15 cm); **K** Ancistrus (15 cm);*
***L** Megalodoras (70 cm); **M** Hypostomus (15 cm); **N** Pimelodus (30 cm); **O** Arapaima (150 cm);*
***P** Pseudoplatystoma (120 cm); **Q** Vandellia (4 cm).*

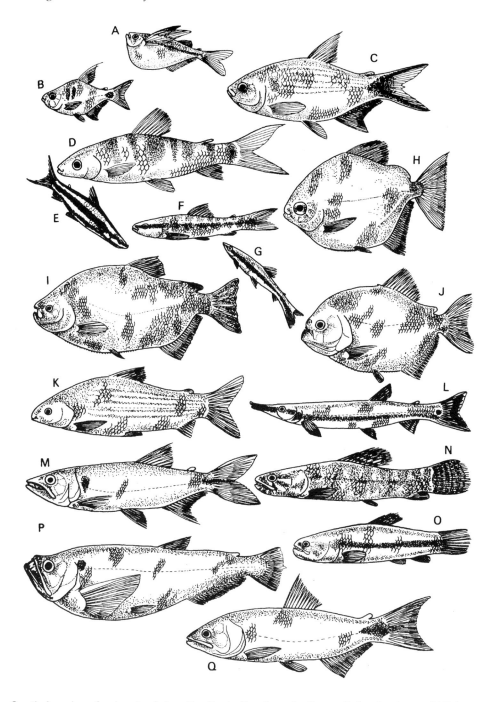

South American freshwater fishes II – illustrating the adaptive radiation in characoid fishes.
A *Gasteropelecus (6 cm);* **B** *Tetragonopterus (12 cm);* **C** *Brycon (50 cm);* **D** *Leporinus (30 cm);* **E** *Anostomus (12 cm);* **F** *Characidium (4 cm);* **G** *Poecilobrycon (4 cm);* **H** *Metynnis (12 cm);* **I** *Colossoma (50 cm);* **J** *Serrasalmus (30 cm);* **K** *Prochilodus (40 cm);* **L** *Boulengerella (45 cm);* **M** *Acestrorhynchus (20 cm);* **N** *Hoplias (30 cm);* **O** *Hoplerythrinus (25 cm);* **P** *Hydrolicus (60 cm);* **Q** *Salminus (50 cm).*

The Geological Survey headquarters in Georgetown, which included our house within the compound. The buildings were on stilts because of the danger of flooding at high tides. The Botanic Gardens are in the distance.

forest, to Karanambu airstrip, where Tiny McTurk in his ancient jeep, and local Amerindians seated on bullocks, awaited the plane.

These savannas, which when seasonally flooded from July to September, connect the Essequibo and Amazon river systems. They were very dry at this time of year, so fishes were easy to seine from isolated ponds where they had accumulated as the floods receded. We were searching for fishes that might be useful for controlling water weeds in the boundary trenches of the sugar estates. Seining these ponds was a wonderful introduction to a whole new fish fauna: cichlids (coming into breeding condition at this time of year), living among numerous catfishes, including armoured loricariid males carrying eggs, and characids of many families. We were surprised to find stingrays so far upriver, and caught electric eels amongst the gymnotoids.

I immediately fell in love with this open savanna country and its wide views of distant blue mountains, and arranged to return here many times to study the ecological groupings of the fishes and the effects of the seasonal cycles on them as they moved into the swamps with the rains. These flooded swamps connected the northward–flowing Essequibo river system with the southwest-flowing Ireng River on the Brazilian border, which in turn joined the Rio Branco which flows, via the Rio Negro, to the main River Amazon. What fishes managed to cross this divide?

So I became attached to the Fisheries Division of the Department of Agriculture – at the princely sum of $1 a year, incremental date April 1st (April fool's day) – as wives could not be 'gainfully employed'. But I had working space in the Freshwater Fisheries Laboratory at the back of Georgetown's very beautiful Botanic Gardens. As I cycled between our house and the laboratory I passed islands in the trenches covered with tall trees where nine species of egret and heron roosted each night. Six of these species were nesting here and this provided a wonderful opportunity to study these beautiful birds. I also passed the small zoo with local animals, many of which I came to know as individuals, and where 'snail hawk' kites (*Rostrhamus sociabilis*) made spectacular displays while nesting on the tall trees on the islands. They also perched on territorial posts along the trenches while spying out the large pomacean water snails on which they fed. The snails were grabbed from the water with long claws and piles of empty snail shells accumulated below their posts. Snails were also carried to feed their screeching young in their nests high in the trees. Dragonflies patrolled territories along the trenches. Manatees (*Trichechus latirostris*) also lived in these trenches where they had been introduced in order to clear water weeds. We experimented on how fast they did so, and I even had to bottle feed a small orphan manatee.

We had many interesting biologists visiting us, mainly from North America. Abundant wading birds also arrived from there to feed on the coastal mudlflats frequented by fiddler crabs (*Uca* species). An interesting happening at this time was the establishment of cattle egrets (*Bubulcus ibis*) in the heronries on the botanical garden islands. How did they do this? I spent hours watching them to see how their relative numbers varied from year to year according to

Dr Hickling (right) examining Tilapia mossambicus *while on his visit to Guyana. With him is Bertie Allsopp, the local Fisheries Officer.*

the duration of the two rainy seasons here on the coast. Cattle egrets were then undergoing a worldwide population explosion and had recently appeared in Florida heronries too. In the 1950s they were not yet to be seen in the Rupununi and it seemed that the forest had been a barrier to their dispersal to that area. A few first appeared there in the early 1960s and they then became very abundant on the dry savannas. As 'dry-feet' feeders, cattle egrets did not compete for food with the 'wet-feet' feeding local herons, but they did compete for nesting sites in the heronries.

Later, I also became biologist to the research ship RV *Cape St Mary.* Originally built for work off West Africa, when Ghana became independent the research ship crossed the Atlantic for a two year trawl survey of fishes on the continental shelf off BG between Venezuela and Surinam. Here we found, landed on the ship in all their glorious colours, some two hundred species of tropical marine fishes representing seventy families. We also found a fascinating assortment of invertebrates which came up in the trawl, collections of which were later studied at the BM(NH) in London. Sciaenid fishes (of over twenty five species) predominated in catches over soft bottoms. Croakers and drums were landed amidst a noisy cacophony. Their seasonal movements, breeding seasons and how they shared food resources made a fascinating study. Towards the edge of the shelf (at 100 fathoms) fossil corals, which grew here when the sea level was lower during the ice ages, tore the trawl net but produced colourful representatives of fishes now found on West Indian island coral reefs. Years later, goggling off Tobago, I swam with many of these beautiful fishes among the large gorgonian seafans.

The upper Mazaruni River.

A typical hand-dug sugar estate canal in Guyana.

Amidst this splendid feast of colourful fishes I did not entirely forget tilapia. In 1954 the BG Fisheries Division established breeding ponds for imported *Tilapia mossambica*, from which thousands of fingerlings were distributed around the country, to farm ponds, sugar estate flood-fallow fields, schools and demonstration ponds. Carp were also being tried for pond cultivation but with less success. In the 'flood-fallow' fields (i.e. fields which were flooded before the new crop was planted) these tilapia were mainly gobbled up by numerous indigenous piscivores, especially the characid huri (*Hoplias malabaricus*), which gained access to the fields from the surrounding canals, and by caymen and herons. We were surprised to hear from one school that bats were catching the tilapia we had just stocked – as indeed they were. Later I watched by torchlight fish-eating bats (*Noctilio*) scooping up small fish from Rupununi pools with a tearing sound as their claws trailed the water surface. In freshwater ponds the tilapia yields were not very rewarding, but tilapia grew and thrived abundantly in the brackish water of coastal plain swamplands. Floods caused by continuous heavy rain, backed up by tidal rise, distributed teeming tilapia populations from the ponds, into miles of brackish-pasture swamps. Here tilapia made up about 95% of the cast-net catches until the swamps almost dried up some two months later.

Establishment of an experimental and demonstration station for brackish water fish culture had been recommended by the International Bank for Reconstruction and Development in their report on Economic Development of British Guiana. So Bertie Allsopp went to study fish culture operations in the Far East and Surinam, and then set up such a station on 100 acres of tidally flooded land at Onverwagt in Western Berbice. These ponds were stocked with indigenous mullet (*Mugil* species), snook (*Centropomus*), sciaenid *Micropogon* and *Cynoscion*, Tarpon (*Megalops*), prawns and *Tilapia mossambicus*. The tilapia grew best in mixed ponds where piscivores controlled the excessive numbers

The RV Cape St Mary which was brought from West Africa to work on the Guyana Shelf.

of small tilapia, and also provided relief from predation for the more desirable mullets. The tilapia also cleared *Najas* and *Ruppia* plant beds, as well as filamentous algae which sheltered the larvae of malaria-carrying mosquitos. Argulid parasites attacked many of the fish, especially in the dry months of higher salinity water, but diminished when the pond water became fresher. To aid transport around the ponds, a horse was purchased, which the auditors queried, declaring it 'a second-hand horse', unaware that this mare contained a 'first hand horse' inside it, which enlivened some bureaucratic correspondence!

From BG I visited the Bamboo Grove Fish farm in Trinidad, run by Fisheries Officer Jake Kenny. From this farm and other ponds *Tilapia mossambica* had escaped into the Caroni Swamp in the mid-1950s floods. The swamp was noted for its roosts of brilliant scarlet ibis (*Eudocimus ruber*) amongst its rich bird fauna in the mangroves, a marvellous place to visit. Here Jake showed me *T. mossambica* males staying by their spawning plaques despite the tidal rise and fall in water level. His 1995 memoirs described bringing the first tilapia material to the West Indies in 1949.

The person responsible was Dr Hickling, the idea born of the need to produce fish to feed the masses of rural poor in the Colonies. Tilapia is one of the easiest species to culture. It breeds readily (far too easily), is tolerant of over-crowding, resistant to disease, can be maintained without artificial feeding and is generally of acceptable form and taste. The main drawback was the prolific breeding, producing many small fish rather than a few large ones. At Bamboo Grove in one small breeding pond the process went from 2 cm long fingerling to 9 cm breeding adult in six weeks. Dr Hickling convinced the Colonial Office that tilapia culture was a potential solution to the general problem of chronic protein shortage in tropical colonies, so in 1949 the first tilapia material was shipped to the West Indies, not from Africa but from Malaya, by slow aircraft taking several days via London to St Lucia. Here they bred in specially constructed ponds in the Botanical gardens, from where numerous fingerlings were moved to Jamaica and Trinidad.

We had many interesting visitors while we were in BG, including another Oxford Expedition, led by A.J. Cain, accompanied by Robin Liley who collected

A fishery adviser's visit to Onverwaget, the brackish water fish culture station.

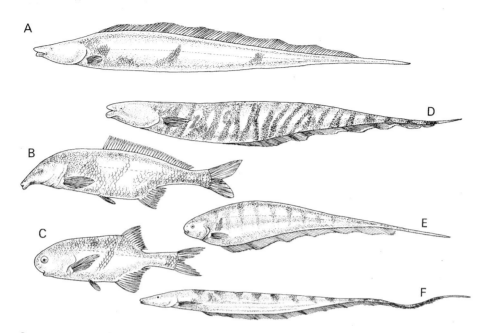

*Convergent evolution in two unrelated groups of electric fishes: the mormyrids of Africa (A, B, C) and gymnotoids of South America (D, E, F). Convergence occurs in types of electric discharge, ecology and body form; propulsion is by undulations of a long unpaired fin in many cases. Mormyrids: **A** Gymnarchus niloticus (100 cm); **B** Mormyrus kannume (60 cm); **C** Petrocephalus catostoma (9 cm). Gymnotoids: **D** Gymnotus carapo (30 cm); **E** Eigenmannia virescens (25 cm); **F** Gymnorhamphichthys hypostomus (15 cm).*

Hans Lissmann using his apparatus for detecting electric discharges from the fishes he has caught.

fishes from the Essequibo, Chris Perrin who studied birds, and half a dozen others. David and Barbara Snow from Beebe's New York Zoological Laboratory in Trinidad came to study manakin displays and University of Toronto people used mist-nets to collect bats. Lear and Margaret Grimmer from Washington Zoo came to investigate the diet of hoatzins (*Opisthocomus hoazin*), large ungainly birds which flopped around in the pimpler thorn bushes alongside the lowland rivers. Their young dived into the water below when danger threatened, then scrambled out using a special claw on each wing. The novelist Evelyn Waugh came to relive his 1934 hilarious *Ninety two Days* description of riding up the cattle trail to Brazil (reprinted in his book *When the Going was Good*). The elderly Colonel Richard Meinertzhagen, veteran of the First World War campaign in Tanganyika arrived wanting 'to see the Kaieteur Falls before he died'. He came with Theresa Clay from the BM(NH) (author with Miriam Rothschild of *Fleas, Flukes and Cuckoos*) who was looking for bird parasites as an aid to determining bird family relationships.

Meanwhile my Richard organised a Symposium of Caribbean Geologists, with field trips into the interior, attended by geologists from many countries. It was a very busy and interesting time.

I was most involved with Hans Lissmann from Cambridge University who came to study the gymnotoid electric fishes, after I had written to him describing the delights of watching the ethereal ballets of these nocturnal fishes in the clear water of Rupununi streams. The first historic test of a gymnotoid-detection apparatus was made in a trench in the Botanic Gardens on a Sunday afternoon as soon as he arrived. The equipment was intended to locate the fish by listening to their discharge frequencies and was linked to a tape recorder. We reeled back in surprise as we first received loud Indian music followed by 'Eat more Marmite'. The apparatus had picked up the local radio station! But the device did prove very successful for detecting gymnotids in the many types of water visited, as described in his classic papers (1958, 1963). Lissmann distinguished Type 1 'tone' (later called 'wave' EODs) signals from specimens living in fast-flowing streams and open water (with discharges up to an unbelievable 1600/sec in *Porotergus* which lived in the fastest-flowing water). Type II 'pulse' discharges were common among sluggish-water and bottom-living forms (with basic discharges of 5 to 190/ sec in undisturbed fish, increasing when they became excited). In Africa Lissmann had previously found both types of discharge, Type I in the large mormyrid *Gymnarchus*, which lived solitarily along swamp fringes, and Type II pulses in many other small mormyroids.

In BG some gymnotoid species (*Sternopygus, Gymnotus, Apteronotus, Hypopomus*) were living solitary lives. Others such as *Eigenmannia* occurred in small schools. In the Botanic Garden trenches they were hiding away under a bridge till dusk, then fanning out with clockwork precision to feed. In the

Rupununi, individual solitary *Apteronotus albifrons* were belligerent in defence of their hiding places. The elongated transparent young of *Gymnorhamphichthys* lived buried in the bottom sand of the streams during the day. Tank experiments showed how the electric field is used to sense the environment (and in the Rupununi pools they backed into crevices at great speed) and to detect food and predators. Later work also showed the social significance of these discharges, males 'wolf-whistling' (as it were) to passing females. Playback experiments in the field showed that *Sternopygus* males could distinguish their own and also send out courtship signals to passing females. The Rupununi Moco Moco creek produced eleven species of gymnotoids, four producing Type I (tone) signals and seven emitting pulsed signals.

Visual and chemical communication in fishes: **A.** Astynax bimaculatus *which bears the humeral and caudal dark markings characteristically found in many midwater schooling fishes;* **B.** Pristella riddlei *in which the black spot on the dorsal fin acts as a social releaser for schooling;* **C** Pterophyllum scalare *a cichlid in which the pelvic fins become conspicuously light in colour and are jerked to 'call' the guarded young;* **D** Corynopoma riisei *a glandulocaudine characid in which the male wafts a pheromone from the caudal gland to the following female; note the extreme sexual dimorphism including opercular extension paddles of the male.*

A selection of Rupununi fish from a drying pond. They include piranas (right), Cichla ocellaris, *a striped catfish and* Hoplias malabaricus *(top left).*

Baron Humboldt, on his early travels to Venezuela (1800), had recorded how the electric eel *Electrophorus electricus* could stun horses. In addition to a slow regular discharge, this very large species has developed a voluntary discharge of up to 550 volts used to stun prey and deter enemies. As Richard Keynes, from a special unit at Cambridge University needed *Electrophorus* for laboratory experiments, he accompanied Hans on one of his visits to BG. With Bertie Allsopp we had a high old time collecting electric eels for him, at one time landing five in one seine haul; I kept well to the rear during this operation!

There is now a huge literature on these electric fishes, which have been found to be very abundant throughout South America, both in deep river channels (where they made up a surprisingly large proportion of experimental trawl catches) and in the floating meadows of white water rivers. They also occur in the terra firma streams (Albert & Crampton 2005).

All too soon, in 1962, Richard's tour of duty in British Guiana came to an end when he reached retirement age and we returned to the UK. Despite the separation from Africa during this period I had gained enormously wide experience of a huge variety of fish that were new to me and I had been privileged to participate in projects ranging from pond culture to marine surveying. I also acquired a very wide network of colleagues in various branches of aquatic ecology, many of whom have remained lifelong friends.

Back to home base –
The Natural History Museum in London.

This photograph shows the staff of the Fish Section in the Fish Gallery
(as it was then) at the British Museum (Natural History) on the occasion of
Geoffrey Palmer's retirement in 1978.
From the left: Gordon Howes, Oliver Crimmin, Ethelwynn Trewavas, Peter
Whitehead, Maggie Clarke, Geoffrey Palmer, Mary Connolly, Humphry
Greenwood, Keith Bannister, yours truly, Alwynn Wheeler and Jim Chambers.

*I have always enjoyed having visitors to our home in Sussex. This group of
visiting scientists from Malawi, via Southampton University, were no doubt glad
of the warmth on our south-facing terrace. Since Barton Worthington lived
nearby we also shared visitors. Here (below) he is with Professor Hiroya
Kawanabe and Yukiko Kada in the 1990s.*

Looking north from the shore of Lake George to the snowcapped Rwenzori Mountains about 1969. There is now evidence that the glaciers are retreating.

The compound of the IBP Lake George team looking eastwards to the escarpment across the two islands that lie on the west side of Lake George.

Some of the IBP team working at Lake George in Uganda. Standing: Mary Burgis and Gideon (lab assistant); seated from the left – Ian Dunn, Lesley McGowan, George Ganf, Asanassio the cook, Joseph the house boy and Lakana the gardener.

Chapter 7
Home base –
Sussex and the BM(NH)

When Richard retired from the UK Overseas Geological Survey in 1962 we came to England to live on a ridge just behind the South Downs in Sussex. From then on (until 2004) my base of operations was in the Fish Section of the BM(NH), the British Museum (Natural History), now known simply as The Natural History Museum, in London. This was very congenial as Ethelwynn Trewavas, Humphry Greenwood, Peter Whitehead and other former colleagues were on the staff and fish researchers from all over the world came to consult them. Moreover, there were libraries with long runs of current journals to consult, an especially important consideration in pre-computer days. Also, the fish collections I had made in Africa and South America were deposited here and there was still much work to be done on them, such as describing new species. In many cases this involved sending material to specialists in museums elsewhere in the world and there was often a long wait while they sat on the lab bench of some busy scientist before they could be named. This information had to be retrieved for publication in scientific journals and information from many sources then collated into books such as *Fish Communities in Tropical Freshwaters* 1975 and *Ecological Studies in Tropical Fish Communities* 1987. As an Associate of the BM(NH), in addition to working facilities and the use of excellent libraries, I was awarded seven shillings and sixpence (= about US$1!) an hour on a diary-kept basis. This was a system introduced for retired staff who continued to work on the collections, until payments were discontinued due to financial cuts.

These books were a much more useful contribution than my efforts at teaching, although I did examine doctorate theses, mostly from universities overseas, with bibliographies which helped keep me up to date. I gave courses on tropical fish and fisheries at Makerere University in Uganda in 1967 and Salford University (UK), and for Sussex University I dreamed up a Further Education course on 'Environment Concern', long before this was a fashionable subject. In it we discussed issues like pollution and overpopulation.

During these years based at the BM(NH) I was also involved in several long-term overlapping projects, many of which involved editing multi-authored volumes after specialist workshops. These projects included the International Biological programme (IBP 1964–74) and the Tropical Group of the British Ecological Society, for which, as Honorary Secretary for about five years, I organised twice-yearly meetings on various aspects of tropical biology and an International Symposium on *Speciation in Tropical Environments* (1968).

NETWORKING
FROM SUSSEX AND LONDON

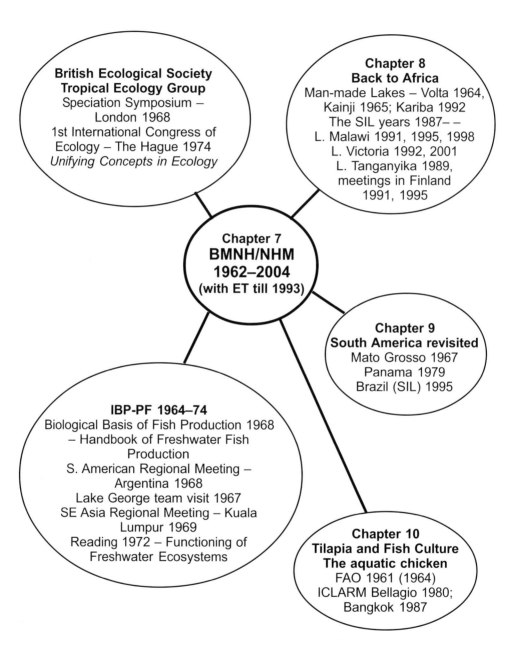

British Ecological Society
Tropical Ecology Group
Speciation Symposium –
London 1968
1st International Congress of
Ecology – The Hague 1974
Unifying Concepts in Ecology

Chapter 8
Back to Africa
Man-made Lakes – Volta 1964,
Kainji 1965; Kariba 1992
The SIL years 1987– –
L. Malawi 1991, 1995, 1998
L. Victoria 1992, 2001
L. Tanganyika 1989,
meetings in Finland
1991, 1995

Chapter 7
BMNH/NHM
1962–2004
(with ET till 1993)

Chapter 9
South America revisited
Mato Grosso 1967
Panama 1979
Brazil (SIL) 1995

IBP-PF 1964–74
Biological Basis of Fish Production 1968
– Handbook of Freshwater Fish
Production
S. American Regional Meeting –
Argentina 1968
Lake George team visit 1967
SE Asia Regional Meeting – Kuala
Lumpur 1969
Reading 1972 – Functioning of
Freshwater Ecosystems

Chapter 10
Tilapia and Fish Culture
The aquatic chicken
FAO 1961 (1964)
ICLARM Bellagio 1980;
Bangkok 1987

*The BM(NH) was an ideal base for meeting people and as a catalyst for ideas and
information. This led to my recruitment for numerous projects involving everything
from basic fieldwork overseas to editing conference proceedings. (Not bad for
someone who 'hasn't had a job since 1953!' – as Ro said when presented with the
Linnean Medal for Zoology by the Linnean Society of London in 1997 - Ed.)*

With Ethelwynn Trewavas in her office at the BMNH.

As tilapia became increasingly important in warm water fish culture throughout the tropics, tilapia studies continued in association with Ethelwynn Trewavas who was completing her *magnum opus* on *Tilapiine Fishes*. I visited the Food and Agriculture Organization (FAO) to help edit papers for the Warm-water Fish Culture conference held in Rome in 1961, and worked with ICLARM (= International Center for Aquatic Resources Management based in the Philippines) at a workshop at Bellagio on Lake Como in Italy (1980). This culminated in a much-used text *The Biology and Culture of Tilapias* (1982), and a follow-up meeting in Bangkok in Thailand which concentrated on *Tilapia Genetic Resources for Aquaculture* (ed. Pullin1988).

From 1962 Richard and I lived very happily in the home base we created in the small village of Streat in Sussex, with its wide views of the South Downs, fifty miles south of London. In the following years we entertained numerous overseas visitors and had very good parties, joined by local friends who had lived in South America or Africa, including the Worthington family, now neighbours in Sussex. Richard took me with him to many International Geological meetings. As a structural geologist, whose initial doctorate was with Professor Lugeon at Lausanne University based on field work in the Alps, it was an exciting time as the mid-ocean Atlantic ridge was just being explored. This was very relevant for understanding connections between South America and Africa. I learned so much from Richard's long-term views of life on earth, and these visits also provided splendid opportunities to visit field stations and universities. In Israel I met Adam Ben-Tuvia at Jerusalem University, Lev Fishelson in Haifa, and saw some of the experimental pond culture of tilapia. I stayed with Colette Serruya at the Lake Kinneret field station on the Sea of

Richard (right) with Barton Worthington (left) at Barton's house, not far from ours in Sussex. Barton's wife Stella, their dog and some IBP visitors.

Galilee, where they were studying 'Saint Peters Fish' *Sarotherodon galilaeus* and we watched *Tilapia zillii* spawning in the sunny sandy shallows near the laboratory. While Richard was visiting the Sinai peninsula I looked at coral fishes in the Gulf of Eilat. At the International Geological Congress in Prague, I was introduced by IBP contacts to the University and Museum, but unfortunately the congress was disrupted by the arrival of Russian tanks, a source of many vivid memories and a very sad time for the Czechs.

Richard was too busy with his international geological activities to come to the many meetings on ecology and animal behaviour which I attended, and he tended to develop a glazed look when discussions became too fishy. We shared the enjoyment of music and theatre, and of goggling to watch fishes on coral reefs in tropical seas. Richard's main loves were still mountains and skiing. He and Barton Worthington became good friends and had many skiing holidays together. These were too cold for me, and I had already broken an ankle on our skiing honeymoon in Switzerland. Once bitten, twice shy!

Meanwhile Richard had also set up 'The Richard Bradford Trust to explore the relationship between the methods of scientific investigation and artistic creation in literature, the visual arts and other art forms'. Thus he was busy with his own life and we have ensured that the Trust has continued after he died. Amongst other activities the Trust supported a series of lectures (1975-

78) given by Kenneth Clark, H.D.F. Kito, Jacquetta Hawkes, Peter Medawar, David Samuel, Glynne Wickham and Ernst Gombrich, under the auspices of the Royal Institution in London. These were edited into the book '*Art, Science and Human Progress*' published in 1983.

All this scattered activity left me free to travel, mostly on fishy business, so to my great joy I was able to revisit Africa and South America and explored new venues in tropical Asia and Australia. The hands-on fieldwork in Africa included pre-impoundment studies for new man-made lakes being created behind hydroelectric dams in West Africa in 1965 and 1966 (see Chapter 8). Later, in the 1980s and 1990s I made many visits to see the progress of research on the African Great Lakes Victoria, Malawi and Tanganyika (Chapter 8). In between I revisited South America as a member of the Royal Society and Royal Geographical Society 1967–69 Expedition to the Mato Grosso in Central Brazil in 1967 (Chapter 9).

Ecological Concepts

A symposium on *Speciation in Tropical Environments*, held in London in 1968, was organised by the Tropical Group of the British Ecological Society and The Linnean Society of London. The sixteen papers on animal and plant groups included contributions from Ernst Mayr on 'Bird Speciation', Robert

George Coulter (left) and (right) Gordon Howes with Bernice Brewster, colleagues at the BM(NH), in our garden which faces south looking out to the scarp slope of the South Downs behind Brighton in Sussex.

H. MacArthur on 'Patterns of communities in the tropics' and Paul W. Richards on 'Speciation in the tropical rainforest and concept of the niche'. In my paper I compared the diversity of fish communities in the very stable environments of the African Great lakes with those in seasonally fluctuating tropical rivers. Summing up, A.J. Cain stressed that the constant round-the-year supply of foods (such as large insects and fruits) not available in temperate climates, allows more specialization and richer faunas. He commented that the common European thrush (*Turdus philomelos*), in the course of a single year, passes through ecological niches appropriate to many different families of South American birds. He also queried whether dry seasons are less drastic than cold ones in their ecological effects. The symposium showed how much studies in tropical ecology were needed and as the book was widely used for teaching it helped to stimulate tropical studies. It was rather a landmark as it stressed that tropical ecology demands some different approaches from those applied in the temperate zone. Also that data from fish studies can make a significant contribution to ecological theory. Most early generalizations on tropical ecology had been based on bird and insect studies, and many ecologists were unaware of the huge amount of data available from fisheries.

Current ideas on relationships between diversity, stability and maturity, both in natural ecosystems and in those influenced by human activity, were hotly debated at the First International Congress of Ecology held in the Hague September 1974. This gathering of leading ecologists, including R.P. Odum, G.H. Orians, R. Margalef, R.H. May and some twenty others, discussed the flow of energy between trophic levels, comparative productivity in ecosystems, and strategies for management of man-made ecosystems. Although the science of ecology was not yet able to formulate rules for every management problem there seemed to be sufficient information to warn against the exploitation of natural resources without a sound evaluation of the consequences. Professor W.H. van Dobben of the Netherlands and I edited the 1975 book of plenary session papers as *Unifying Concepts in Ecology*. (It was later translated into Spanish.)

In 1978 the Zoological Society of London organised a symposium on phenology ('The temporal aspects of recurrent natural phenomena in relation to weather and climate'). By then, abundant data were available on ecological aspects of seasonality of fishes in tropical waters and showed a spectrum in which seasonality (caused mainly by seasonal injections of nutrients), varied greatly from the marked annual rhythms in floodplain rivers to relatively aseasonal conditions in equatorial lakes and coral reefs. It seemed that at the seasonal end of the spectrum, fish populations fluctuate greatly, both through the year and from year to year, whereas at the 'aseasonal' end populations remain stable. Under seasonal conditions this is achieved by migration, seasonal breeding cycles and growth rhythms. High fecundity, rapid development, early maturity and short life cycles, result in high production/

biomass ratios and few age groups in the populations. Seasonal mortalities are high and the fish have to be facultative feeders. Under more aseasonal conditions, fishes may spawn throughout the year, but biotic pressures (such as competition for nest sites) may impose seasonality. In species with large demersal eggs (such as cichlids) which produce small broods of guarded eggs and young, maturity tends to be delayed and fecundity reduced. Marine reef species with pelagic eggs are more fecund, whether total or fractional spawners (i.e. whether they spawn once a year or at intervals throughout the year). Aseasonal conditions allow great trophic specialization ('adaptive radiations') and produce more diverse communities in which fishes show the most complex behaviour and interactions (territoriality, complex social systems, symbioses in reef fishes, anti-predator devices such as camouflage, poisons etc). Predation pressures are high and availability of living space helps to limit fish numbers. Man-made lake studies (discussed in Chapter 8) have provided large scale experiments demonstrating how seasonal riverine communities become changed to less seasonal lacustrine ones.

Looking back from 2005, how true are these generalisations? (See Lowe-McConnell 1987.) Was I very brave (naïve?) to make them? Ecological theory then suggested that the fast-turnover '*r*-selected' populations produced under

Attributes of extreme types of seasonality in tropical waters		
Conditions	**Very seasonal**	**Aseasonal**
Examples	Floodplain Pelagic upwelling zone	Lacustrine littoral Coral reef
Fish populations	Fluctuating	Very stable
Migrations	Long migrations	Local migrations
Spawning	Seasonal, total	Aseasonal, multiple
Life cycles	Short	Longer
Production/ Biomass ratio	High	Lower
Feeding	Facultative	Specialized
Behaviour	Simple	Complex
Selection	r type, biotic and abiotic agents	Mainly K type, mainly by biotic agents
Community Implications	Rejuvenated/Cyclical ?resilient	Very mature/unchanging ?fragile

seasonal conditions in the tropics should be very resilient, whereas 'K-selected' species in communities characteristic of less seasonal habitats may be very fragile. This has important implications for the development of fisheries and conservation of fish stocks.

IBP-PF The International Biological Programme: Production in Freshwaters

The setting up of the International Biological Programme had been stimulated by the International Geophysical Year of 1957–8, although it was realized that biological problems need more than one year to solve. So, after preliminary discussions in 1959, IBP was launched for the decade 1964–74 and limited to basic studies related to biological productivity and human welfare. Aspects were chosen which were calculated to benefit from international collaboration and were urgent because of the rapid rate of changes taking place in environments throughout the world. Throughout the decade the freshwater productivity (PF) section of the IBP had its headquarters in London, where Barton Worthington was its Scientific Director.

Perhaps my best contribution to the IBP was to propose Dr Julian Rzóska to be Convenor of the Productivity of Freshwaters (PF) section. An active hydrobiologist conversant in many languages (including Russian), Julian was a colourful character who came to England to work with Charles Elton in Oxford when Poland was invaded during the war. After the war he led research on the River Nile from the University of Khartoum before returning to London, where he taught at the Sir John Cass College and trained many students who followed in his limnological footsteps. He was just about to retire from the College when IBP started.

The IBP set out to obtain internationally comparable observations of basic biological parameters for inter-calibration of suitable methods for measuring productivity in natural ecosystems. One of its most useful products was the series of IBP methodological handbooks, such as the *Handbook of Freshwater Fish Production* produced by the PF group. This was a success scientifically and financially. The first many-authored edition (1968), edited by W.E. 'Bill' Ricker of the Fisheries Research Board of Canada, was reprinted in 1971. It was later revised under the editorship of Tim Bagnold of the FBA. To produce this handbook an international team of nineteen scientists spent an enjoyable two days before and two days after an International Symposium on *The Biological Basis of Fish Production* hammering out the chapters. We were staying in Whiteknights Hall, a student residence at Reading University, where we were joined by 150 scientists from 19 countries for the symposium. This conference was memorable for many hilarious incidents, among them Karl Lagler's lost manuscript which turned up in the fridge. I remember a Japanese participant, who ten minutes or so before he gave his paper asked me to 'please

An aquarium display of cichlids from Lake Malawi.

*The colourful Neon tetras (*Cheirodon axelrodi*), from the upper reaches of the Amazon, are very popular with aquarium enthusiasts.*

The very colourful Hemichromis bimaculatus, *used in many aquarium experiments, is a West African forest river species.*

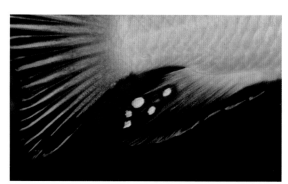

Egg spots on the anal fin of Pseudotropheus socolofi, *a Lake Malawi species. These spots attract females who try to take the 'eggs' into their mouth but instead receive a squirt of sperm which fertilise the eggs already there.*

A very colourful male Cyathopharynx furcifer *on its distinctive sand-castle spawning plaque in Lake Tanganyika.*

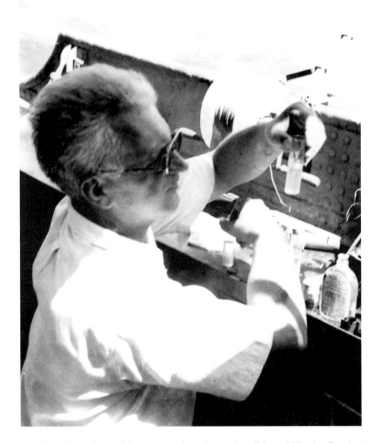

*Julian Rzóska taking samples from the River Nile in Sudan
in 1953. (Photo by J.F. Talling.)*

correct my English', then having delivered his rather incomprehensible paper
very politely and publicly thanked me for 'having corrected his English'.

The papers prepared by international contributors before the meeting
initiated discussions on the vital statistics of fish populations, the relationships
of fish populations to their food supply, competitive and behavioural factors
influencing production, predation and exploitation by man, and the
contribution of freshwater fish production to human nutrition and well-being.
The proceedings were edited by Shelby D. Gerking.

The history and development of the PF section of IBP was described by
Julian Rzóska (1980). It contained 232 projects from 42 countries by 1969 and
was later enlarged and totally modified in the USA. Julian described his job as
PF Co-ordinator as one of persuasion, diplomacy, human tact and travel round
the world to visit those biologists who had shown some interest in IBP ideas.
He likened the IBP to a stone thrown into a pond which would go on leaving

*The group photograph of those who met at Reading University
to write the IBP-PF Handbook on Freshwater Fish Production.*

ever larger ripples. Some people were highly critical of such international co-operation and it took time before a network of collaborators could be established. I had the fun of accompanying Julian to two regional meetings, the first of Latin American biologists in Santo Tomé on the Paraná River in Argentina in March 1968, then to the Southeast Asian Regional Meeting, as part of a symposium on *Biology of Inland Waters* held at the university in Kuala Lumpur in May 1969. In Argentina, for three or four days we listened to sonorous speeches in various forms of Spanish, delivered by delegates from Mexico to Chile in a beautiful conference room, but nothing came out of the meeting 'because of coherence and regional jealousies'. The Southeast Asian Regional Meeting 'did bring about co-operation between Japan and local scientists'.

Before this Argentine meeting I was able to visit the Limnological Laboratory at Santa Fé on the Middle Paraná River, where Dr Bonetto's team were doing splendid work studying the variations in fish communities in the local oxbow lakes (as recounted in Lowe-McConnell, 1987). Starting in 1961 they had tagged some 40,000 fishes of 25 species to discover how fast and how far they moved up and down the river on their reproductive and trophic migrations. Recaptures indicated that there were rapid reproductive migrations upriver and more leisurely trophic movements downriver. The most spectacular were of the characids *Prochilodus platensis* moving 780 km upriver at 8.7 km a day, *Salminus maxillosus* 237 km upriver in 11 days (21 km per day) and downriver 610 km at 5 km per day. During the IBP meeting we were very kindly invited to an Anglo-Spanish evening. Expecting only coffee and cakes, we were taken aback to discover that we had to eat a huge dinner (having prepared by having an early dinner in the hotel). I fell on what I hoped would be an anglophone 'Mr Williams' only to find he only spoke Welsh and Spanish.

While at the IBP meeting in Malaya we also visited the fish culture station at Malacca which was directed by Gerald Prowse. Here we saw the follow-up from Dr Hickling's project in the 1950s, including a 'latin square' of ponds being used to test the most promising crosses of tilapia species to produce mono-sex supplies for pond culture. We also visited a Malayan fish culture station over the hills in the highlands, where Gaythorne Medway (who much later, as Lord Cranbrook, became the President of UK WWF), was studying birds, and Adrian Marshall (who later took over from me as secretary of the BES Tropical Group) was making fascinating observations on very slender bats which lived in bamboo stems. Sadly, after the meeting, Kuala Lumpur burst into flames during pre-election riots due to conflict between indigenous Malayan people and the many Chinese active in the country. Julian and I escaped in time to continue our journey to India, but the Russian delegates were caught there for some days.

In India, where we were guided round an IBP trail, we were due to go to Kashmir, but floods prevented this, so instead we drove up to the very beautiful Kulu valley where I was introduced to the cyprinid 'snow trout' (*Schizothorax*) living in rushing torrents. We also discovered some ephemeropteran nymphs with phoretic *Simulium* larvae attached to them, which I collected for David Lewis at the BMNH. We had previously found these in East African rivers when the search was on for the whereabouts of the *Simulium damnosum* larvae that caused river blindness. These were later

Fish culture ponds visited in South-East Asia.

One of the numerous cartoons by Ian Efford of the Canadian IBP team that were 'approved' by Julian Rzóska and duplicated for those who attended the final IBP-PF conference in Reading in 1972.

discovered to live phoretically on freshwater crabs, and when Mount Elgon streams were treated with DDT, the crabs just got out of the river until the chemical had passed by.

Julian's judgement of the final two IBP-PF meetings, one in Poland and one in Reading (September 1972) concluded that the Reading one was controversial and not very inspiring. An illicit booklet of cartoons of the personalities involved was very funny indeed. Scientifically the net results were a large collection of reports, publications and opinions which then had to be collated by David Le Cren and myself, which was not published until 1980. Since David had just been appointed Director of the FBA, this editing proved to be quite a chore for me as about 54 authors were involved, some of whom kept updating their sections, while others did not. The resulting book was a compendium of sections on the effects of physical variables on freshwater production, chemical budgets and nutrient pathways, primary and secondary production, organic matter and decomposers, trophic relationships and efficiencies, estimations of productivity in lakes and reservoirs and dynamic models of lake ecosystems (with a generous section on Soviet IBP studies, then little known in the West). Nothing on rivers. I wonder how much this volume has been consulted?

Apart from this editing, throughout the IBP period I was also involved as a member of the Royal Society committee planning the team which made a five year study of the biology of the equatorial Lake George in Uganda. After initial discussions it was decided to concentrate on this one equatorial lake, rather than move to other African lakes such as Lake Tanganyika. This decision turned out to be a good one, as the team accumulated an impressive amount of basic scientific information from Lake George (as already described in Chapter 4).

The equatorial Lake George had extremely large populations of algae throughout the year. The lake is shallow (only three metres deep), and the seasonal changes were so slight that the lake biology was dominated by twenty four hour cycles bringing nutrients up from bottom mud daily rather than in a seasonal succession as at higher latitudes. The waters, which were pea-green with algae throughout the year, supported mainly herbivores: *Tilapia nilotica* which was then the basis of an important fishery, a smaller *Haplochromis* species and a cyclopoid copepod *Thermocyclops hyalinus*. The team appointed in December 1965, with advice from Professor Leonard Beadle, who had recently retired from the Chair of Zoology at Makerere University, consisted initially of five young biologists: Mary Burgis and Lesley McGowan, Tony Viner, Ian Dunn, and George Ganf. The team was later expanded to include Christine and David Moriarty, Johanna Darlington, Mike Tevlin and James Gwahaba. After a training period in the UK, including time spent at the FBA and BM(NH), the first members of the team started work in western Uganda

Lesley McGowan trimming Leonard Beadle's hair in the garden at IBP Lake George during my stay there in 1967. Lucy Leake, a visitor, and Ian Dunn are on the left, George Ganf and Mary Burgis on the right.

in late 1966. As their base they rented a derelict Uganda Fish Marketing Corporation building, at Kasenyi on Lake George which had been damaged by an earthquake. Nothing had been done by the time the first team members arrived so they had to start by building their laboratory and living accommodation. The team worked in collaboration with some Makerere University staff, and had many international visitors to the laboratory.

At the end of five years the scientific work of this team produced quite a comprehensive picture of how the ecosystem of the lake worked at that time. This has formed a baseline for more recent work on the fisheries of Lake George. One discovery which now has world-wide application is that of Dave and Chris Moriarty who demonstrated that *Tilapia nilotica* are able to digest blue-green algae (cyanobacteria) (see Chapter 4). After this it is was clear that tilapia could be cultured in nutrient-rich pond water, feeding on blue-greens and other algae (see Chapter 10).

The delights of watching tropical freshwater fishes – in aquaria and the field

In the last fifty years the aquarium fish trade has brought ever increasing varieties of colourful and curious fishes from tropical waters to homes worldwide as this fast-growing hobby expanded. Where do these fishes come from? In the 1930s my father's passion for fishes had included a 'tropical fish' aquarium, so I grew up with one heated by a gas flame (*sic!*) on the telephone table in the dining room. Here for many years lived generations of colourful live-bearing rainbow fish (*Lebistes*) which became conditioned to rising for food when the telephone bell rang. Other prize inhabitants included South American Angel fish (*Pterophyllum*) and small catfishes which helped the pond snails keep the glass clear of algae. All were kept happy with guidance from *The Handbook of Exotic Fishes* by Wm Innes (published in 1935, followed by 18 editions over twenty years). Even then, a special small plane was already taking fishes from South America to New York. Other tropical fishes were also being imported to Europe from Asia and Africa. From this trade escapes were inevitable; even the tilapia that first appeared in South East Asian waters were said to have originated from an aquarium shipment to Hong Kong (see Chapter 10) in pre-WWII days. Some popular aquarium species have thus become widely distributed. For example in Bangkok markets I visited in the 1960s I saw many live *Symphysodon* the South American cichlid discus fish, for sale, and some escapes have caused problems.

Since those early days the aquarium trade has exploded, with an accompanying plethora of beautifully illustrated books and magazines containing photographs of the vast array of tropical fishes now for sale, both freshwater and marine. Bringing comfort and delight to viewers, typical domestic tanks of 'tropical fishes' probably contain neon tetras and other small characins (of South American origin) schooling in mid-water, with minnow-

The discus fish Symphysodon.

like barbs and gorami (of Asian origin). Often there are a few small long-whiskered or armoured catfishes hiding away from the light, and cichlids (from the Neotropics or Africa). Perhaps these are dwarf cichlids, and others including substratum-spawners from South America, or mouth brooders of African origin. There may even be some 'mbuna' from Lake Malawi (such as *Pseudotropheus* species) or the remarkably convergent rock fish (*Tropheus* species) from Lake Tanganyika. The export trade from the East African Great Lakes developed enormously. In the 1990s we visited Pierre Brichard's large export facilities in Bujumbura on Lake Tanganyika and Stuart Grant's at Salima Bay on Lake Malawi, where some of the more popular species were being bred for export to conserve the wild stocks. In Sussex, local dealers offering specialist books on different fish groups tell me they now get supplies 'from Singapore or Czechoslovakia' where tropical fishes are bred for export. Big business!

At the BM(NH) Ethelwynn Trewavas had close connections with the British Cichlid Association, helping members with identifications and learning much from them about the lives of these fishes. Many of the members had made fish-watching safaris to the African lakes. In Lake Malawi Africa's first underwater nature trail in the Cape Maclear National Park, now cited as a UNESCO World Heritage Site, has a *Guide to the Fishes of Lake Malawi National Park*. Ethelwynn also had close contacts with the American Cichlid Association, which published the *Tropical Fish Hobbyist* (T.F.H) magazine, and with the editors of the popular German *Buntbarsch Bulletin*.

Examples of parental care in freshwater fishes: **A** *Male* Loricaria *guarding eggs (in some species these are attached to an elongation of his lower lip);* **B** Pterophyllum *pair guarding young attached to a water plant;* **C** *Oral incubation of eggs in* Tilapia; **D** Tilapia *young returning to the mouth of female parent.*

In the 1950s the developing science of ethology discovered what useful subjects cichlids were for studying mechanisms of behaviour (see Baerends and Baerends van-Roon 1950). Elaborate experimental work in aquaria (now often combined with DNA studies) has continued in many countries, including North America, Japan, Germany and at Leiden in the Netherlands. At Hull University (UK) George Turner and Ole Seehausen have confirmed the hypothesis that the females of Malawi and Victoria haplochromine cichlids choose males according to their breeding colouration, a mechanism involved in keeping the many cohabiting species distinct. Furthermore, in Leiden, the HEST group found that decrease in underwater visability in the Tanazanian waters of Lake Victoria, caused by recent eutrophication, had led to some hybridization. Although tilapia have been used for some behaviour experiments in Israel, most species grow too large for convenience and are not colourful enough for the hobbyist.

However, the smaller and more colourful rock-dwelling haplochromine cichlids from Lakes Tanganyika and Malawi are very much in demand. Among the numerous books on cichlids, many contain superb underwater photographs of all the then known cichlids from these lakes (see Brichard and Konings, commissioned by H. Axelrod for T.F.H. Press). Cichlid Press books, including *Tanganyika Secrets* (1992) and *Malawi Cichlids in their natural habitat* (1992) – are based on Ad. Konings scuba observations over many years. They describe the different communities of cichlids, on wave washed shores, living amongst rocks, or over sandy bottoms. The lives of the more recently discovered cichlids living offshore in the open waters of Lake Malawi have been described by George Turner (1999) and Ole Seehausen (1996) has produced a comparable Cichlid Press book on the ecology of the more recently discovered flock of nearly a hundred colourful rock-dwelling cichlids in Lake Victoria (discovered by HEST, see Chapter 9). Known to local fishermen as 'mpipi', these have life styles convergent with those of the 'mbuna' in Malawi. We now know much more about cichlid ecology and behaviour from underwater scuba studies. In particular, there is now better understanding of how so many closely related cichlid species manage to coexist in these rocky communities, sharing feeding and breeding territories thanks to the classic underwater studies made from 1972 onwards in Lake Tanganyika by Professor Hiroya Kawanabe of Kyoto University, with his teams of Japanese and African biologists. In aquaria one can control experimental conditions, but it is much more fun to watch the fishes in their natural environments and I too spent many absorbing hours in the field just watching behaviour (with many unexpected interruptions from other fauna appearing!).

Observations in my numerous field notebooks, combined with a wealth of information from the BM(NH)'s excellent libraries, were later woven into two books: *Fish Communities in Tropical Freshwaters* (1975) and, when this was out of print, it was replaced by *Ecological Studies in Tropical Fish Communities* (1987, reprinted 1991,1995, and translated into Portuguese for use in Brazil). For this later text the publishers asked for a section on marine fish studies. It was very stimulating to collate the abundant work on underwater observations of coral reef fishes, and note how these resembled and differed from those of the rocky shores of African lakes. It was also interesting to compare demersal and pelagic fish studies in freshwaters and the sea. Sadly, this meant that the chapters on reactions of fishes to conditions in tropical freshwaters, their trophic relationships and breeding adaptations, and communications between fishes, from the earlier text had to be omitted. This 'lost' section considered the reactions of fishes to conditions in tropical waters that affected their growth rates and trophic relationships, such as the sharing of the available food resources and plasticity in feeding habits. Also discussed were the ecological effects of seasonality in reproduction and adaptations of breeding behaviour with so many species showing some form of parental care which is unusual among Teleosts as a whole, yet so frequent among the tropical fish I have studied. Field observations of communication between fishes had stressed the significance of certain markings and colours in the diurnal species (for example for schooling and or young following their parents in substratum-spawning cichlids), as well as more transient breeding colours. Sound production (produced in different ways) was important (as well as electric signals) in many of the nocturnal fishes (catfishes, sciaenids, pirana and even some cichlids), and those living in turbid water. As yet we know very little about chemical communications. These sorts of observation also had much to contribute to the general discussion then in vogue amongst ecologists on possible reasons for the high species diversity at low latitudes compared with temperate regions.

Observations made over my six years in the field in South American tropical waters, after the years I had spent in Africa, provided a marvellous opportunity to compare how the seasonal and year-to year changes in ecological conditions affected the relative abundances, lives and behaviour of the numerous fish species sharing the different habitats, the devices that had evolved to enable them to use all the available food sources, to rear their young, how they communicated, and managed to avoid the very numerous predators. How much were these communities structured? And how much was determined by chance, enforced by extraneous factors such as local and long term climatic variations, and increasingly by anthropogenic factors such as clearance of forest, and other changes in the watersheds leading to pollution, hydroelectric schemes etc. Comparative studies brought out differences between lacustrine and riverine faunas, with studies of fish ecology in the new man-made lakes behind hydroelectric dams (Chapter 9) providing experiments on how riverine faunas became changed to lacustrine ones. Also the effects of differences between the faunas available in the different continents, for instance, the absence of cyprinids from South America, but a great radiation of characoid fish families.

Chapter 8
Back to Africa

In the postwar years studies of man-made lakes became increasingly fashionable as they formed behind dams created for hydroelectric power in many parts of the world. In Africa new lakes were formed first on the Zambezi, where the Kariba dam was closed in December 1958, then on the lower Volta River, in Ghana behind the Akosombo dam which closed in 1964. In the same year, Lake Nasser-Nubia was formed on the River Nile when the high dam at Aswan was completed, followed in 1968 by the Kainji dam on the River Niger in Nigeria. These four big hydroelectric dams caused over 7000 square miles of country to be inundated, from which some 200,000 people had to be resettled. For each dam project an integrated lake basin development programme was needed, including preparations for the development of new fisheries. My first opportunity to return to Africa from the BM(NH) was on preimpoundment studies of the two new lakes being created in Ghana and Nigeria.

Man-Made Lakes

In 1965 at the instigation of Barton Worthington, who was Scientific Coordinator of the IBP, the Institute of Biology in London organised the first symposium on man-made lakes. This brought together over two hundred delegates – biologists, hydrologists, engineers, sociologists, and those interested in medical and other aspects of new lakes. I was given the jolly job of editing the resultant volume *Man-Made Lakes* which provided a good introduction to the problems of these new lakes. The papers included several

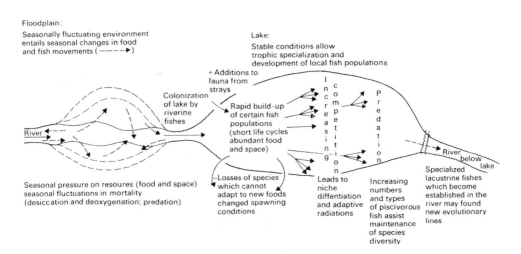

Summary diagram of the changes which take place when a running water community is changed to more lacustrine conditions.

on the hydrology and development of fisheries on Lake Kariba (by Derek Harding and Peter Jackson) and the explosive development of the exotic South American water fern *Salvinia* that had occurred as the lake filled. For the Volta Lake the progress of limnological investigations in 1964–5 was reported by Professor D.W. Ewer of the Volta Basin Research Project, University of Ghana. Medical problems, caused by insects such as the blackfly, *Simulium damnosum,* which transmits onchocerciasis, the cause of river blindness, mosquitoes carrying malaria, and aquatic snails carrying bilharzia, were considered by D.S. Lewis and W.E. Kershaw and population resettlement plans by T. Scudder from California. These new lakes also presented large scale natural experiments on how riverine fish communities evolve into lacustrine ones.

Volta Lake Studies

In 1965, after dam closure at Akosombo, the Volta River began to fill what was to become the largest man-made lake in Africa (8,500 km^2) extending from 6° to 9° N. Here a rainy season in May was followed by floods until October. There was then a maximum drawdown of 3 metres and an annual

An aerial view of the construction site at Akosombo on the Volta River in Ghana 1965.

The lake beginning to form behind the dam on the Volta River, Ghana in 1965.

outflow to volume storage ratio of 1:4. The UNDP (United Nations Development Programme) sent a mission to Ghana consisting of Bobby Beauchamp, George Marlier (former director of the Belgian research station at Uvira on Lake Tanganyika) and myself. We were based at the beautiful (Cambridge-inspired) campus of the University of Ghana in Accra hosted by Professor Ewer and his zoological wife Griff. His staff were studying the hydrology and fisheries of the lake basin. From here we visited the dam site at Akosombo by helicopter to view the extent of the filling lake and had meetings with doctors and engineers concerned with the effect of the new lake on onchocerciasis, malaria and bilharzia. We also visited the resettlement areas, where the displaced families were each given a house site with one room completed and building material for them to construct the rest. Food aid had to be provided until their new gardens could produce crops.

At the University Tomi Petr was already studying changes to the fish populations in the lake basin, based on catches by local fishermen and experimental fishing. The Volta River had many of the same nilo-sudanian fishes found in Lake Albert, but also some which were specifically distinct. There had been a lot of discussion on how much of the high forest needed to be cleared (a costly operation) before the reservoir flooded, to make fish landings, also on how to avoid an explosion of floating aquatic plants as had happened on Lake Kariba. In the Volta basin little riverine forest had been cleared and rapid deoxygenation occurred due to decomposition in the new lake. This led to fish deaths as the lake filled, which it did very gradually until 1971, mainly from the Volta River which flowed in at the northern end of the lake where conditions remained more riverine than near the dam wall. Inflows were low in nutrients so the standing crop of phytoplankton was low, and algae growing in association with microorganisms on the drowned trees formed the main basis of the food webs.

Fish catches in the early years after impoundment at first comprised species which migrated upriver to spawn, especially at the north end of the lake (*Alestes, Citharinus, Distichodus, Labeo*), and which relied heavily on the floodplains as feeding areas during the rainy season. *Lates niloticus* spawned in the lake annually, and tilapia, which became increasingly important in catches at the southern end of the lake, throughout the year. The predominance of insectivorous fishes from the River Volta gave way to mainly herbivorous and plankton-eating fish in the lake. The numerous mormyrid species, mainly feeding on benthic insects in the river bottom, almost completely disappeared from the south end of the lake. Tilapias flourished and fairly rapidly became the dominant fishes in the lake, where *Sarotherodon galilaeus* was found to feed mainly on phytoplankton, *O. niloticus* on epiphytic algae and *T. zillii* on submerged grass and debris.

Local people and their canoes among the trees drowned by the rising waters of Lake Volta behind the Akosombo Dam. (Photo Tomi Petr.)

The bark of the flooded trees developed a rich growth of periphyton, and the burrowing nymphs of the mayfly *Povilla adusta* became exceedingly abundant in the dead trees. These provided food for species that had been river bottom-feeders, mainly on insect larvae, such as the small catfishes *Schilbe* and *Eutropius*; a good example of generalized feeders taking to a more specialised source of food in the new environment. It proved beneficial to the fisheries that the trees were not all cleared, as these drowned trees, with their periphyton and *Povilla*, were a major element in the unexpectedly high yield of fish. Volta Lake produced about ten times the weight of fish as did Lake Kariba on the Zambezi in the early years after impoundment. A small native freshwater clupeid *Pellonula afzeliusi* (a zooplanktivore occupying a niche comparable with that of the clupeids in Lake Tanganyika) became very abundant in the open waters of the new lake where it formed the major food source for Nile perch (*Lates niloticus*) and the smaller common predatory cichlid *Hemichromis fasciatus,* as well as some other fishes. Species which bred within the lake extended their breeding seasons and rapidly became very abundant. Subsequent FAO reports showed that the Lake Volta fish yield, in which tilapia became an important part of the catch, rose steadily to almost 62,000 tonnes in 1969 – the highest yield recorded for a man-made lake – followed by decline and stabilization at around 40,000 tonnes (FAO, 1995; Petr, 2004).

While in Ghana we borrowed the Zoology Department's laboratory truck to visit the small steep-sided Lake Bosumtwi which is probably an impact crater lake. It is inhabited by a subspecies of *Sarotherodon galilaeus* (*S.g. multifasciatus*) of which the biology was later studied by Whyte (1975). This revered lake was subject to a local superstition which did not allow any boat on the lake, so local fishermen floated about on banana logs while fishing for tilapia with hooks. The lake was such a striking site that Bobby Beauchamp remarked that it would be a lovely retirement home for hydrobiologists. Alas, we evidently did not propitiate the local gods properly and found that we were unable to get the truck out of the crater. We then had to walk out and hitch hike back to Accra on an overloaded 'mammee wagon'. And we were not at all popular with the Department staff who then had a long journey back to collect their truck.

In 1965 an Institute for Aquatic Ecology was set up in Ghana for long term hydrobiological studies. Staffed by Ghanaian nationals, this was directed by Dr Letitia Obeng who organised a well-attended *Man-Made Lakes: the Accra Symposium* in Ghana in November 1966. The ensuing book contained numerous useful papers on the progress of research in many African man-made lakes, including Tomi Petr's assessment of fish population changes in Volta Lake and several papers by EAFFRO staff. These included Bobby Beauchamp on 'Hydrobiological factors affecting biological productivity: comparison between the Great Lakes of Africa and the new man-made lakes',

Fisherman using banana logs as a float on Lake Bosumtwi where boats were not allowed.

Robin Welcomme who summarised the effect of rapidly changing water levels in Lake Victoria on the commercial catches of *Tilapia* and J.M. Gee who compared the biology of *Lates niloticus* in endemic and introduced environments in East Africa. Other papers reviewed human schistosomiasis in the newly formed Volta Lake and of *Simulium*-carried onchocerciasis in the Volta basin, which was a major health hazard in this area.

Later, another symposium, attended by 550 scientists, engineers and managers, on *Man-made Lakes: their Problems and Environmental Effects* was held at the University of Tennessee, Knoxville in May 1971, at the headquarters of the TVA (Tennessee Valley Authority), which had created so many barrages and thus artificial lakes. Before and after the meeting we had field excursions up, then down, the Tennessee valley looking at the numerous dams. I greatly enjoyed travelling with Letitia Obeng from Ghana but was appalled at some of the reactions to our appearance together in a hotel in the Deep South. The 800+ page book was published by The American Geophysical Union in 1973.

Lake Kainji, Nigeria

My visit to Lake Kainji, from July to September 1965, was much more hands-on, identifying and dissecting large samples of fishes as a member of the Lake Kainji Biological Research Team which carried out a pre-impoundment survey of the 1,280 km² lake to be formed when the hydroelectric dam across

When the Akosombo
Dam was closed the
River Volta flooded
adjacent forest as the
new lake formed
(above). The decision
had been taken to leave
most of the trees in
place. They then (right)
provided a substrate for
periphyton and insects
on which fish fed for
several years.

The team working on Lake Kainji lined up outside their headquarters in 1965.

Professor Ukoli, the parasitologist on the team at Kainji working outside their headquarters building.

Local assistants testing the fishing gear as the water rises in the new Lake Kainji formed by damming the River Niger.

the River Niger at Kainji was closed. This survey, led by Eddy White from the University of Liverpool, and organised jointly with Ife University in Nigeria, was made by eight scientists from the UK with six from various Nigerian universities. Together we studied the river water chemistry, algology, zooplankton, fish and their parasites (F. Ukoli and J. Awachie) and fisheries (Mike Holden, John Banks and me), the *Simulium* problem (W.E. Kershaw), aquatic and marsh plant communities (by C.D.K. Cook, who was about to become a Professor of Botany in Switzerland) and a supporting staff of Nigerian field assistants. We worked from a new research station provided by the Niger Dams Authority near Shagunu on the west bank of the River Niger, 56 km north of the Kainji dam.

The River Niger here has two floods a year. A 'black' flood arrives in November when the river rises as water, which has already deposited its sediments arrives from annual rains in countries thousands of miles upriver. A 'white' flood arrives six months later, with suspended sediment from local rains in Nigeria. Which would most affect fish breeding seasons? The survey started in July as the local rainy season was only just beginning. The river was at its minimum level with extensive sandbanks exposed. It was so low in fact that for our initial sampling near our camp, we used an inflatable rubber

Members of the Kainji research team (John Banks left and Mike Holden with back to the camera) mending nets etc. with their staff outside the laboratory at Shaguna.

dinghy, believing that we were setting forth on a deep river. It was a great surprise when a white heron suddenly landed and stood fishing in the middle of the river. Here, over the sandy bottom, castnets expertly thrown by locals caught large numbers of the tilapia *Sarotherodon galilaeus*. There were several pools, isolated by rocky outcrops, which became part of the river as it rose.

When the rains arrived the road became almost impassable with mud so we were cut off from the world. But we had plenty to do, examining fish catches from our seines, castnets, gillnets of various mesh sizes, longlines, hooks and the D.C. electric fish-shocker machine used to sample fishes in the inflowing streams. We had arrived without mosquito nets, as in theory the living quarters were 'air-conditioned', so initially our electric fish shocker generator also had to be used to try to get some air circulation. While preparing a field key for identifying the fish, and examining their guts to see what they had eaten and whether they were in breeding condition, I shared a lab with Nigerian colleagues from several universities. Since English was their common tongue, I was able to listen in to their heated political arguments between Ebo and Mid-West supporters. This was an interesting time, predating the forthcoming Nigerian war.

In the new lake the ratio of annual outflow to lake storage volume would be 4:1, with an annual drawdown of 10 metres, so it would remain much more riverine than Volta Lake. It would also flood Foge Island, a large sandy area in mid-river due west of our base. This was reputed to be the location of an important tribal shrine to ancestors; would this be moved when the island flooded? We also examined African catches from fish traps set in the vegetation alongside the main river, and visited the local market. But the Fulani people

Before the dam closed one way of catching fish from the river was to use a cast net.

bringing goods for sale were cattle people not fishermen. The market had beautifully made things, including rice sieves of woven plant fibres, small phials made out of cowhide for kohl eye shadow and exquisitely designed iron hoes. I was privileged to be in the party that had an audience with the ancient Emir living in his thatched palace at Old Bussa, at the north end of the new lake, which was to be relocated before the waters rose.

We sampled a large number of sites both in the main River Niger and affluent streams to prepare a field key to the fish species. Many were the same as in the Volta Lake, and later an illustrated key for the two lakes was published in Ghana. Over a hundred fish species occurred in the Kainji area of which we caught 58 in gillnets. At the end of the dry season the majority had quiescent gonads and many fish stomachs were empty. Although cichlids were not abundant, it was anticipated that the tilapias would become so in the new lake, with *O. niloticus* predominating in the open water. Mike Holden therefore attempted to determine its growth rate as he had already studied this species in northern Nigeria.

Compared with the East African lakes, this West African fauna had many large species, such as the mormyroid *Gymnarchus niloticus* (together with 14 smaller mormyroid species), the osteoglossid *Heterotis occidentalis* (a detritus feeder which grows well in ponds), many large catfishes (*Clarotes laticeps*, two species of *Auchenoglanis* and *Chrysichthys nigrodigitalis*), two *Distichodus* and two *Citharinus* species. There was also a fascinating array (eleven species) of abundant and distinctively marked *Synodontis* catfishes, including counter-shaded ones which floated down the river ventral side uppermost feeding on surface organisms and zooplankton. These *Synodontis* later provided material for a fascinating study into how they shared resources.

During the Kainji dam construction a coffer-dammed channel of the River Niger was emptied of fish, presenting an unusual opportunity to assess the fish fauna in the main river. The 82 species collected from the channel represented 18 fish families: 19 mormyroid species, 18 mochokid catfish species, 8 characids, 7 bagrids, 6 cyprinids, 5 citharinid/distichodontids, with 16 representatives of other families (including species of *Polypterus, Heterotis, Gymnarchus, Microthrissa, Malapterurus, Lates* and *Lutjanus*. The cichlids *Oreochromis, Tilapia, Hemichromis* and *Pelmatochromis* were also present but numerically cichlids were scarce in these river faunas.

Immediately after impoundment fish catches rose far above the estimated 10,000 tonnes a year to a maximum of 28,000 tonnes in 1971, stabilising in 1974–75. The 4500 tonnes in 1978 represented a catch of 35 kg per hectare, very similar to that from the floodplain. Early high catches were predominantly of *Citharinus,* a floodplain spawning species which flourished as the waters rose. Tilapia populations took longer to build up than in Kariba and Volta, perhaps inhibited by the greater annual fluctuations of water level in the littoral zone of Kainji where they spawned. But the *S. galilaeus* population did build up in the flooded bush and by 1972 were common in castnet catches. By 1976 tilapia had become the main component in catches from inshore waters with a standing crop of 104 kg per hectare with *S. galilaeus, O. niloticus* and *T. zillii* caught in a ratio of 16:5:1. *S. galilaeus* was an algal and detritus feeder here, *O. niloticus* took some worms and insects along with algae and *T. zillii* fed on macrophytes (see Imevbore 1971).

Lake Kariba

This was the first man-made lake in Africa but, although the experience of others gained from work on Lake Kariba provided a template for work on other man-made lakes, I was not able to visit there until much later, in December 1992. This 4,300 km² lake on the Zambezi River, its waters shared by Zimbabwe and Zambia, had been studied in great detail by Balon & Coche (1974), followed by many others (e.g. Machena *et al,* 1993). As Kariba filled it featured frequently in the international news as 'Operation Noah' rescued elephants and other large game animals stranded on islands by the rising water. There was also the infamous explosive growth of the South American water fern *Salvinia,* which soon covered much of the lake surface, causing deoxygenation of the water beneath. Riverine fish species predominated at first, but from 1970–74 characids and cichlids made up 90% of gill net catches, largely of the tiger fish *Hydrocynus vittatus* and the tilapia *Oreochromis mortimeri* (with the predatory cichlid *Serranochromis codringtoni*). Other tilapia here included *Tilapia rendalli,* and later some *O. macrochir* appeared, and now it seems *O. niloticus* has also arrived in the lake.

Peter Jackson (2000) had proposed the stocking of the tilapia *O. macrochir* from Lake Mweru into Kariba as this species was the most openwater-living, adults penetrating into deep water and many kilometres offshore. Moreover, in Mweru it had adapted to coexisting with the piscivorous tigerfish. Unfortunately, when the Kariba stocking was carried out, in March 1959 using fingerlings bred at Chilanga fish farm, the fish culturist had bred *O. macrochir*

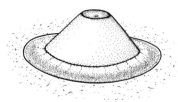 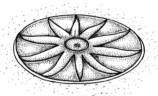

The breeding plaques of Oreochromis macrochir *(left) from the Kafue river system, and* O. mweruensis *(right) from Lake Mweru. (From Fryer and Iles 1972.)*

A lift net designed for catching the 'Tanganyika sardines' that were introduced to Lake Kariba after the dam was closed. The fishing vessel is approaching the shore where many launches are gathered in 1992.

stock from the Kafue river (as this was nearer and therefore cheaper than Mweru), a form which would not go out into open water and had never known how to avoid tiger fish (absent from the Kafue system). These were later recognised as two separate species, most readily distinguished by the cone shaped breeding plaque in the Kafue species *O. macrochir*, and the star shaped plaque in the Lake Mweru form *O. mweruensis*. This is a good example of the need for taxonomic work to ensure that the right tilapia species is stocked.

In all 23.6 tonnes of tilapia fingerlings were stocked into the new Kariba lake (in the ratio of two *O. macrochir* to one *T. rendalli*). Jackson recalls how he watched the Kafue fingerlings being attacked and consumed by young tigerfish as soon as they were poured into the lake. He concluded that this tilapia stocking was debatable. *T. rendalli* may have built up from those already present. The *O. macrochir* disappeared until much later, when they reappeared in small numbers in the catches, perhaps from individuals which had survived the long drop over the Victoria Falls from the Upper Zambezi. The Middle Zambezi species *O. mortimeri* (related to the Lower Zambezi's *O. mossambicus*), already in this stretch of the river, was the one that became most plentiful in Kariba.

Lakes develop more zooplankton than do rivers, so to utilise this and boost fish catches from Kariba, zooplankton-feeding sardines (clupeids) were introduced from Lake Tanganyika. Of the two Tanganyika clupeids *Limnothrissa miodon* came to support an important fishery and also spread down the Zambezi, appearing in Cabora Bassa, another new lake created lower down the Zambezi when the second dam was closed in 1974. The effects of these introductions on the fisheries of Lake Kariba were summarised by Brian Marshall in *The Impact of Species changes in African Lakes.*

When I visited Lake Kariba I was attending the African Fisheries Society meeting in Harare and was hosted on Lake Kariba by Digby Lewis. I also visited various other man-made lakes with Brian Marshall who had been involved with the Tanganyika sardines fishery on Lake Kariba. By that time there were three well-established research stations on the lake and the commercial fishery for the introduced clupeids was very important. I arrived at the end of long drought when elephants had been driven to eating pot plants in the staff gardens but they vanished into the bush as soon as the rains arrived. When I tried to identify an odd 'bird?' in an artificial waste-water pool behind a house, binoculars revealed this to be the twitching ears of a hippo sitting in this small tank.

The SIL years – back to the African Great Lakes (1987–2003)

After more than thirty years of sharing a happy life with Richard, sadly he died in 1986. Despite being rather restricted in our activities during his final years, fortunately he was able to remain at home. We both completed books on our respective interests during that period and read a lot of proofs for other people.

At the SIL (International Limnological Society) congress in New Zealand, in February 1987, I found myself 'volunteered' to be Convenor of the newly formed African Great Lakes Group of the International Limnological Association (known as SIL), which involved many overseas conferences and revisiting these lakes, as already described in *Freshwater Forum* 20, 2003.

SIL's triennial Congresses are gatherings of freshwater scientists from all over the world and provide an excellent opportunity to meet colleagues and make new contacts. At the New Zealand congress the new African Great Lakes Group was formed in response to George Coulter's concern that drilling for oil had started on the shores of Lake Tanganyika. This could endanger the priceless endemic faunas, fisheries and water supplies for the four riparian countries (Burundi, Tanzania, Zambia and Zaire), so the first task I was given was to organize an International Symposium on *Resource Use and Conservation of the African Great Lakes.* This was held at the University of Burundi in Bujumbura in 1989. What a task! Being an independent researcher I had no departmental backup and as a notably bad linguist I did not even speak respectable French. Who would help me raise funds for the meeting, choose delegates to invite, make all the arrangements for this meeting, in a francophone African country where I had never worked? Other members of SIL's African Lakes Group were all far away: George Coulter was based in South Africa so, in the political climate of the time, could not organise a meeting

Great Lakes Organisations

My involvement with the African Great Lakes Group of SIL led on to contacts and participation in a raft of other groupings and their conferences concerned with the Great Lakes.

IDEAL – International Decade of the East African Lakes which was primarily concerned with examining the history of the lakes through sediment cores and geological analysis.

SIAL – Speciation in African Lakes. These meetings were originally organised from the Royal Museum in Brussels.

PARADI – A series of conferences organised by French scientists which provided invaluable contact between those working in Franco-phone and Anglo-phone Africa. We met first in Senegal and later in South Africa.

GLOW – Great Lakes of the World, an organisation started in North America but initiating conferences in many different locations.

At the PARADI conference in Senegal in 1993 I met up with Melanie Stiassny who had moved from the BM(NH) to the American Museum of Natural History in USA many years previously – a joyful reunion.

in Burundi. Prof Hiroya Kawanabe who had students working on Lake Tanganyika, was back in Japan, but when I phoned him about dates his wife, who answered the phone, spoke only Japanese and French. I visited Paris to try to get help (and funds) from UNESCO and ICSU (International Council of Scientific Unions), with which SIL had a connection. Everyone was charming, but no help was forthcoming.

We had already discovered that in this fast-growing town on Lake Tanganyika, Bujumbura officials had consulted a Swiss firm about where to site the pipeline to bring in more drinking water from the lake, unaware that other town authorities had consulted an Austrian university about where to put the sewage outfall pipe. Both had worked out answers from George Coulter's map of lake currents, which brought them within about fifty metres of one another. The oil companies were notably discrete about their plans, so finding out about the oil threat proved a headache. Other practical problems loomed too, such as how could I possibly carry in enough money to pay the *per diem* food allowances for the African delegates? Travellers cheques would not enable them to get food in Bujumbura, as the organisers of a later conference discovered. I was saved from this dilemma when Mary Burgis phoned to say that a Dutchman 'good at all languages' had offered to help.

Thus began a long and fruitful association with Frits Roest of the Fish Section of the IAC (International Agriculture Centre) at Wageningen in the Netherlands. His help and the backing of his institute were vital for this

Talking to Frits Roest (left) and Ruud Crul alongside racks of Tanganyika sardines drying in the sun on the shore of Lake Tanganyika.

John Balirwa in his office at EAFFRO during my visit in 2001.

Left: George Turner and his wife Rosanna, now at the University of Hull, measuring fish on board the Ethelwynn Trewavas during work on Lake Malawi and (right) me aboard the ET in 1991 with a huge catch of cichlids, many of still unknown species.

Conferences are always a good opportunity to meet old friends and make new ones, particularly on excursions. Right: bird watching on an excursion to the Ruizizi delta was obviously a welcome distraction for these delegates of the SIL meeting on The Great Lakes of Africa, held in Bujumbura in 1989.

With Professor Kawanabe (left), Carl Hopkins and Denis Tweddle (right) during the PARADI meeting held in Senegal in 1998.

The new generation: Frans Witte (right) and Jan Wanink of the HEST team with their new student, Mary Kishe-Machumu who is learning the techniques for new work on Lake Victoria in 2005.

Delegates at the SIL African Lakes Group conference in Bujumbura 1989.

symposium. Frits had formerly been based in Bujumbura as an FAO Fisheries Officer and had numerous contacts there and in many other parts of Africa. The IAC sent three people (Frits, Ruud Crul and an administrative officer) to help. They transported the cash and a huge volume of papers prepared for the meeting. Even this had problems, as Air Sabena on which we were booked to fly to Burundi, suddenly had no planes available. So George Coulter and I had to travel via Paris, where the Dutch team were to join us on a French plane departing at midnight. Their connection was delayed so there was no sign of them! We envisaged arriving for the meeting sans money and papers. What to do? But on our dawn stopover at Nairobi airport, they miraculously appeared through the mist. Rarely have I been so pleased to see anyone.

This SIL Symposium, proved a great success. Attended by over a hundred people from 21 countries, it brought together for the first time people to discuss fish stocks and fisheries, water quality and vulnerability to pollution in the African Great Lakes, the scientific value of the lakes and conservation measures. Some agricultural experts from the USA who happened to be in Bujumbura advising Burundi, joined the meeting and seemed quite surprised to hear that the chemicals they were advising for land use would end up in the lake. Jenny Baker, a consultant on oil spill problems worldwide, arranged for a Nigerian ex-Minister, then tackling oil problems in the Niger Delta, to show us graphic photographs of oil spill fires encountered in their early explorations. The recommendations from this symposium were then used to help apply for international funds for fisheries and diversity projects on African lakes.

The Biodiversity Convention, signed at Rio de Janeiro in Brazil in 1992, enabled United Nations agencies to set up Global Environmental Facility (GEF) funds for such projects. So the 1990s saw a veritable explosion of research on the three great lakes, Tanganyika, Malawi and Victoria. As I have already described and discussed these projects in *Recent Research in the African Great Lakes: fisheries, biodiversity and cichlid evolution* published as Special Issue 20 of the FBA's *Freshwater Forum* (2003), I give here only a summary of recent changes encountered when I revisited each of these lakes.

Lake Malawi revisited

In 1991 Denis Tweddle, Fisheries Research Officer at the Monkey Bay Research Station, invited me to see how conditions had changed since my 1945-47 survey. Peggy Varley came with me and we stayed in the Tweddle's guest rondavel on the edge of the lake in their beautiful garden, a recognized meeting place for any hydrobiologists visiting Lake Malawi. We arrived in time for Rosanna Turner's birthday party, an excellent introduction to the local community and visiting biologists. George Turner was stationed here as part of an FAO team studying the sad decline of tilapia catches. Rosanna was using scuba to study the behaviour and ecology of 'mbuna', rock-dwelling cichlids. Other visitors included Jay Stauffer, an ichthyologist from the USA. The Monkey Bay station had all the records of catches from the north end of the lake, and we accompanied the experimental trawl fishing on the research vessel *RV Ethelwynn Trewavas*, which caught hundreds of pounds of haplochromine cichlids, many of them as yet unnamed species. Could such trawl catches, of cichlid species that produced so few young at a time, continue to be so bountiful?

After 1962, when the first colourful 'mbuna' cichlids were exported from Lake Malawi, the ornamental fish trade expanded so rapidly (to over 4,500,000 fish annually by the mid-seventies) that a survey of the rocky shore cichlids was undertaken by Tony Ribbink and his colleagues from the J.L.B. Smith Institute in Grahamstown, South Africa. Scuba had by then revolutionised underwater observations of fish behaviour and ecology in these clear lakes. In 1980 the Cape Maclear Peninsula, separating the southeast and southwest arms of the lake included an underwater National Park. It has published a guide and has an underwater nature trail to delight the many visitors (Lewis *et al* 1986), a number of whom have written books illustrated with magnificent underwater photographs of the numerous brightly coloured cichlids and with a wealth of observations on their ecology and behaviour in their home waters (see Chapter 7). In 1991 Denis took Peggy and me to visit the Salima headquarters of Stuart Grant's impressive aquarium fish export facilities where, in addition to having a team of Africans trained to collect fishes from different part of the lake, there were tank facilities to rear the cichlid species

Left: Peggy on board the RV Ethelwynn Trewavas on Lake Malawi in 1991 when she came with me on a visit there. Right: Ro talking to Stuart Grant, the main exporter of cichlids from Lake Malawi to the aquarium trade. He rears them in captivity to conserve the stocks in the lake. Denis Tweddle is behind him.

much in demand, so helping to conserve the wild stocks. From here Malawi cichlids were being shipped all over the world.

We also visited the Government Experimental Fish Culture project at Domasi, where Lake Chilwa tilapia (*Oreochromis shiranus chilwae*) were being grown in ponds in association with various farm crops. This species tended to dwarf in response to the restricted pond conditions, and many of the tilapia had a black spot parasite in the body tissues.

The effects of fisheries in changing the fish populations in this lake were well summarised in *The Impact of Species changes in African lakes* – a useful symposium held in London in 1992. As tilapia catches from the lake were declining, attempts to find another source of fish led to a technologically very advanced survey of the open waters. This had not hitherto been possible because it required a large craft to work far offshore on this often stormy lake, for which a specially equipped 15 m long catamaran the *RV Usipa*, was being built at Monkey Bay. Requested by the three riparian countries, Malawi, Tanzania and Mozambique, this was financed by UK's Overseas Development Administration in 1985.

*One of the fish ponds of the Experimental Tilapia Culture project at
Domasi incorporating fish ponds into farms 1991.*

In 1994 I revisited Lake Malawi again to see the progress of this UK/SADC
Pelagic Fish Resource Assessment Project based at Senga Bay. Directed by
Andy Menz, a team of a dozen scientists (among them Graeme Patterson,
Ken Irvine, Eddie Allison, Ben Ngatungu and Tony Thompson), aided by
state-of-the-art computer and satellite links, had produced an impressive
picture of the limnology, water chemistry, plankton, lake fly and fish ecology,
and fisheries potential of the pelagic zone of the whole lake. When the survey
began in 1987, they had expected to find that the little pelagic cyprinid 'usipa'
(*Engraulicypris sardella*) might be abundant enough offshore to support a fishery
comparable with that for the endemic sardines on Lake Tanganyika, together
with the zooplankton-feeding 'utaka' cichlids already fished by local
fishermen. In the event, the 'utaka' were found to be restricted to areas of
upwelling near rocks, and adult 'usipa' were scarce in open waters. However
their pelagic larvae, widely distributed in the open lake, were an important
food for piscivorous cichlids, together with the larvae and pupae of the lake
flies (*Chaoborus edulis*) of which the adults swarm in huge smoke-like clouds
from the surface of this lake. The great surprise was that the fleets of
experimental gillnets set in the open lake, at different depths down to the
limit of dissolved oxygen (*c* 200 m), discovered a number of new cichlid
species, mainly of zooplanktivorous *Diplotaxodon* and piscivorous
Rhamphochromis species, each living at their own particular depths. These had
evidently evolved in open water in the absence of large piscivorous fishes.

On my next visit to Lake Malawi in 1999 the Senga Bay laboratory facilities
were occupied by the SADC/GEF Lake Malawi/Nyasa Biodiversity

Conservation Project (financed by the World Bank, 1997–2000) directed by Tony Ribbink. We accompanied Tony and Fabrice Duponchelle when they were scuba diving for 'mbuna' to determine cichlid relationships from DNA samples. We also had to keep a 'crocodile watch' while they fixed underwater light sensors. Harvey Bootsma's study of inputs from the drainage system affecting water quality in the lake, and of how the seasonal inflow of turbid Lintippe River water affected the fishes, was also an important contribution. Jos Snoeks from Tervuren also had a team at Senga Bay which discovered many new demersal haplochromines, including *Lethrinops* species.

More recently (1998–2002) the Senga Bay facilities were used for another large multidisciplinary survey on the trophic ecology of the demersal fish community. This involved biologists from many institutions, financed by the European Community. Using a combination of stable isotope and stomach analyses, this study found evidence that benthic algal production contributed to the energy requirements of the offshore fishes. These fish occupy depths between 10 and 30 m, and it was also confirmed that the lake fly *Chaoborus edulis* is a food source for benthic fishes. There was also evidence for resource partitioning among the benthic haplochromines with apparently similar diets, feeding behaviour and depth preferences.

Lake Malawi has attracted many projects from various parts of the world and Tweddle's *Twenty years of fisheries research in Lake Malawi* (1991) provided a useful summary of these, as did Crul's bibliography prepared for UNESCO. When I returned to the lake in 1995 and 1999, it was heart-rending to see so many local people on the beaches awaiting fish from the seine net catch and so few, mostly small, fishes in the net. 'Yes, we know we should not catch fish before they breed, but our families are hungry and must eat'. The human population pressures, plus illegal and unchecked use of increasingly small meshed seine nets had led to a serious decline in the tilapia and other fisheries. Deforestation in the hills had also altered the river flows, hastening the decline of 'mpasa', *Labeo* and other river-spawning species. Experimental, then commercial, trawling was introduced for the huge biomass of small cichlids (mainly of still undescribed species) over the sandy bottoms of the southeast and southwest arms, but cichlids produce only small batches of young, so for how long would these catches be profitable?

Malawi Fishery Department records show that in the southeast arm of the lake plus the Upper Shire River and Lake Malombe, 'chambo' (endemic tilapia) catches were highest in the early 1980s, then declined to negligible amounts after 1996. As so many people were involved in the various aspects of the fishing industry, the significance of this decline for the country's economy has stimulated the Malawi Government towards serious attempts to restore 'chambo' production with a 'Save the Chambo campaign'. A 'Chambo Restoration Strategic Plan' now aims to restore 'chambo' to its peak production of 6000 – 8000 tons harvested pre-1990. But could this be done? The demise of 'chambo' was attributed to a complex mixture of illegal fishing methods, poor enforcement of fishery regulations, destruction of habitats, and inadequate involvement of users in decision-making. Sociological reasons included the open access regime, lack of both property rights and a taxation system on use of the resource.

Lake Tanganyika revisited

In addition to the conferences held in Burundi in 1989 and 1991, we also had two workshops with Professor Osse Lindqvist's team at the University of Kuopio in Finland. Between 1992 and 1998, with FAO they conducted a lakewide Lake Tanganyika Research (LTR) project on Production and Potential for Optimal Management of the Pelagic Fisheries. This involved many international scientists and produced an impressive amount of basic limnological data, despite wars in Bujumbura and the Congo which made working conditions difficult. To some extent this project overlapped with the UNDP/GEF Lake Tanganyika Biodiversity Project (LTBP) (1995–2000) which dealt with pollution control and other measures to protect biodiversity.

In addition to the findings from these two surveys, I was especially interested in the Japanese/African underwater scuba studies (1977–2004), initiated by Prof H. Kawanabe of Kyoto University. These were studies of the ecology and behaviour of the littoral cichlid fishes, which have revealed so much about resource partitioning in these very diverse fish communities. In shallow waters off rocky littoral shores, their 20x20 m quadrats contained about 7000 individuals of some 38 fish species, mostly cichlids. These showed intense inter- and intraspecific competition for breeding and feeding sites, also examples of cooperative behaviour and many unusual breeding strategies. Unlike most other African lakes, Tanganyika has substratum-spawning as well as female mouth-brooding cichlids. The early Japanese studies have been described in a special number of *Conservation Biology,* in *Cichlid Fishes: behaviour, ecology and evolution,* edited by Keenleyside 1991, and by Kawanabe and others in *The fish communities in Lake Tanganyika* (1997). Many of Lake Tanganyika's colourful aquarium fishes, mainly cichlids, exported from several centres, are now well-known worldwide.

The view from 2005, prepared for the GLOW IV International Symposium on the state of Lake Tanganyika (and Lake Victoria), in Tanzania shows that the fisheries of these two lakes have grown remarkably over the past decades to become the largest lake fisheries in the world. But although catches on both lakes were originally limited by effort, there is now concern about the sustainability of the current catches as effort continues to increase. In Lake Tanganyika the industrial fishery period (1975–1984) was marked by high total landings of pelagic fishes which included a high proportion of *Lates.* Since then the artisanal period (post 1984) has had relatively low catches and these have continued to show wide and unpredictable fluctuations which cause problems to the fishery. These fluctuations arise from variable recruitment to the fishery, affected by complex interrelated physical, biological and fisheries related factors. A three year lake-wide survey of climate variability (CLIMLAKE 2001–2005) in Lake Tanganyika has shown significant changes in environmental conditions, including decreased production of diatoms (on which the clupeids feed) in the last decades. These changes are thought to be caused by the observed increase in surface temperature of the lake and reduced wind speed, associated with climate change in this region of Africa. The warmer surface temperatures appear to have resulted in a sharpening of the thermocline, which increases water column stability, reducing upward mixing of nutrients from the hypolimnion with consequent decreasing productivity of the surface waters. It seems that Lake Tanganyika is becoming more oligotrophic in response to the warming climate. Overfishing has probably added to the decline of *Lates* in the catch.

Lake Victoria: the Great Experiment

Changes to the ecology and fisheries of Lake Victoria have been the most spectacular, providing a large scale, though unintentional, experiment on environmental factors affecting cichlid communities. These have been recounted in numerous publications by the HEST team from Leiden University, who were working from their laboratory near Mwanza at the south end of the lake when the Nile perch *Lates niloticus*, originally introduced into Ugandan waters in the mid 1950s, first arrived there in the early 1980s.

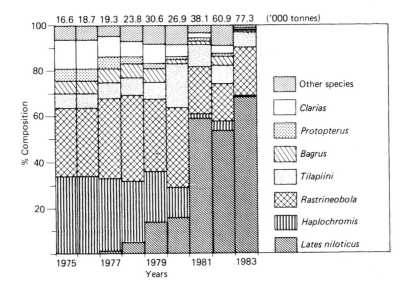

Changes in the fish catches from Lake Victoria.

Humphry Greenwood (left) and Frans Witte discussing the work on Lake Victioria cichlids during a consultation visit of the HEST team to the Fish Section of the Natural History Museum in London. (Photo K. Barel.)

I happened to be working in the Fish Section of the BM(NH) in London the day that members of the HEST team arrived, making one of their frequent visits to identify Lake Victoria haplochromines with Humphry Greenwood. They brought colour slides of their trawls, suddenly full of large immature Nile perch, the advance party of the *Lates* irruption in those waters. Very soon these fish were breeding there. What would this exotic piscivore do to the haplochromines and other endemic fishes? Introduced into Ugandan waters in the mid-1950s, Nile perch moved round the lake, appearing in Kenya waters in the 1970s, taking until the early 1980s to reach the Mwanza area.

In Tanzanian waters in the 1980s more than 500 haplochromine species, which originally made up more than 80% of the demersal fish biomass, were most severely affected, and many other fish species disappeared. Within ten years the haplochromines in this area had almost vanished from the catches in the sublittoral and offshore waters. HEST estimated that lakewide some 200 species had probably disappeared. Assessed as 'the greatest extinction of vertebrate species in modern times', a paper in *Nature* (1985) by thirteen fish biologists (including me) drew attention to this 'Destruction of fisheries in

Africa`s lakes'. But to what extent was this loss of an estimated 200 haplochromine species due to *Lates* predation, overfishing, or associated limnological changes, including eutrophication and deoxygenation of the bottom waters of the lake?

Surprisingly, in both Lake Kyoga, then in Lake Victoria, fish catches rose (changes which stimulated the symposium on *The impact of Species changes in African lakes* with its many papers on Lake Victoria). In the 1960s Victoria's fisheries based on indigenous species had sustained a production of ca.100,000 tonnes a year, although there were already signs of overexploitation. After 1979, catches were augmented by the exploding Nile perch (*Lates*) population. By the early 1990s the fisheries produced over 500,000 t annually. But these fisheries were much simplified and dominated by three species: Nile perch, the introduced Nile tilapia *O. niloticus* (which had replaced the endemic *O. esculentus*) and dagaa, the small endemic cyprinid *Rastrineobola argentea*.

In Lake Victoria, Nile perch became the mainstay of the fishery, attracting very large numbers of fishers such that boats on the lake increased from 22,700 in 1990 to 42,500 in 2000. Nile perch processing factories developed to absorb about 122,000 tonnes of wet fish annually and the combined exports from the region were worth about US$ 220 million annually. Research essential for sustaining these fisheries was financed by the European Union as a Lake Victoria Fisheries Research Project (LVFRP) that worked in collaboration with the fishery institutes in the three territories, and from 2001 with a resuscitated Lake Victoria Fisheries Organisation (LVFO). But despite scientific advice on available stocks, the building of so many factories to process Nile perch fillets for export, from all three countries, has now led to serious concern that the Nile perch are overfished.

The 2005 view estimated annual fish catches from Lake Victoria as about 840,000 tonnes (with a beach gross value of nearly 350 million US$). This is twice the peak of approximately 400,000 t estimated in the early 1990s. The bulk of current production (62%) is however made up of 'dagaa' (*Rastrineobola argentea*) and haplochromines, with a beach value only 20% of all fish landed. Frame survey data also indicated widespread use of destructive illegal fishing equipment. It was questioned whether Western consumption of Nile perch from Lake Victoria is sustainable. Exports to the EU (European Community) seemed to have reached their maximum in 2003 and then declined, which could have been due to subsequent competition from cheaper exports of fish from Asian countries.

Is Nile tilapia replacing Nile perch in Lake Victoria? If so what are the consequences? Studies of biomass and distribution of *O. niloticus* collected by trawls between 1997 and 2000, 2004 and 2005, showed that Nile tilapia, which constituted less than 1% of catch in the 1980s to 90s, now contribute more than 25% to catches from the lake, and are now caught up to 20 m deep

*The headquarters of the new Lake Victoria Fisheries Organisation in the EAFRO
compound at Jinja (2001). The most noticeable change for me is the security
fencing which was quite unnecessary in the old days.*

(whereas they were previously distributed in water less than 10 m deep).
Length frequency distributions and maturation sizes depict a stable tilapia
population with a high proportion of mature fish, unlike the Nile perch of
which more than 60% of the catches were juveniles. This spread of Nile tilapia
into deeper water and increase in biomass was attributed to declining stocks
of predatory Nile perch, availability of suitable food, and probability of
occupying vacant niches left by reduction in indigenous species, especially
haplochromines. The contribution of Nile perch to the catch has been reduced
from 90% in the 1990s to 52% in 2005, a decline mainly attributed to
overexploitation and ecological changes to the lake. Dramatic changes in the
multimillion dollar export industry of Nile perch will have serious economic
consequences.

What has happened to the tilapia fishery? Members of the HEST team,
who researched the plight of the tilapiine fish stock of Lake Victoria before
and after the Nile perch upsurge, described how, thirty years after its
introduction, *O. niloticus* was the most successful tilapia species. It replaced
the indigenous tilapiines almost completely *before* the Nile perch came to
dominate the ecosystem of the lake. Reduced fishing pressure on the tilapiines
in the 1980s, when the local fishery used larger-mesh gillnets for Nile perch,
resulted in an increase in the *O. niloticus* stock, an increase in the average fish
size, and *O. niloticus* landings also increased. The stock of indigenous tilapiines
declined to extremely low levels or vanished from the main lake, although
some still occur in satellite lakes from which *O. niloticus* is absent. Nile perch
do feed on *O. niloticus* but the limited overlap in distribution between the

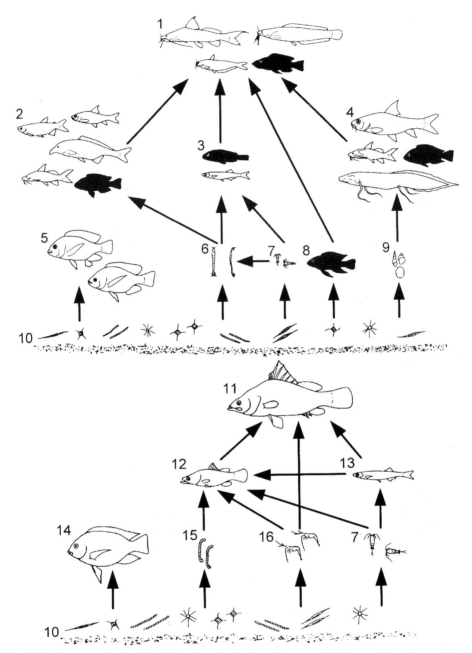

The fish fauna and simplified food webs in the Mwanza Gulf sub-littoral zone (6–20 m deep) during the 1970s before the arrival of Lates *(above), and in 1989 after the* Lates *irruption (below). Only those organisms known to form a major component of the diets of the main fish species are depicted. In the 1970s Haplochromines (coloured black) dominated both the biomass and number of species in all groups except the piscivores. Later,* O. niloticus *(14) replaced the indigenous tilapias (5) and Nile perch (11) the top predator, cannibalised juvenile Nile perch (12) and* Rastrineobola *- 'dagaa' (13). (From Witte et al. 1992.)*

piscivorous Nile perch and *O. niloticus* of consumable sizes is probably an important factor in explaining their coexistence. The team concluded that the disappearance of the native tilapiine species seems to have been due primarily to competitive dominance by *O. niloticus*.

In addition to changes in fish species composition, other great changes have occurred in the whole ecosystem. Following a marked increase in the human population in the drainage basin, the lake has become increasingly eutrophic. Soil runoff, eutrophication and phytoplankton blooms led to a decline in dissolved oxygen concentrations and water transparency. Oxygen no longer circulates to the bottom waters, restricting fish distribution, and HEST experiments have shown how reducing transparency interferes with cichlid breeding behaviour, when females can no longer select the right males. However, in the late 1990s, by when fish factories were exporting huge numbers of Nile perch fillets from the lake, HEST found a resurgence of some haplochromine species. Some of these had changed their feeding habits, and some appear to be hybrids.

Though the HEST team had recorded the decline and loss of so many endemic haplochromine species at the south end of the lake, they also discovered a whole suite of previously unrecognized zooplanktivorous haplochromines in these waters. In the 1990s they found another hundred species of cichlids living on rocky shores with life styles comparable with those of 'mbuna' in Lake Malawi. So this amazing species flock, thought to have evolved in a mere 14,000 years since the lake refilled, was even more amazing. This has stimulated much recent, ongoing, research on the possible origins of this species flock in East African waters.

Whether there is inevitably a conflict between developing fisheries and the conservation of biodiversity was much discussed at an International Conference on 'Lake Victoria 2000: A new Beginning', held in Jinja, Uganda in 2001. Balirwa and ten other authors (including me) thought that maintenance of the lake's biodiversity could help to sustain the fisheries.

It was quite an emotional visit for me to return to Jinja after all those years. I had been kept in touch with what was happening to the lake and the research being carried out, but it was a long time since I had been back to the place where it all started. EAFFRO had a large staff of African graduates, directed by Fred Bugenyi until he left to become Professor of Limnology at Makerere University. He was replaced by Richard Ogutu-Ohwayo until he moved to the LVFO, when John Balirwa took over.

Chapter 9
South America revisited
– my other life

My five years as a biologist in British Guyana, while Richard was Director of the Geological Survey there, had been so utterly delightful (as recounted in *Land of Waters* and Chapter 6) that with alacrity I seized the opportunity to return to that part of the world. In April and May 1968 I spent two months doing fieldwork in Brazil as a member of the Royal Society and Royal Geographical Society expedition to the Mato Grosso in central Brazil. This came about when the Brazilian authorities began building a highway through the Mato Grosso, a vast, remote, and almost unexplored region, as part of a great South America highway system. They invited several countries including Great Britain to send teams of scientists to study the area in the vicinity of this road. The RGS and Royal Society in London were quick to respond to this generous invitation, which brought botanists, zoologists, geographers and soil scientists from universities, museums and other institutions in the UK to work together in a two-year programme. It was a rare opportunity to study a habitat in its pristine condition in a fast developing country. After a reconnaissance in 1966, between July 1967 and 1968 an Anglo-Brazilian exercise involved forty-four British and twenty Brazilian scientists, some for a few months, others for the whole time. Base Camp, about 800 road kilometres from Brasilia, became a small temporary field research station in the midst of a large area then little disturbed by man and his animals. Subcamps allowed anthropological and medical studies much further afield along the Suia Missu and Xingu rivers, a refuge for the dwindling Indian tribes who once lived throughout the Mato Grosso.

The Mato Grosso streams on which we were to work are tributaries of the mighty Amazon, where lived some of the same species (or their ecological equivalents) I had already encountered in the Rupununi District of Guyana in rivers flowing south to the Rio Negro, a blackwater tributary of the main Amazon river (see Chapter 6). The Amazon basin, which drains 6.5 million km^2, has the world's richest freshwater fish fauna of probably more than 1500 species, 85% of them characiforms and siluriforms. To the north, the Amazon system connects to the Orinoco system through the Casiquaire Canal which alternates its direction of flow seasonally. It also connects to the Essequibo system across the seasonally flooded Rupununi savannas of Guyana. To the south there were former connections with the vast Paraná-Paraguai system, and many of the larger fish species are now widely distributed from the Orinoco to the Paraná-Paraguai. The main Amazon river presents an ecological barrier to smaller fish species, but around the central basin ecological

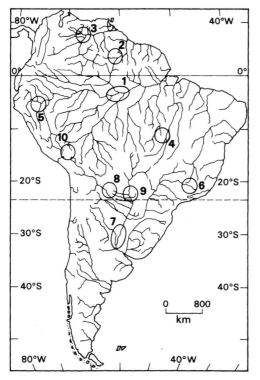

A map of South America showing the locations of various fish studies:
1. Manaus, Central Amazon (Brazil);
2. Rupununi District (Guyana - see chapter 6);
3. Orinoco tributaries (Venezuela);
4. Mato Grosso streams (Brazil);
5. Andean Amazon tributaries (Peru);
6. Rio Mogi Guassu (Brazil);
7. Middle Paraná (Argentina);
8. Pilcomayo (Bolivian waters);
9. Paraguaian Chaco (Paraguay);
10. L.Titicaca.

conditions in the peripheral streams are much alike and share similar fish faunas, suggesting that a primitive fauna spread around the main river basin (then possibly a marine gulf and later large lakes). The proto-Amazon drained westwards to the Pacific before the rise of the Andes reversed the drainage, probably in Miocene times. The waters were later dammed to form a huge lake or lakes before they broke through to the Atlantic in the Pleistocene. During the Pleistocene glacial phases, when the sea level was lower, the rivers would have run in deep valleys, so conditions as the fishes evolved must have been very different from those prevailing today. The key to Amazon fish ecology lies in their mobility which enables them to move from rivers in to and out of lateral lakes and forest that is flooded for months with the changing water levels. This relates to changing oxygen levels, and to trophic, breeding and dispersal migrations. So the fish communities are very dynamic, the relative abundances of different species continually changing, the fishes having to adjust their feeding regimes to what is available seasonally. This is all a great contrast to communities in the more seasonally stable conditions of the Great Lakes of Africa. With the exception of the high Andean Lake Titicaca, South America lacks deep lakes.

The central Amazon now has seventeen tributaries more than 1600 km long joining the main 'white water' river, full of sediments from Andean tributaries, known as the Solimões above its confluence with the 'blackwater'

Rio Negro at Manaus. The Andean streams, swollen by September to June rains and snow meltwater, carry vast loads of sediment which are deposited alongside the main river forming the varzea floodplain of fertile soil allochthonous to the central Amazon region, with numerous lateral lakes on the floodplain. Left bank tributaries, such as the Rio Negro its 'black water' stained tea colour with humic acids, rise in the uplands of Guyana and Colombia, well north of the Equator, so have high water in June. Right bank tributaries (including the Xingu and Tocantins) have 'clear waters' that drain the hard crystalline rock of the Brazilian plateau. Their headwaters, far to the south of the Equator, reach high water in March or April and they have a predominant, though delayed, influence on the level of the lower Amazon. The commercial fishing seasons vary with the rhythm of the inundations, occurring mainly at low water, from June to February in the middle Amazon.

Getting to the Mato Grosso Expedition headquarters was quite an adventure as I had to travel from Argentina following the IBP meeting in Santo Tomé, after which Julian Rzóska and Professor Arthur Hasler from the University of Wisconsin and I stayed overnight in Buenos Aires. As VIPs they were being collected from our hotel in a Government car to take them to the airport early next morning so they kindly offered me a lift. But at 6 am Julian suddenly realised that as they were going to Lake Barraloche in the Argentinian Andes they would be leaving from the internal airport, whereas for Brazil I had to fly from the international airport on the other side of town.

Sometimes one has to test the depth of the water before continuing along a flooded road or crossing a stream in the Mato Grosso.

So I was unceremoniously bundled, with all my gear, from their VIP car into a passing town taxi. The driver seemed to have little idea of how to get to the international airport, which we viewed from some miles away at the scheduled departure time. Catching this plane was essential as my complicated journey entailed flying to Rio de Janeiro, changing airports for a small plane to Brasilia, the new capital then under construction. I was to overnight there, then go on by bus from Brasilia to Goiana where I was supposed to arrive in time to catch a small plane to Xavantina, where the expedition had rented a house by the ferry over the Rio das Mortes (= River of the Dead). Here I was to be met by the lorry taking supplies to Base Camp, which only visited Xavantina once a fortnight, for the drive north on the embryonic road along the Sierra do Roncador (= Snoring Mountains). The whole sequence depended on catching that plane from Buenos Aires! Relax, relax: by great good fortune when we finally got there we found that they were still sweeping out the international airport for the arrival of the plane.

When I eventually reached Xavantina, illuminated by flashes of lightning, the small plane landed in a splitting thunderstorm, and the road was under water. This was in April, towards the end of the rains when much of the country was flooded. But the journey had been very pleasant as people were so friendly and helpful. The children on the bus and planes took turns to sit by me to practice English from my Portuguese phrase book and tutor my faltering Brazilian. This skill was much needed in a camp where our field work was made possible with the help of a band of cheerful 'Brasiliero' assistants, people of Amerindian/Negro/European descent steeped in bush lore.

Base Camp was isolated in the wilderness in a small clearing created by the road builders, a couple of kilometres off the main road at the junction of two small but permanent streams. This happened to be on the border of the 'cerrado' (open bush/grassland), stretching to the south, and the forest which continued away to the north, an excellent location for botanists and soil scientists. It also proved to be so for the fish studies as these two streams, within only about two kilometres of meeting one another, were headwater tributaries of two quite different drainage systems. One flowed northwest through more open country into the Rio Suia Missu, where the water flooded into lateral lakes, thence to the Rio Xingu. The other flowed northeast, shaded by riverine forest, through more broken, mountainous country to the Araguaia River, hence to the Tocantins entering the Amazon estuary at Belem. The Xingu and Tocantins thus entered the Amazon many hundreds of miles apart from one another.

The team leader and camp organiser, Ian Bishop and his wife Angela, presided over what was a very happy place, set among a chorus of colourful birds, insects and other creatures. It was inhabited by a changing mix of specialists, each working hard to make the most of the marvellous

Above: Arriving at the Mato Grosso Base Camp after an expedition into the forest in 1968.

One of the camp assistants fishing on the Rio Suia Missu.

A selection of fish caught in the Rio das Mortes in the Mato Grosso.

Detecting electric fishes with Ian Bishop in a pool near Base Camp during the Mato Grosso expedition of 1968.

opportunities to discover new things. One could wander into the surrounding forest very freely by day or night (with no lions waiting to pounce). There was always something new to see, and after dark the communal evening meal in the light of pressure lamps attracted an array of bizarre insects. In the two months of living in camp together we made good friends and there were fascinating discussions between scientists of different disciplines and very varied tropical experiences.

Measuring the catch during the Mato Grosso expedition.

The soil scientists (from Newcastle University), who spent most days surveying and sampling in hot deep pits, included two whom the Brasilieros speculated were probably my sons. David Moffatt was blond, slight and quick of movement, who after the expedition married Ruth Jackson who was completing her PhD here on the mammal fauna. The other was the sturdier, dark-haired Peter Seale. When the tall, red headed and bearded Jim Ratter, from the Royal Botanic Gardens Edinburgh, arrived (a vegetarian who fared well on the traditional Brazilian diet of fejon black beans and rice), he announced: 'The usual question: is she your mother? I answered yes, it was so much easier than trying to explain relationships'. Other botanists there included Ray Harley (interested in pollination mechanisms, together with a Brazilian scientist) and David Philcox, both from Kew Gardens. The forester David Gifford, from Edinburgh, had a passion for the numerous butterflies and was an authority on butterflies in Malawi. Later came the rainforest botanist Prof Paul Richards from Bangor University in North Wales, whose older brother Professor Owain Richards from Imperial College, also a deeply revered tropical ecologist, was here concentrating on the Hymenoptera which are so varied and abundant in South America, with his student W.H. (Bill) Hamilton and his wife Christine. For Bill this must have been a very formative period when he was developing his ideas on kin selection. They needed to collect (often from high trees or over a swamp) the beautiful and distinctive wasp nests, with all their wasps inside, to enable them to determine relative numbers of breeding individuals and sterile workers. For this they received numerous stings, as their swollen faces in the expedition photographs testify. The other freshwater ecologist, Professor Jim Green from London had to delay his visit until after I had left, but he then discovered how important the rain was in bringing nutrients (probably from forest fires) into these low-nutrient headwater streams.

We all enjoyed the colourful birds and Hilary Fry from the University of Aberdeen, during his later two months mist-netted 940 birds of 161 species, recording another 102 species by observation alone. The cerrado yielded 60 species (only five of them endemic) and gallery forest 33 endemic species. He found all five of South America`s large kingfishers here along rivers and streams in gallery forest. Hilary concluded that Brazil`s endemic avifauna is

Fish from the pool near Base Camp in the Mato Grosso.
Clockwise from the bottom the genera are: Gymnotus, Sternopygus, Callichthys,
Aequidens, *2* Hoplias, *another* Callichthys *and a small* Moenkhausia *in the centre.*

The camp doctor netting a large Hoplias malabaricus *from a clear pool. It was too full of parasites for him to let us eat it!*

richer than that in Africa and (like me) he was very impressed by convergence in form and life style between unrelated families in the two continents. For example, the South American jacamars are directly comparable with African bee-eaters. In my case the comparison was between the electric fishes: gymnotoids in these neotropical streams with mormyroids in African waters. The medics were mostly concerned with diseases amongst the indigenous population. All of us in camp at that time were involved in a 24 hour experiment to test the stress hormones in our urine, not only when compared with samples from local people, but when tested again when we were back in England. This revealed how all but one couple were more stressed in England than under jungle conditions.

My letter to Anthony Smith describing fish collecting experiences for his Mato Grosso book summarised the delights of working from base camp. I did a lot of fishing at night, as experience in Guyana had taught me that this was the most productive way to get fish with the limited gear I had with me. Certain fish groups (cichlids and most characoids) were active by day and hid away motionless by night, often along the river bank, while others (the many types of catfish and gymnotoids) were nocturnal. Fishing with a good torch at night one could bail out the sleeping fish with a dip net and also take nocturnal fishes as these had by then emerged from crevices where they hid during the day. Their gleaming eyes, red, orange or silvery yellow, caught

Lagoa Leo, a virgin pool where native fish were so easily caught on hooks they had never seen before.

the torch light and gave their presence away. The numerous freshwater prawns also had bright gleaming eyes, and the innumerable spiders, some of which used to run over the water surface at night while others lined the river banks, had eyes glinting like diamonds. The eyes of nightjars hovering around shone like candles in the torchlight, also reflected in the dark water.

I was delighted to find that base camp was on a complex of streams with clear pools so I was able to pop in and out, watching and catching fishes at all times of night and day. It was surprising what large fishes appeared at night, such as 15 inch long gymnotoids (*Sternopygus* and *Gymnotus*) slid backwards and forwards with equal ease, with their long slim bodies held rigid, for the electric field around them to sense the surroundings. We rigged up a tape recorder to pick up their electric signals, each of a specific frequency, which showed that we had three species in the camp stream (one *Gymnotus* later proved to be new to science). At night the 15 cm long armoured catfish *Callichthys* searched among the leaves carpeting the pools searching for ephemeropteran nymphs and other food items like a terrier after a rat. *Callichthys* proved to be a remarkably tough fish that climbed out of bowls in the lab, lived out of water for a long time, and wriggled across the ground with tail flexures and pelvic fins. The *Aequidens* cichlids in these stream headwaters were also very tough, able to withstand lower oxygen concentrations than most of the other fish. Many of these species have accessory respiratory devices that cope with the low oxygen content of these streams, decomposing leaves and the very acid conditions. Several of the nocturnal fishes, and some others such as pirana, made characteristic sounds, squeaking when caught.

Kids playing on the beach at the edge of the Rio das Mortes river where the expedition had a house whose effluent attracted small trichomycterid catfish which are reputed to enter orifices of unwary bathers.

A selection of Suia Missu fish, 1969.
From the bottom: piranas, Boulengerella, striped catfish, Cichla sp.

I was wet through from chest downwards most of the time as I always worked in clothes, a habit developed in Guyana where pirana were numerous, so I kept cool while soil scientists in their pits were finding it very hot. Sitting on muddy river banks to examine the catch in sopping wet trousers got clothes into an indescribable state, and wet cloth splits easily. Drip dry materials were a great help. Sweat bees used to swarm to the damp fish as I measured them, stingless but mixed in with few feral 'Europa' bees with dangerous stings. Small midges, *Simulium* blackflies and mosquitoes also frequented some streams.

One snag about my work was the amount of gear that had to be carried to catch the fish and preserve them before they went bad, as they did very fast in the hot climate. In this uninhabited country there were no local villagers (as in Africa) to help carry things. I traipsed through the bush looking like the White Knight, slung about with equipment. Many of the camp Brasilieros were very skilful fishermen and enjoyed this very much, but most of them were very noisy in the bush compared with the Amerindians in Guyana. It was hard work physically as we had to improvise, even setting gillnets by swimming in the absence of any boat, and with circumspection, being well aware of what electric eels and pirana can do. But in many places the water was clear enough to observe the fish through polaroid glasses and assess what was there before trying to catch them.

Using dipnets, a small mosquito-mesh seine, small gill nets, traps and hooks we collected over 150 species from this small area. These included about 88 characoid species of 12 different families, 38 siluroid catfishes of eight families, seven gymnotoid electric fish of four families, only sixteen species of cichlids and eight species of seven other fish families. A number of species were new to science, others rather atypical from type specimens collected from other areas. At this time of year the water levels proved too high to make comprehensive catches, as would be possible from dry season pools. Professional fishermen in Xavantina reputedly caught big catfishes and characoids from the larger rivers when they move upstream and the water is low, but at high water the fish were widely distributed over the landscape. Many of the fish bred during the rains, and as the waters fell, spectacular swarms of young characins migrated upstream along the river banks. The resident fishes in the headwater streams and the camp pool were mostly species that are widely distributed throughout much of South America. Many were known to me from Guyana and to aquarists, such as *Hoplias malabaricus*, here growing very large, *Hoplerythrinus unitaeniatus* and *Callichthys callichthys*, hardy species which can withstand periods of low water. *Gymnotus* and *Sternopygus* electric fishes were also found, along with *Leporinus friderici* and the smaller *Moenkhausia oligolepis*. The very common *Aequidens 'xavantina'* (a new cichlid species) closely resembled the widespread *A. tetramerus* in life style, living in small family parties in the camp pools.

The eastward flowing upper Araguaia system tributaries with their steeper gradients had a restricted fauna compared with the westward flowing Xingu tributaries, the differences in topography leading to different ecological conditions. Many fishes shared food items, dashing for whatever foods, insects and plant bits, dropped on to the water surface from the surrounding vegetation. The wet season lakes were particularly rich in species and numbers of fish, and the Suia Missu (Xingu basin) floodplain oxbow lakes housed larger fish species. In streams across the open cerrado, naïve cichlids which had not yet met hooks, immediately got hooked. Seasonal effects were very marked, with spectacular upriver dispersal migrations of small fishes, mostly characins, as water levels fell. The study showed how varied ecological conditions are in these tropical streams, both seasonally and spatially.

The numerous scientific papers from the diverse studies carried out during this expedition were published in widely scattered specialist journals, but for the RS/RGS Anthony Smith produced a very readable account of the expedition in his book *Mato Grosso*. The original plan had been to protect the 20 km² of forest/cerrado studied in such detail as a reference site, but even before this could be gazetted, locals moved in and cleared the forest. Revisiting the site later, Anthony Smith saw huge development in this area, a centre for cattle and soya bean cultivation, with Xavantina grown into a considerable town. And when flying from São Paulo to Manaus in 1995 we could see from the air the monumental clearing of this Mato Grosso landscape.

Barro Colorado

Another Neotropical field station I very much enjoyed was the Smithsonian Institution field station on Barro Colorado island in Gatún lake in the Panama Canal, which I visited with Tom Zaret after chairing a session at the Society for Tropical Biology symposium in Panama in 1979. The symposium was held in Panama parliament's main hall in a huge modern building in Panama City. This was available as parliament was 'closed', but the audience was tethered at the back of the vast auditorium by the simultaneous Spanish/ English translation apparatus. After the meeting Tom and I escaped on the little train which crosses the isthmus, alighting on a bare platform alongside the canal where the Smithsonian launch collected us and took us to their Barro Colorado island field station. This was an amusing ride in such a small launch alongside the vast liners making their way between locks in the Panama Canal. On a later visit by Professor John Maynard Smith and his wife, the launch driver must have been drunk for he left them abandoned on the platform for a most uncomfortable night.

Barro Colorado was a most stimulating place as visiting scientists from many countries were working on such different projects, including ecological and behavioural studies of many animals from leaf-cutting ants to howler monkeys. A small tame tapir hung about hopefully outside the communal dining room, and a charming little silky anteater was brought in for study.

Introduced Cichla ocellaris *from the Panama Canal.*

Holding a large specimen of Cichla with Bob Wetzel, who was then General Secretary of SIL. We were on the excursion to Manaus which followed the SIL Congress in São Paulo, Brazil, in 1995.

The excursion boat on the Rio Negro upstream of where it joins the Solimões to form the main River Amazon at Manaus.

The meeting of the waters. The clear, dark water of the Rio Negro is quite distinct from the silt laden water of the main Amazon.

A beautiful pest in its South American homeland – the water hyacinth Eichhornia crassipes *which floats on the surface of the water and forms thick mats preventing light reaching the water below and often causing it to become deoxygenated.*

The introduction of Eichhornia *to Lake Victoria in Africa was disastrous for those attempting to earn their living from lakeside villages. It also caused major obstructions to boat traffic on the River Nile in Sudan and further downstream in Egypt. Fortunately researchers have found a weevil which will control its growth.*

This photograph (left) shows mangled masses of Eichhornia *after passing through the turbines in a dam on the Teite River in Brazil, which we visited on a mid-Congress excursion from Säo Paulo, in 1995. Above the dam, water hyacinths were piled up in a floating mass a metre deep.*

Tom was interested in whether ultraviolet light, known to guide insects to certain flowers, could also be perceived by surface living fishes. We also spied out a suitable incoming stream for Mary Power's later field experiments on loricariid catfish distributions. Before I left we were all co-opted for a census of howler monkeys on the island. This involved each of us going out into a designated part of the forest before dawn, armed with a compass to record the direction of the howler morning choruses. Some amusing confusion in the dark resulted in one party boated round the island being inadvertently landed on a floating mass of plants. I disgraced myself when alone in the dark spooky forest I found comfort by climbing a ladder propped against a tall tree, not realising it was a metal ladder which deflected the compass bearings. Not a useful contribution.

At Barro Colorado Tom Zaret and his colleagues had been investigating the effects of the introduction of the piscivorous *Cichla ocellaris*, an old friend of a species that I had studied in Guyana. It is the largest South American cichlid (which can grow to 70 cm long, 7 kg in weight). A hundred fingerlings had been introduced by fishermen for a sport fishery in the Chagres River in Panama in the early 1960s. These multiplied and spread down the river into Gatún Lake in the Panama Canal. Here they led to the disappearance of many indigenous fishes and simplified the food web through secondary effects on the zooplankton, insects and vertebrates, including the many fish-eating birds. Most of the small indigenous fishes (atherinid *Melaniris chagresi*, poeciliids and small characins) were wiped out from the lake, although they survived in the river where there was more plant cover. However, a large indigenous cichlid, *Cichlasoma maculicauda* increased, attributed to the elimination by *Cichla* of species that formerly fed on *Cichlasoma* fry.

While in Panama I also visited the Smithsonian's two marine stations, one at the Pacific end of the canal, the other by flying across to the San Blas Islands off the Atlantic coast. Here a team of scuba divers were studying the behaviour of coral reef fishes, including territorial pomacentrid damsel fishes which defended their algal gardens against the mobs of wandering mixed species groups that arrived to crop their algal patches. Most intriguing. While living on the beach of these delightful islands the main food item available was the delicious lobsters awaiting export to the mainland.

São Paulo and back to the Amazon

In 1995 Peggy Varley (Peggy Brown of EAFRO days) and I attended the XXVI International Congress of Limnology held in São Paulo Brazil, a most eventful trip with field excursions during and after the meeting. We were well looked after by many Brazilian colleagues and friends, especially Miguel Petrere (whose PhD on Amazon fishes I had examined in the early 1980s in the UK). The University of São Paulo had previously arranged for my

Itaipu reservoir above the dam on the Rio Paraná, just north of the Iguaçu Falls. It is the largest dam in Brazil.

Cambridge University Press book *Ecological Studies in Tropical Waters* to be translated into Portuguese, with additional chapters by Brazilian authors. These included the excellent studies of fish and fisheries in the many huge new man-made lakes developed as part of Brazil's hydroelectricity schemes (many directed by Angelo Augustinho and his students), and also on studies made in Brazil's coastal waters. As this book was much used for teaching in Brazil, I had many contacts there, and at the SIL General Assembly, to my complete surprise, I received the Nauman-Thienemann Founders medal, mainly for work in Africa.

The field trips included a visit to Dr Manuel Pereira de Godoy living near the Cachoeira de Emas rapids on the Mogi Guassu tributary of the Upper Paraná. Here, between 1954 and 1963, he had tagged some 27,000 fishes. Returns showed that the characoid *Prochilodus scrofa* made a 600 km up and down river migration, from spawning in huge aggregations in the shallows below the Cachoeira de Emas barrage, upriver to feed in the lower reaches of the Pardo and Grande rivers (Godoy 1967). But in 1995 few of these fishes were to be found, due to barrages and pollution in these rivers. We also visited the Brazilian (IBAMA) Training and Research Center for Aquaculture (CEPTA) founded in 1979 at Pirassununga where they were culturing the large indigenous characoid 'tambaqui' (*Colossoma macropomum*) and various hybrids in ponds. Some were in polycultures with tilapia species, already widely distributed in Brazil. For this SIL Congress, the Brazilian Academy of Sciences produced a very useful survey of *Limnology in Brazil*.

For me the highlight of the SIL trip was a long-anticipated visit to the INPA Research Station in Manaus which has for long been the main centre for ecological research in the central Amazon. It was the base for Dr Harold Sioli's team who had carried out classic studies of 'black water' and 'white water' Amazonian sites. In the 1960s, as Secretary of the Tropical Group of the British Ecological Society, I had invited him and a colleague to London for a stimulating meeting with biologists working on African lakes so I already knew some of the people but had not been to their headquarters before.

Carlos Araujo-Lima laid on a delightful post-congress excursion for fifteen or so SIL delegates living on one of two vessels. On our boat we first visited the Rio Negro archipelago of islands, accompanied by the very knowledgeable Wolfgang Junk. The vegetation was clearly reflected in its darkly stained, brown (mosquito free) waters. We then crossed the 'meeting of the waters', where these dark Rio Negro waters run alongside those of the turbid 'white' waters of the main Amazon stream, here called the Solimões, which has abundant mosquitoes. En route we visited the Harold Sioli floating laboratory, after we had found it – it had been towed away to another site as the river

Reminiscing with Peggy about our trip to Brazil ten years on – 2005.

level was falling. Here there were displays of fish adaptations to low oxygen tensions, and nearby we saw work in progress on rates of production of swamp vegetation, very relevant to work in Africa (but here they had another species of the floating water hyacinth *Eichhornia*). Another highlight was fishing for electric fish with Cristine Cox Fernandes (our kind hostess in Manaus) when at dusk we landed a huge catch of one species of electric fish (*Rhabdolichops*) which must have been hiding below a log waiting to emerge to feed as the sun went down. On this voyage I also learned much from vetting the proofs of *The Central Amazon Floodplain: Ecology of a Pulsing System* which Wolfgang Junk was editing for Springer (1997).

Peggy and I had many other visits full of incidents, ending with a pilgrimage to the spectacularly beautiful rainbow-ringed Iguaçu Falls on the Paranã River where Brazil and Argentina meet. The falls are just below the hydroelectric barrage built in 1982, behind which the huge, 170 km long, Itaipu Reservoir has formed. On the Upper Paranã River there are more than 130 major reservoirs which have inundated the river floodplain system. The effect of these dams on the fish and fisheries has been studied in great detail since 1986 by Angelo Antonio Agostinho and his 'NUPELIA' team based at the University of Maringa.

*Iguaçu Falls on the Paranã River which here forms
the border between Brazil and Argentina.*

Chapter 10
The aquatic chicken

While based at the BM(NH) from 1962 I continued my research on tilapia, working with Ethelwynn Trewavas until she died in 1993, and indeed until the present time. Related activities included examining a number of theses and supervising two Open University students who were studying the ecology of *Tilapia mossambica* in the Sepik River floodplain in Papua New Guinea, where these introduced tilapia had spread and come to support the main fishery (Coates 1987). Tilapia workers from far and wide visited the Fish Section to consult ET and the collections. Among them was Thys van der Audenaerde who was working on Congo tilapias with Max Poll from Tervuren. From the Zambezi system came Graham Bell-Cross and, from South Africa, Peter Jackson, Mike Bruton and Paul Skelton. Visitors studying tilapia behaviour in aquaria included G.P. Baerends, from the Netherlands, Lester Aronson from the USA and Lev Fischelson from Israel. All this interest in tilapias was a crescendo compared to when only a handful of us studied these fish. Now thousands of people around the world do so as they have become a major food fish stocked in lakes and dams, and cultivated in ponds throughout the warmer regions of the world. How did this all come about?

In spring 1963, when Richard was abroad skiing, I was surprised to be phoned in Sussex from FAO (= Food and Agricultural Organization of the United Nations) to ask if I could come to Rome for two months to help edit papers submitted for the First World Congress on Warm-Water Fish Culture. So I went, and from this experience learned a great deal, made new friends, enjoyed Rome and the Italian countryside and had an inside view of working for FAO. Surprisingly few tilapia papers were actually submitted for this meeting because tilapia had not then become as fashionable as carps. In 1964 when I returned to Rome to participate in the conference, the hotel where the delegates were all staying said there was no room for me – ' Had not I had their telegram?' No, so what to do? On finding I was a woman, it was suggested I could stay with the nuns who were running a girls school behind the hotel and have meals with the others in the hotel. So I was led away, up a flight of steps from the garden, to a lofty room with three beds in it – and the Cardinal's personal effects. They were an Argentinian Order and this was the Cardinal's room. A great honour, but its massive key, produced in support of my payments for rounds of drinks, caused considerable amusement among the hotel waiters!

At this FAO Symposium on Warmwater Fish Culture the emphasis was on using Indian and Chinese carps. As I have already described (Chapter 4), the advantages of using tilapias for warmwater fish culture had much earlier been espoused by the Belgians in the Congo and, in the 1950s, by Dr C.F.

Hickling, whose studies in Malaya, of tilapia male monoculture and hybridisation, had inspired similar studies in many parts of the world. The use of tilapias as the warmwater culture fish *par excellence* was later given prominence in 1979 when Roger Pullin, who joined the newly formed ICLARM (International Center for Aquatic Resources Management – based in the Philippines), was advised to make tilapia research the mainstay of ICLARM's aquaculture programme. After that the idea really took off.

ICLARM's first major event was to organise an International Conference on *The Biology and Culture of Tilapias* in September 1980. It was held in the Rockefeller Foundation Conference Centre at Bellagio, a beautiful old house full of treasured vases and pictures, on an island in Lake Como, Italy. The Proceedings of this meeting is still a much-used source of information. Twenty five participants from different countries had prepared reviews on what was then known about tilapia biology, physiology, and prospects for their culture in ponds or cages. The Biology Session (which I chaired) opened with a paper by Ethelwynn Trewavas on 'Tilapia Taxonomy and Speciation' in which she explained why the genus *Tilapia* had now been divided into three genera. The substratum-spawning, plant-eating species were still known as *Tilapia* (s.s), but the mouthbrooder, microphagous species (formerly in a subgenus

Tilapia from fish ponds at Kisumu for stocking into Lake Victoria.
Bottom left is Tilapia melanopleura.

Sarotherodon) were now recognised as two new genera: the paternal/ biparental brooders species as *Sarotherodon*, the maternal mouth-brooders (lek spawners) as a distinct genus, *Oreochromis*. Tilapia speciation has evidently occurred allopatrically by geographical isolation in different river systems as in the cases of the nilo-sudanian *T. zillii* and *T. rendalli* (formerly included in '*T. melanopleura*') and in the many tasselled tilapias surrounding the rift valley (including *O. variabilis*, and the Malagarasi species), but sympatrically in the case of the Malawi species flock.

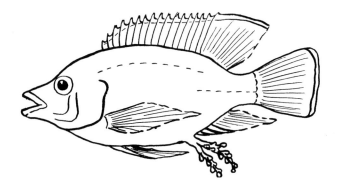

Tilapia karomo *from the Malagarasi showing the male tassels. These encourage the female to think they are eggs and thus when she tries to pick them up, sperm goes into her mouth and fertilises any eggs already there.*

A masterly summary by two Belgium biologists (J-Cl Philippart and J.Cl. Ruwet) gave maps of tilapia distributions in Africa's river systems and analysed the physical and chemical factors influencing where they thrived (such as tolerances to different water temperatures, salinity and oxygen etc, and choice of microhabitats for feeding and breeding). They also listed transfers of tilapia within Africa and worldwide, of the species then most used in fish culture: *O. mossambicus, O. hornorum, O. niloticus* (and the closely related *O. aureus*), *T. zillii* and *T. rendalli*.

Taking an evolutionary perspective of tilapia life histories, D. Noakes and E.K. Balon pointed out that 'stunting' (then a great problem for pond culture) was a misunderstood phenomenon. 'Dwarfing' is a better term, because growth is not stunted; there is just a shift to earlier maturation at a very small size. This enables populations to build up speedily, as they do when dried up floodplains are repopulated. Tilapiine fishes were almost certainly derived from fluvial ancestors and some species still retain their adaptive ability to invade newly created marginal habitats. Since stocking fishes in ponds replicates these conditions, tilapia react by maturing early at a very small size and age.

My own paper summarised findings on tilapias in fish communities. In Lake Malawi the endemic tilapia species share resources but remain distinct by breeding at different depths and seasons, aided by different male breeding colours. In Lake Victoria the two endemic species, formerly the mainstay of the gillnet fisheries, had been ousted by introduced nilo-sudanian tilapias. During the same period, the clear waters of the Malagarasi and Kyoga swamps had allowed me to make observations of *Oreochromis* spawning behaviour in the wild, and new species had been discovered in the Pangani system. I showed that floodplain tilapias tend to have seasonally fast growth, early maturity, high fecundity. They produce small eggs and several broods in quick succession, all characteristics of 'r-strategists' as usually found in pioneer habitats, like floodplains which open up each year. In contrast, the more 'K selected' lacustrine species which evolved in the large lakes have a delayed maturity (2-4 years) and final size, reduced fecundity producing only one or two broods a year, with few relatively large ova and young brooded to a larger size.

This production of numerous very small fish, the major discouragement to raising tilapia in ponds, had stimulated many lines of research into the use of monosex cultures, or multi-cultures with some piscivores to control their numbers. At the Sagana fish farm, dwarf male *T. nigra* had been shown to continue growth when moved to less crowded ponds but dwarf populations in natural waters are known to occur in most tilapias. As already mentioned (Chapter 4) Iles considered that this represented an adaptation towards survival under extreme physical conditions, for small tilapia are very hardy and have a higher temperature tolerance than do the adult tilapia or other small cichlids. Furthermore, breeding size is reduced to an even greater degree than final size, giving very low values for maturity/total length ratios. These precocious breeders can mature in less than three months (compared with 2-4 years in lake populations), speeding up the whole life cycle. This enables them to withstand very high mortality rates, such as when numerous wading birds descend on pools that are drying up, and swamps. Iles thought that tilapia might be unique in this cumulative effect of a combination of a marked increase in relative growth rate, increase in brood frequency and decrease in egg size.

However, Pauly (1984) later suggested that the change from growth to reproduction probably results from diminishing oxygen supply per unit body weight. In all growing fish this serves as the master factor in inducing the transition from juvenile to adult, and Pauly suggested that any stress (such a high temperature, crowding, osmotic cost) which raises the maintenance metabolism would result in a reduced final size. The conditions under which we had found dwarf populations of tilapias supported this view. The Lake Albert lagoon populations were very stressed and in Lake Turkana the dwarf tilapia collected by Worthington from the crater lakes on Central Island had little food and space. When later studies found that those in Ferguson's Gulf,

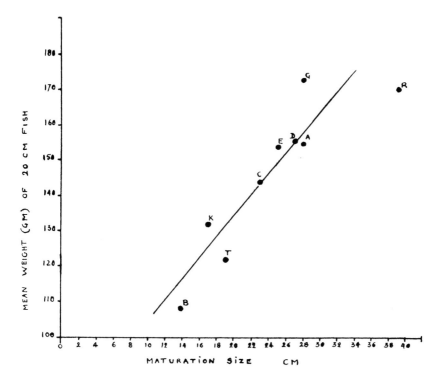

This shows that Tilapia nilotica *in good condition (high weight for length at 20 cm TL), such as those in Lakes George (G) and Rudolf (R), mature at a larger size that do those in poor condition living in the lagoons (B, K and T).*

which produced the enormous 1976 boom, appeared very well fed on a rich phytoplankton bloom from newly flooded land, Kolding (1992) postulated that low or fluctuating oxygen conditions probably resulted from this bloom and caused the dwarfing.

Since the studies already discussed in earlier chapters, much additional information had become available from other parts of Africa. For example from Mike Bruton's study of the ecology of *O. mossambicus* in its natural home in Lake Sibaya, in southern Africa, where breeding was seasonal (after the water temperature first exceeded 20°C). Here the small fry fed in the warm shallows and scale studies showed that males grew faster than females after the first year. The females bred after one year when 11–12 cm, the males at 17 cm after one to two years (largest female 18 cm, male 29 cm TL). Adult fish had to live in deeper waters where they had less nutritious food than was available in the sunny shallows inhabited by the young and this led to precocious breeding, after which growth decelerated.

The ecology of tilapias in the Zambezi system had been studied as part of the pre-impoundment surveys for hydroelectric schemes at Kariba and Cabora Bassa, also on the Barotse floodplain and Kafue Flats. The Zambezi has a series of tilapia species, the brackish-water tolerant *O. mossambicus* in estuarine reaches, the very similar *O. mortimeri* in the middle Zambezi (where the Kariba dam was being built), with *O. macrochir* and *O. andersoni* in the Upper Zambezi . There are also several large piscivores in this system and the tilapia are used to living with them, especially the tiger fish *Hydrocynus vittatus*. The story has already been told (Chapter 8) of how the wrong species came to be stocked into Lake Kariba which demonstrated so clearly the need to understand the species ecology before interfering with natural communities.

Many new tilapia species had also been discovered. For example, the small crater lake Barombi Mbo (in Cameroon) had been found by Ethelwynn Trewavas to have four endemic species of *Sarotherodon* evolved sympatrically in the lake. Later a species flock of small *Tilapia* species was discovered in Lake Bermin, Cameroon (Stiassny *et al* 1992). The Kenya Rift soda lakes (ph 10.5) also have dwarf *Oreochromis* species living very close to their inflowing hot springs (43°C) and other dwarf species have since been discovered in these lakes by Seegers & Tichy. Among studies of tilapia introduced into exotic communities, an interesting case was *O. mossambicus* stocked in Plover Cove, Hong Kong, an arm of the sea converted into a freshwater reservoir What adaptive and fascinating fish tilapias are proving to be!

Data on tilapia production and yield from the Kafue floodplain and Lake Kariba showed that only a small part of the total biological production can be cropped as yield from natural waters, in contrast with ponds from which,

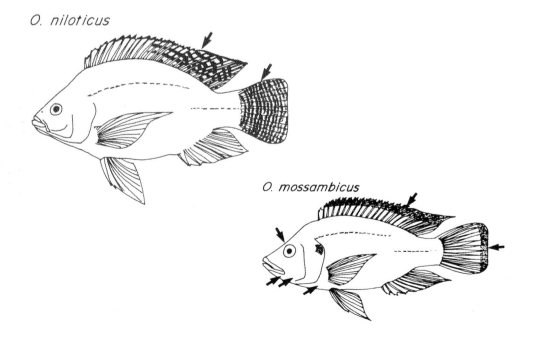

O. niloticus

O. mossambicus

when drained, almost the whole production can be removed, The turnover rate (production/biomass ratio) was higher in the substratum-spawning *T. rendalli* than in the associated mouth-brooding *Oreochromis*. In the equatorial Lake George (see Chapter 4), which once produced the highest yield of tilapia

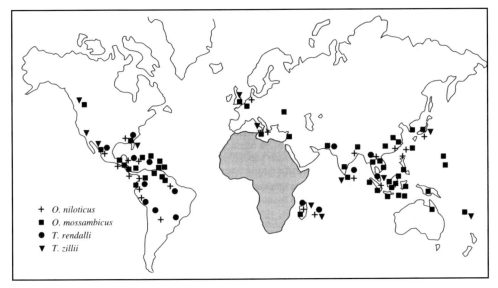

+ *O. niloticus*
■ *O. mossambicus*
● *T. rendalli*
▼ *T. zillii*

The current world distribution (outside Africa) of the four species of tilapia illustrated below and opposite. (From various sources.) The arrows point to characteristic features.

Tilapia zillii

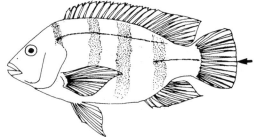

Tilapia rendalli

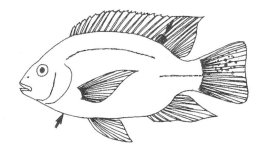

from any natural water body, this was comparable with those from unfertilised ponds. Despite this, the high yield represented less than 1% of the very high primary production of bluegreen algae on which these tilapia fed.

Review papers given in the 'Culture' sessions at the Bellagio meeting had produced evidence of introgression of Asian stocks of *O. niloticus* with *O. mossambicus*, and as there was a clear need for specimens of known strains of tilapias for research and culture work, recommendations were made as to how these should be collected. This subject was considered further in the follow-up ICLARM workshop held in Bangkok in March 1987, the year when the first direct transfers of pure stock from Africa to ICLARM (later renamed the WorldFish Center) were made.

But before this, in February 1981, I accompanied Ethelwynn Trewavas to Kenya to seek out some tilapias species of interest for fish culture, including *O. spilurus niger* (the 'T. nigra' used in the monosex experiments at Sagana Fish Culture station, which Peggy and I had visited in 1951). Stocked tilapia always seemed to escape into river systems, where they hybridised with other species, making it increasingly difficult to find pure stocks for breeding and growing the best strains. In 1981 when Ethelwynn and I, together with knowledgable local people, searched the Athi river (the original home of *O. spilurus niger*) all we could find were hybrids with species escaped from stocked dams. The trip was enlivened for me by having to deliver an African baby – a fine healthy boy, born breach presentation on to my bath towel at the side of a dusty road. The mother was helped by the women of the village holding her in midair, for a gravity-assisted birth, which seemed very sensible. This was an enlightening experience: I wondered if he would grow up to be a future Premier of Kenya?

While in Kenya ET and I also visited the Bamboo commercial fish farm at Bamburi near Mombasa. This was part of a rehabilitation programme for a disused fossil-coral limestone quarry being developed by Rene Haller (from Switzerland), assisted by Fishery Officer John Balarin, in an attempt to utilise the abundant water resources. Here the growth performance of ten species of tilapia (including the new species from Lake Jipe) were tested in raceways and concrete circular tanks, where yields of 100–200 kg m^{-3} a year were made possible by a continuous water flow and intensive feeding with nutritionally balanced, pelleted food. The fry were produced in a hatchery which exploited the 'arena' breeding behaviour of *Oreochromis*. Fingerlings were then on-grown in raceways before being graded and transferred for growth in circular tanks. Here constant circulation of the water prevented the males from establishing territories, and so from breeding, a method then a closely guarded 'commercial secret'. I was persuaded to sit in this large tank with goggles on to watch the tilapia behaviour. But oh how awful I smelt when I emerged! I felt very sorry for the fish having to live in such water. The end product of this tank culture was large tilapia, weighing over 250 gm, for the hotel and restaurant trade; smaller fish found a ready outlet in local rural markets. Another memory is of a little reef heron slinking around the tanks catching one of the 'carefully guarded' strain of tilapia then dropping it into an adjacent tank.

All this was in the gorgeous hot sunshine near the palm-fringed Kenya coast, where ET and I were lent a company house (plus cook and night watchman). It was right on the beach where local fishermen landed fish fresh from the sea that were most excellent to eat. These included many exciting species we had never seen before, except in the BM(NH)'s jars of alcohol, after they had lost their glowing but fast-fading colours. I introduced ET, then in her eighties, to the joys of goggling (her first time), out on the reef from a very wobbly canoe. She was ecstatic, but as the tide fell while we were on the reef we had a difficult passage back trying to avoid the long-spined sea urchins that are so abundant on these Kenyan reefs.

About this time (1982) ET attended the First International Symposium on Tilapia in Aquaculture (ISTA I) that Israeli scientists had organised in Nazareth. Attended by about 200 people representing 48 countries, this demonstrated the growing interest of tilapia as a food fish, as well as for scientific study. The 624 pages of the proceedings included numerous papers on tilapia biology and ecology, physiology and pathology, reproduction, genetics, nutrition, management and production. A fascinating paper by Lev Fishelson on 'Social behaviour of tilapia fish in nature and in captivity' summarized his comparative observations on the behaviour of *T. zillii*, *O. niloticus* and *O. aureus*, and *S. galilaeus*, made from 1947 over several years. He used a face mask and snorkel, together with observations through clear water in the Tiberias Sea (= Lake Kinneret, the Sea of Galilee), the inflowing river and in captivity. He found that in the substratum-spawning *T. zillii*, the female joins the male in defending a large breeding territory against conspecifics within a breeding colony and that pairs may remain together for several years. Whereas in the *Oreochromis* species (*O. niloticus*, *O. aureus* and *O. hornorum*), in which males develop spawning colours, competitive interactions become ritualistic postures and the nest territories are just small spawning plaques crowded into leks. Here a visiting female, spawning 600 to 1000 eggs, may visit several nests in turn, then pick up and carry away in her mouth spawn fertilised by two to four males, moving up to 80 m away from the lek site. In *S. galilaeus*, in which males and females are of a similar colour, the pair swims together closely and both sexes may mouth brood eggs.

Following The Second International Symposium on Tilapia in Aquaculture in Thailand in March 1987, ICLARM tackled problems raised at the 1980 Bellagio meeting, in a two-day workshop on *Tilapia Genetic Resources for Aquaculture* (edited by Pullin 1988). The opening session by Thys van der Audenaerde reviewed the natural distribution of tilapias and its consequences for the possible protection of genetic resources (with useful maps), and I reviewed the ecology and distribution of tilapias in Africa that are important for aquaculture.

Session II summarised the status of wild and cultured tilapia genetic resources in various countries, including eight contributions from Africa (presented by representatives from Cameroun, Ivory Coast (brackish and freshwaters), Ghana, Madagascar, Malawi and Zimbabwe), three from Asia (Philippines, Thailand and Singapore/Malaysia), and other countries including Israel and USA . This clearly showed how wide interest in tilapia culture had become. Session III, on research methods used in tilapia identification and genetic research, included reviews of electrophoresis by Pullin, tilapia blood groups by Villwock, multivariate analysis of morphometric/meristic data by Ms Pante; taxonomy by Thys and me, and estimation of genetic parameters and evaluation of culture performance by G.W. Wohlfarth from Israel. Session IV on gene banks and culture collections included a paper on cryopreservation as a tool (by B.J. Harvey), and one on broodstock collection in the Philippines. There was also a general discussion leading to the formulation of recommendations on documentation and conservation of tilapia genetic resources, their evaluation and use, culture collections and gene banks, and international research cooperation and funding. Two other appendices collated information on 'Genetic Improvement of Tilapias: Problems and Prospects' (by Pullin and J.B. Capili), and on genetic considerations in acquisition and maintenance of reference populations of tilapia (by R.O. Smitherman and D. Tave from Alabama Agricultural Experiment Station, Auburn University, Alabama USA). It became clear that many hybrid tilapias were becoming important in aquaculture.

Roger Pullin's chapter in *Cichlid Fishes; behaviour, ecology and evolution* was based on a meeting we had at Vancouver University. It summarised the excellent attributes for aquaculture of tilapias, dubbed 'aquatic chickens' by ICLARM. Unfortunately the first species spread throughout the world for aquaculture (*O. mossambicus*) had poorer growth and breeding characteristics than most other cultured species. Rapid developments resulted from a change from *O. mossambicus* to *O. niloticus* in the Philippines, and this became the favoured species throughout the world for tropical fish farmers, though other species remained locally important like the more cold tolerant ones (such a *O. spilurus nigra*) at higher latitudes and altitudes, or more salinity-tolerant species (such as the West African lagoon species *S. melanotheron*) for brackish ponds.

The prolific breeding of tilapias in confined ponds, thereby overpopulating the pond with undersized fish, still remained a stumbling block. Clearly this allows wild fish to populate new environments very rapidly, as when dried-up lakes become refilled and are recolonized from residual stocks in streams. A major factor seems to be space. For example, *O. mossambicus* may mature at

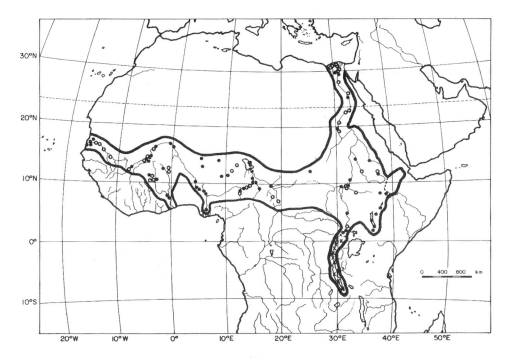

The natural distribution of O. niloticus *as illustrated in the proceedings of the Bangkok meeting.*

5 g in aquaria, but at hundreds of grams in lakes. This problem led to much further research, eg on monosex culture, hybridization or hormone treatments.

Despite the difficulties of making realistic estimates, FAO statistics at that time indicated tilapia culture produced c 250,000 tonnes a year, but it was thought that this might be doubled by 1999 as more farmers in Third World countries become aware of the benefit of incorporating aquaculture into mixed faming systems. Cichlid aquaculture had progressed much more in Asia than in Africa and other regions, but there was great scope for cooperation, particularly between Asia and Africa, to assist the development of aquaculture from Asian experience, and to spur tilapia genetic improvement world-wide from African genetic resources.

The demand for fish has increased worldwide and it is now clear that most wild fish stocks have been overexploited or have reached their maximum sustainable yield due to over fishing, habitat deterioration and pollution. Against a production of 93.2 million tonnes of food fish in 1997, it was estimated that the demand for fish will increase to over 130 million tonnes by 2020. There is room for increasing aquaculture through better farm management, but to meet these global demands genetically improved strains are necessary, as in the case of crops and livestock (see also Petr, 2004).

From FAO statistics for 2002, it was a surprise to learn that China had become the world's largest tilapia producer, producing 706,000 tonnes, mostly on small family farms. Eighty percent was consumed domestically, 20% exported (frozen whole or as fillets) mainly to the USA. The Philippines produced over 122,000 tons from ponds and net cages for the domestic market, Thailand 100,000 tons mostly from ponds, of which 90% were consumed domestically. Of Taiwan's 90,000 t from ponds, many tilapia were sent frozen to Europe and Japan. Indonesia, too, exported 25% of its 50,000 t from ponds and cages to the USA, consuming the rest at home. Across the Atlantic, Mexico and Brazil produced 110,000 and 75,000t respectively from tanks, raceways, cages, ponds and reservoirs, for their domestic markets. The 'aquatic chicken' had become (and is still becoming) increasingly useful and is now established as a key domestic species in the service of mankind.

But not everyone is so happy with the spread of tilapia, and once introduced they are impossible to eradicate. In Madagascar they led to the decline of scientifically valuable endemic cichlid genera. In Queensland, Australia it was feared they would interfere with indigenous river fishes, and in the Hawaiian Islands, where they were introduced as bait for tuna long lines, they are said to have affected mullet cultivation. Tilapia are also spreading in the southern rivers of Florida.

The University of Stirling in Scotland, organised the next major multi-authored synthesis on *Tilapias; Biology and Exploitation* which was edited by Malcolm Beveridge and Brendan McAndrew. In my chapter on 'The role of tilapia in ecosystems`, I pointed out that since all tilapia species are basically herbivores or detritivores they occupy an intermediate position between primary producers and piscivores. They thus have two main ecological roles in fish communities: helping the circulation of the nutrients on which the primary production of their planktonic food depends, and supporting fish-eaters, including other fishes, birds or man. As they are such important food fish, research has concentrated mainly on the latter role. Their success as widely dispersed and abundant fish in African waters appears to be due mainly to their use of algae, aquatic plants or detritus; food sources which are rarely limiting (though varying in quality). Relatively few freshwater fish feed directly on living plants or detritus, and in many African waters tilapia make up a large share of the ichthyomass (60% in Lake George and 74% in Sokoto River pools in Nigeria for example). Most freshwater fish feed predominantly on invertebrates and small fishes and for them the main problem is to obtain an adequate quantity of food at a minimal cost in time and energy. By contrast, tilapia food is generally present far in excess of their ability to consume it, but the quality of the food is highly variable (especially its protein content) and this affects tilapia growth and life history strategies. Tilapias have an important limnological role in the circulation of nutrients needed to keep water bodies

Fish ponds in a valley in Kigezi, southwestern Uganda. The steep hills of this district are covered with fertile volcanic soils which are intensively cultivated. This photograph was taken in the early 1970s. The government of Uganda is still encouraging people to grow fish in ponds , but they complain that the cost of buying the fingerlings is so high that no one can afford to buy the final harvest.

Above and right: Fish ponds in Israel, where they were already growing tilapia when these photographs were taken in 1968.

The enormous heated barn where Tilapia UK are growing thousands of fish in tanks.

Tilapia UK –
The more natural grey-
coloured tilapia are preferred
by some customers. In
London, and perhaps some
other cities in UK, you can
apparently buy them alive
over the counter.

Most of the tilapia grown in the
UK are sold as fillets. Apparently
the pink coloured form of
O. niloticus *is preferred.*

And now… British tilapia!

Tilapia are a delicious high quality food, but their transport to Britain from the warmer regions of the world is unsustainable and undesirable as it adds to the 'food/miles' cost. Commercial scale experiments are now under way to farm tilapia in the UK to supply the home market direct.

At a farm near Cambridge, a huge insulated barn is heated to 26-28 degrees C to warm the concrete tanks in which UK Tilapia Ltd are raising half a million fish. The fry are from stock bred in the USA and are hybrid red tilapia (cf. *niloticus*), which are actually a pale pinkish colour, as this is apparently preferred by customers. A smaller number of natural grey coloured fish are reared with them for the specialist ethnic market. The fish are YY 'super males' that grow exceptionally fast as they do not divert energy into growth of eggs. They reach market size in about 5 months, but have to be sorted regularly to avoid the larger individuals out-competing the smaller ones for food, leading to a variable-sized product. Perhaps selective breeding will one day help to standardise size and growth rates, as it has done for many species in domestication for a longer time. The YY hybrids are derived from a parental generation, which were themselves the progeny of fish that were manipulated by hormonal treatment. Thus the fish for human consumption are not GM and are also two generations away from anything that has had hormone treatment. This must make them more acceptable in our increasingly discerning markets. Selection of appropriate foods and rearing conditions will make fully organic production feasible too.

Since tilapia are basically herbivores, feeding them on pellets made from vegetable material must not only be less expensive than an animal protein diet, but must always be energetically more efficient than raising carnivorous species like salmon and trout. The tilapia are reared to about 350g, and sold gutted at about 270g each. The annual yield is about 75kg wet weight of fish per cubic metre of water.

The fish farm has a huge biological filtration mechanism to treat the water in a similar way to the tanks of tropical fish kept in the home. Waste ammonia and nitrites in the water are converted to nitrates by microorganisms cultured on thousands of floating perforated plastic blocks. These jostle each other continuously in the water flow, avoiding clogging the filter. The waste water produced might one day be diverted to hydroponic culture of useful plants such as tomatoes. UK Tilapia's farm has continuous production and supplies of chilled fish are taken daily to the distributors in Grimsby for sale to the supermarkets.

The system is now being franchised to other farmers in East Anglia, so we should soon be seeing this tasty and nutritious fish on the UK market as 'home grown'. Already Burger King is apparently selling tilapia in Jamaica as a healthy food option.

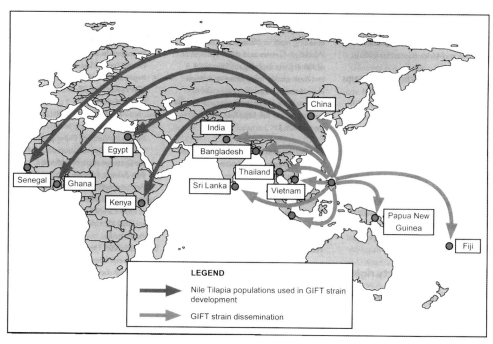

This shows how the germplasm of Oreochromis niloticus *was taken from a number of locations in Africa to the World Fish Centre in the Philippines and then distributed to fish culture centres in other countries. (From the WFC Bulletin 2004; a pity the arrows from Africa point the wrong way!)*

productive, and under tropical conditions where nutrient salts are circulated faster through the biota than by breakdown in bottom sediments, the removal of large quantities of herbivores (such as by a large tilapia fishery) may decrease the overall productivity of the system. This aspect deserves serious consideration in the light of recent declines in tilapia fisheries in natural waters. However, in a Sri Lankan reservoir introduced tilapia (*O. mossambicus*) increased the overall productivity, by being more efficient plankton feeders than the indigenous cyprinids.

What roles have tilapia had when established in ecosystems outside Africa? Lever (1996) devoted 40 pages to the distribution of naturalised tilapias and their ecological and socio-economic impacts on the indigenous fish faunas. Tilapias established in natural waters, often as escapes from fish culture activities, have come to be regarded as either beneficial to local fisheries (and sometimes in control of mosquitoes or aquatic plants), or as pests – viewed as 'stunted' populations or thought to compete with or damage indigenous fish species. Some authors stress benefits, others the negative effects of these introductions.

In many cases tilapia species have become established from introductions of very few individuals, resulting in a small genetic base. For example, Lever said that only three males and one female survived in the batch of *O.*

mossambicus introduced to the Philippines from Thailand in 1949. The Papua New Guinea populations, which came to support an important fishery in the Sepik River basin, originated from only 250 *O. mossambicus* fry sent to PNG from Malaysia in 1954. Those now widely dispersed on Pacific islands appear to have originated from fourteen survivors of a batch of small O. *mossambicus* sent to Honolulu in 1951. Once established, tilapia have proved impossible to eradicate, as has been evident when eradication has been attempted on some islands where they are now living in tidal estuaries, reputedly to the detriment of local mullet populations.

Lever (1996) thought aquarists were responsible for the first tilapia introductions outside Africa. He quotes a 1954 report that O. *mossambicus* came to Hong Kong with aquarium imports pre-1940 from Singapore and the USA. However, he also notes that this species had been found in the wild in Java in 1938/39, and was then widely dispersed as a food fish in Indonesia and Malaysia during the Second World War when it was difficult to get juvenile milk fish (*Chanos chanos*) to stock brackish fish ponds. Post-war experiments at the Malacca Fish Culture station in Malaya, aimed at producing better-growing monosex (male) hybrids for pond culture, had led to imports of other species, including O. *urolepis hornorum* (then called the 'Zanzibar tilapia) and O. *niloticus* (see Trewavas 1983). A Nile delta species O. *aureus* was brought from the USA to the Philippines in 1977, where it hybridised with others already there (*O. mossambicus* from 1950, O. *niloticus* received from Thailand and Israel post 1970). These became established in lakes and rivers.

The success of tilapias outside their natural range, as in African waters, appears to be due mainly to their herbivorous and/or detritivorous feeding habits and to their flexible growth rates and ability to mature at different sizes according to the environmental conditions.

O niloticus, native to Africa, has been introduced to some ninety countries, and in December 2004 I was delighted to receive 'From drawing board to dining table: the success story of the GIFT project' published by the WorldFish Centre (the new name for ICLARM) in its regular Bulletin. This traced the history of the Genetic Improvement of Farmed Tilapia (= GIFT) project intitiated by the World Fish Center and its partners for the development of methods of genetic development of tropical finfish, using Nile tilapia (*O. niloticus*) as a test species, and the dissemination of improved breeds in Asia and the Pacific. After twenty years of meticulous field trials based on germplasm of Nile tilapia collected from May to October 1988, from Egypt, Ghana's Volta River system, Kenya (the Lake Turkana strain *O.n. vulcani*) and Senegal (plus consideration of other stocks from Israel, Singapore, Thailand and Taiwan) O. *niloticus* had been chosen for its relatively short generation time (about six months). It was also identified as an important species for developing countries because of its many desirable traits including hardiness (ability to tolerate shallow and turbid waters), comparatively high resistance to diseases and parasites, and suitability for culture in a wide range of conditions from small waste-fed fish ponds to intensive culture systems.

The numerous recipes for tilapia culture now to be found on the internet testify to its increasing popularity as a food fish in temperate as well as tropical culture systems. Pat Morris has provided an example (see box and photographs) of it being grown in culture in UK!

Looking back, this book was intended to be a celebration of the beauty and intricate relationships of the natural world. Sadly it appears that efforts to provide extra food supplies (whether in agriculture or fisheries) have inexorably led to human populations increasing beyond the carrying capacity of the earth. The real problem is what can be done about the effects of the human overpopulation on this unique and wonderful planet.

The fisheries developed on the African Great lakes became the most important lake fisheries in the world, but are now over fished. In Lake Malawi the chambo fishery has almost ceased, though efforts are being made to try and revive it. On Lake Tanganyika the non-indigenous industrial fishery for pelagic fish discontinued many years ago because it was no longer economically viable. In Lake Victoria the endemic tilapias, and other endemic species, have almost vanished, but here the main fisheries were revitalised by the introduced Nile tilapia and Nile perch, together with the blossoming of the small, endemic pelagic cyprinid *Rastrineobola*. Now the Nile perch catches, which have become so important in the economics of the riparian countries, are dwindling. These lakes are, however, continuing to be excellent laboratories for studies of how new species evolve and coexist.

I have been enormously fortunate to have been around during the last 80+ years. If I had been born earlier I should probably have been less free to follow my yearning for travel and biological exploration. Later, and I should have missed the days when travel to other continents was an adventure which took time and ingenuity as well as some endurance. In those early days we could not just fly to anywhere we chose, but we were not hampered by so many rules and regulations (eg health and safety) as we are now. I hope this book will give those who are interested in any aspect of tropical fish an idea of how our present knowledge was obtained.

Notes and References

To make this book more readable, references have not been cited in the text as in scientific papers. However, since one of the main objectives of writing it is to provide a bridge between past studies and those currently interested in tilapias and other tropical freshwater fish, references to relevant publications are listed below. They are in alphabetical order for each chapter, with occasional supplementary notes. Some are, of course applicable to more than one chapter but, in an effort to avoid repeats, they are listed only under the one to which they are most relevant. A complete list of the author's publications (not included in the chapter lists) is provided separately at the end.

The best place to go for fish references these days is the FishBase web site, where you can search by author, subject or almost any way you choose. Another example of how the world has moved on!

Chapter 1 Liverpool and the Lake District

Fryer, G. 1960. Some controversial aspects of speciation of African cichlid fishes. *Proc. zool. Soc. Lond.* 135: 569-578.

Graham, M. 1929. *The Victoria Nyanza and its Fisheries*. A report on the Fishing Survey of Lake Victoria 1927-28. Colonial Fishery Reports, Crown Agents for the Colonies, London.

Ricardo, C.K. 1939. *Report on the Fish and Fisheries of Lake Rukwa in Tanganyika Territory and the Bangweulu Region in Northern Rhodesia*. Crown Agents for the Colonies, London.

Ricardo, C.K. 1939. The fishes of Lake Rukwa. *J. Linn. Soc. Lond. Zool.* 40:625-656.

Ricardo Bertram, C.K. & Trant, J. 1991. *Letters from the swamps: East Africa 1936–37*. Private publication.

Snoeks, J. 2000. How well known is the ichthyofauna of the large East African lakes? pp 17-38. In: Rossiter, A. & Kawanabe, H. (eds) *Ancient lakes: Biodiversity, Ecology & Evolution*. Advances in Ecological Research vol. 31. Academic Press.

Worthington, E.B. 1929. *A report on the Fishing Survey of Lakes Albert and Kyoga March to July 1928*. Crown Agents for the Colonies, London.

Worthington, E.B. 1932. *A Report on the Fisheries of Uganda investigated by the Cambridge Expedition to the East African Lakes, 1930-31*. Crown Agents for the Colonies, London.

Worthington E B., 1932. The lakes of Kenya and Uganda, investigated by the Cambridge Expedition, 1930-31. *The Geographical Journal*, 79(4):275-297.

Worthington, E.B. 1932. Scientific results of the Cambridge Expedition to the East African Lakes, 1930-31. General introduction and station list. *J. Linn. Soc. Zool.* 38 (no. 258) [The series was continued by various authors, including Trewavas 1933 on Cichlids, till 1936 No 15 Worthington & Ricardo, The fish of Lake Rudolf and Lake Baringo].

Worthington, E.B. 1933. The fishes (other than Cichlidae) of Lake Bangweulu and adjoining regions. *Ann. Mag. Nat. Hist.* Ser. 10 vol.7:34-52.

Worthington, E.B. 1933. The fishes of Lake Nyasa (other than Cichlidae). *Proc. Zool. Soc. Lond.* 1933 (1):285-316.

Worthington, E.B. and Ricardo, C.K. 1937. The fish of Lake Tanganyika (other than Cichlidae). *Proc. Zool. Soc. Lond.* 1936 Pt.4:1061-1112.

Worthington, E.B. 1937. On the evolution of fish in the great lakes of Africa. *Int. Rev. ges. Hydrobiol. Hydrogr.* 35:304-317.

Worthington, E.B. 1954. Speciation of fishes in African lakes. *Nature,* London 173:1064.

Worthington, S. & E.B. 1933. *Inland Waters of Africa.* Macmillan, London.

Chapter 2 Africa here I come

Beadle, L. 1974. (2nd edition 1981) *The Inland Waters of Tropical Africa. An introduction to Tropical Limnology.* Longman, London.

Bertram, C.K., Borley, H.J.H. & Trewavas, E. 1942. *Report on the Fish and Fisheries of Lake Nyasa.* Crown Agents for the Colonies, London

Fryer, G. 1959. The trophic relationships and ecology of some littoral communities of Lake Nyasa with special reference to the fishes, and a discussion of the evolution of a group of rock-frequenting cichlids. *Proc. Zool. Soc. Lond.* 132:153-281.

Fryer, G. & Iles, T.D. 1972. *The Cichlid Fishes of the Great Lakes of Africa. Their biology and evolution.* Oliver & Boyd, Edinburgh, 641 pp.

Jackson, P.B.N., Iles, T.D., Harding, D. & Fryer, G. 1963. *Report on the Survey of Northern Lake Nyasa by the Joint Fisheries Research Organization 1954-55.* Government Printer, Zomba, Nyasaland. 171 pp. [Includes: Hydrology (Harding); an annotated list of L. Malawi fishes and *Bathyclarias* species flock (Jackson); Utaka (Iles) and Mbuna cichlids (Fryer).]

Kalk, M., McLachlan, A.J. & Howard-Williams, C. (eds). 1979. Lake Chilwa: studies of change in a tropical ecosystem. *Monographiae Biol.* 35. Dr. W. Junk Publishers, The Hague, 462pp.

Livingstone, David, 1865. *Narrative of an expedition to the Zambezi and its tributaries.* (Written in collaboration with his brother Charles.) Murray, London.

Morgan, R.P. 1970. The Lake Chilwa Tilapia and its fishery. *Afr. J. Trop. Hydrobiol. Fish.* 1:51-58.

For a huge bibliography of work on Lake Malawi try:
    http://malawichichlids.com/ which says it gives a "Bibliography of Lake Malawi Biology (with emphasis on fish systematics, ecology, and evolution). Compiled by Michael K. Oliver Ph.D." It includes many abstracts and some full texts.

Chapter 3 EAFRO and Lake Victoria

Barel, C.D.N. *et al.* 1985. Destruction of fisheries in Africa's lakes. *Nature, London* 315:19-20.

Corbet, P.S. 1961. The food of non-cichlid fishes in the Lake Victoria basin, with remarks on their evolution and adaptation to lacustrine conditions. *Proc. Zoo. Soc. Lond.* 136:1-101.

East African Fisheries Research Organisation, Annual Reports.

Fryer, G. 1961. Observations on the biology of the cichlid fish *Tilapia variabilis* in the northern waters of Lake Victoria. *Rev. Zool. Bot. Afr.* 64: 1-33.

Fryer, G. and Talling, J.F. 1986. Africa: the FBA Connection. *Freshwater Biological Association Annual Report* 54:97-122.

Garrod, D.J. 1957. An analysis of records of gillnet fishing in Pilkington Bay, Lake Victoria. EAFRO Supplementary Publication No. 2:1-17.

Goldschmidt, Thys, 1996. *Darwin's Dreampond: drama in Lake Victoria.* MIT Press, 274 pp.

Greenwood, P.H. 1966. *The Fishes of Uganda.* The Uganda Society, Kampala. 131 pp.

Greenwood, P.H. 1974. The Cichlid fishes of Lake Victoria: the biology and evolution of a species flock. *Bull. Brit. Mus. Nat. Hist. (Zool.)* Supplement 6, 134 pp.

Jackson, P.B.N. 2000. Freshwater fisheries research organizations in Central and Eastern Africa. A personal recollection. *Trans. Roy. Soc. S. Africa,* 55 (Special Issue). 81 pp.

Lake Victoria Fisheries Service Annual Reports.

Macdonald, W.W. 1956. Observations on the biology of chaoborids and chironomids in Lake Victoria and on the feeding habits of the 'Elephant-snout fish' (*Mormyrus kannume*). *J. Anim. Ecol.* 25:36-53.

Osmaston, Anna, 1991. *Uganda before Amin. Our family life in Uganda 1949-1963.* Privately Published by Henry Osmaston (ISBN 0-9518039-0-5).

Welcomme, R.L. 1964. The habitats and habitat preferences of the young of the L. Victoria Tilapia. *Rev. Zool. Bot. afr.,* 70:1-28.

Welcomme, Robin L. 1966. Recent changes in the stocks of Tilapia in Lake Victoria, *Nature, London* 212:52-54.

Welcomme, R.L. 1967. Observations on the biology of the introduced species of tilapia in Lake Victoria. *Rev. Zoo. Bot. Afric.* 76:249-278.

Welcomme, R.L. 1970. Studies of the effects of abnormally high water levels on the ecology of fish in certain shallow levels of Lake Victoria. *J. Zool. Lond.* 160:405-436.

Witte, F. *et al.* 2000. Recovery of cichlid species in Lake Victoria: an examination of factors leading to differential extinction. *Rev. Fish Biol. Fisheries* 10:233- 241.

Witte, F. *et al.* 2005. Eutrophication and its influences on the fish fauna of Lake Victoria. pp 301-338, In: M.V. Reddy (ed.) *Restoration and Management of Tropical Eutrophic Lakes.* Science Publishers, Inc., Enfield (NH), USA.

Worthington, E.B. & Lowe-McConnell, R. 1994. African lakes reviewed: creation and destruction of biodiversity. *Environmental Conservation* 21(3):199-213.

Chapter 4 Nile tilapia at home

For information on TUFMAC, Uganda Game & Fisheries Department Annual Reports, also Hickling (see below). There is a brief resume of TUFMAC history at http://fao.org//docrep/006/ad147e/ad147e04.htm.

Burgis, M.J. & Dunn, I.G. 1978. Production in three contrasting ecosystems. In: Gerking, S.D. (ed.) *Ecology of freshwater fish production,* Blackwell, Oxford.

Cott, H.B. 1954. The status of the Nile crocodile in Uganda. *Uganda Journal* 18:1-12.

Cott, H.B. 1952. [on fish eating birds] EAFRO Annual Report, 1952: 23-25.

Cott, H.B. 1961. Scientific results of an enquiry into the ecology and economic status of the Nile crocodile (*Crocodilus niloticus*) in Uganda and N. Rhodesia. *Trans. Zool. Soc. Lond.* 29(4):212-356.

Gwahaba, J.J. 1973. Effects of fishing on the *Tilapia nilotica* (Linne 1757) population in Lake George, Uganda over the past 20 years. *E. Afr. Wildl. J.* ll: 317-328.

Hickling, C.F. 1961. *Tropical Inland Fisheries.* Longmans, London, 287 pp.

Hopson, A.J. (ed) 1982. *Lake Turkana. A report on the findings of the Lake Turkana project 1972-1975.* 6 vols (tilapias in vols 5 & 6) Overseas Development Administration, London. 1614 pp.

Kolding, J.P. 1992. A summary of Lake Turkana: an ever-changing mixed environment. *Mitt. Internat. Verein. Limnol.* 23:25-35.

Kolding, J.P. 1993. Population dynamics and life history styles of Nile tilapia *Oreochromis niloticus* in Ferguson's Gulf Lake Turkana, *Env. Biol. Fish* 37:25-46.

Moriarty, D.J.W. 1973. The physiology of digestion of blue-green algae in the cichlid fish *Tilapia nilotica. J. Zool. Lond.* 171:25-39.

Worthington, E.B. 1929. *A Report on the Fishing Survey of Lakes Albert and Kioga.* Crown Agents for the Colonies, London.

Worthington, E.B. & Ricardo, C.K. 1936. Scientific Results of the Cambridge Expedition to the East African Lakes 1930-1. No. 15. The fish of Lake Rudolf and Lake Baringo. *J. Linn. Soc. (Zool.)* 39:353-389.

Chapter 5 Further afield

Bailey, R.G. *et al.* 1978. The ecology of fishes in Nyumba ya Mungu reservoir, Tanzania. *Biol. J. Linn. Soc.* 10:109-137.

Bruton, M. 1994. The life and work of Rosemary Lowe-McConnell: pioneer in tropical fish ecology. In: E.K. Balon, M.N. Bruton & D.L.G. Noakes (eds) 'Women in Ichthyology'. *Environmental Biology of Fishes* 41 .

CSA [Conseil Scientifique pour L'Afrique au Sud du Sahara] 1952. Symposium on African Hydrobiology and Inland Fisheries, Entebbe 1952.

Dadzie, S., Haller, R.D. & Trewavas, E. 1988. A note on the fishes of Lake Jipe and Lake Chala on the Kenya-Tanzania border. *Journal of the East African Natural History Society & National Museum* 78(no192):46-51.

De Bont, A.F. 1954. Station de recherches piscicoles a Elizabethville. Rapports annuels. *Bull. agric. Congo Belge* 45:157-184.

Denny, P. & Bailey, R.G. (eds) 1978. The 1974 biological survey of Nyumba ya Mungu, reservoir, Tanzania. *Biol. J. Linn. Soc.* 10:1-157.

Frost, W.E. 1955. *Observations on the biology of eels (Anguilla spp) of Kenya Colony, E. Africa.* Fishery Publications 6:1-28. Colonial Office, London.

Hitchcock, Griselda (née Worthington). 2004. *The way of emigrants.* Privately published by the author, Australia.

Huet, M. 1957. Dix annees de pisciculture au Congo belge et au Ruanda-Urundi. *Trav. Sta. Rech. Groenendaal (D)*, 22:1-159.

Leakey, R. & Lewin, R. 1996. *The sixth extinction: Biodiversity and its survival.* Orion Books, London.

Paice, E. 2001. *Lost Lion of Empire: the life of Cape-to-Cairo Grogan*, Harper Collins.

Poll, M. 1956. Poissons Cichlidae. *Explor. hydrobiol. Lac Tanganyika (1946-47)* vol. III fasc. 5B, 619 pp.

Poll, M. 1976. Poissons. *Exploration du Parc National de l'Upembe. Mission G.F. de Witte*, fasc, 73: 1-127.

Poll, M. 1986. Classification des Cichlidae du lac Tanganika. Tribus, genres et especes. *Mem. Acad. R. Belg, Cl. Sci.* (Ser. 2) 1-163.

Thys van der Audenaerde, D.F.E. 1968. An annotated bibliography of Tilapia (Pisces, Cichlidae). *Mus. R. Afr. Cent. Doc. Zool.* 14:1-406.

Trewavas, E. 1983. *Tilapiine fishes of the genera Sarotherodon, Oreochromis and Danakilia.* British Museum (Natural History), London. 583 pp.

Lake Nakuru is a soda lake in Kenya, which is primarily known for its spectacular flocks of flamingoes. It is a good example of how the introduction of a tilapia species changed the ecology of a whole lake. Originally there were no fish in the lake, so no fish-eating birds.

The dwarf tilapia Oreochromis alcalicus grahami *which lives naturally in the very hot and alkaline springs on the edge of Lake Magadi was introduced into Lake Nakuru in 1953, 1959 and again in 1962 after the lake had dried up and re-formed. The main effect of their introduction was to extend the food chain to fish-eating birds such as pelicans and cormorants.*

Pelicans feeding in a group on the tilapia in Lake Nakuru. The great white pelican (Pelecanus onocrotalus) *is now the pre-dominant fish-eating bird on Lake Nakuru. It has been estimated that the population removes up to 20,000 kg of fish from the lake each day.*

There are also many other fish eating birds living and breeding at Lake Nakuru, including these white breasted cormorants (left). Altogether about 50 species of new birds have been recorded there since the introduction of tilapia.

Unlike the pelicans which feed at Lake Nakuru but fly away to nest nearby, the cormorants form colonies on the trees along the lake shore. The lake level varies greatly from year to year and when the trees are inundated, as seen below, the trees die because the lake water is so saline.

Van Someren, V.D. 1960. The Inland Fishery Research Station, Sagana, Kenya. *Nature, London* 186 (No 4723):425-426.

Van Someren, V.D. 1962. The migration of fishes in a small Kenya River. *Rev. Zool. Bot. Afr.* 66:375-393.

van Someren V.D. & Whitehead, P. 1959-61. Sagana fish culture experiments with *T. nigra. East Afr. Agric. For. J.* 25:26-27.

Chapter 6 The "marriage bar" and a new life

Albert, J.A. & Crampton, W.G.R. 2005. Diversity and phylogeny of Neotropical electric fishes (Gymnotiformes) pp 360-409 In *Electroreception*, E.H. Bullock, C.D. Hopkins, A.N. Popper & R.R. Fay (eds). Springer Handbook of Auditory Research Vol 21.

Joyce, D.A., Hunt, D.H., Bills, R., Turner, G.F., Katongo, C., Duftber, N. Sturmbauer C. & Seehausen, O. 2005. An extant cichlid fish radiation emerged in an extinct Pleistocene lake. *Nature, London* 435.

Lissmann, H.W. 1958. On the function and evolution of electric organs in fish. *J. Exp. Biol.* 35:156-191.

Lissmann, H.W. 1963. Electric location by fishes. *Scientific American.* 208:50-9.

McConnell, R.B. 1967. The East African Rift System, *Nature, London.* 215:578-581.

McConnell, R.B. 1972. Geological development of the rift system of Africa. *Bull. Geol. Soc America*, 83:2549-2572.

Porter, Jack, 2003. The extraordinary odyssey of R.G. McConnell. *Reservoir, Canadian Society of Petroleum Geology*, vols 30 & 31 (in instalments).

Chapter 7 Home Base: Sussex and the BM(NH)

Baerends, G.P. & Baerends-van Roon, J.M. 1950. An introduction to the ethology of cichlid fishes. *Behaviour*, Supplement 1:1-243.

Barlow, G.W. 2000. *The Cichlid Fishes. Nature's Grand Experiment in Evolution.* Perseus Publishing, Cambridge, Massachusetts, USA. 335 pp.

Bonetto, A. & Pignalberi, C. 1964. Nuevos aportes al conocimiento de las migraciones de los peces en los rios mesopotamicos de la Republic Argentina. *Com. Inst. nac. Limnol, Santo Tome (S Fe).* 1:1-14.

Bonetto, A., Dioni, W. & Pignalberi, C. 1969. Limnological investigations on biotic communities in the Middle Parana valley. *Verh. int. Verein. Limnol.* 17:1035-50.

Coates, D. 1987. Consideration of fish introductions into the Sepik River, Papua New Guinea. *Aquaculture and Fish Management.* 18:231-241.

Downing, J.A. and Rigler, F.H. 1971. IBP Handbook 17. *A Manual on methods for the assessment of Secondary Productivity in Fresh Waters.* Blackwell Scientific Publications, Oxford. (2nd edition 1984.)

Gerking, S.D. (ed), 1967. *The Biological Basis of Freshwater Fish Production.* Blackwell, Oxford, 495 pp. [outcome of the IBP-PF Reading meeting 1966 – includes papers on vital statistics of fish populations; relation of fish populations to food supply; competitive and behavioural factors influencing production; predation and exploitation by man; contribution of FW fish production to human nutrition and well-being.]

Gerking S.D. 1978. *Ecology of Freshwater Fish Production.* Blackwell, Oxford.

Greenwood, P.H. & Lund J.W.G. (eds) 1973. A discussion on the biology of an equatorial lake: Lake George, Uganda. *Proc. R. Soc. Lond. B.* 184:227-346. [contains 4 papers by the Lake George IBP team which summarise their work.]

Greenwood, P.H. 1976. Lake George, Uganda. In. A review of the United Kingdom contribution to the International Biological Programme. *Phil. Trans. R. Soc. London B.* 274:275-554.

Keenleyside, M.H.A. (ed.) 1991. *Cichlid Fishes: Behaviour, Ecology and Evolution.* Chapman and Hall, London.

Margalef, R. 1968. *Perspectives in Ecological Theory.* University of Chicago Press, 111pp

McConnell, R.B. (ed.) 1983. *Art, Science and Human Progress.* John Murray, London.

Prowse, G.A. 1962-1965. Annual Reports of the Tropical Fish Culture Research Institute, Malacca, Malaysia.

Ricker, W.E. (ed.) 1968. *Methods for the assessment of fish production in fresh waters.* IBP Handbook No. 3. Blackwell, Oxford. 313 pp. [3rd edition ed. T.Bagnold.]

Rzóska, J. 1980. History and development of the freshwater production section of IBP. In E.D. Le Cren & R.H. Lowe-McConnell (eds). *The Functioning of freshwater ecosystems.* International Biological Programme 22. Cambridge University Press.

Rzóska, J. 1982. *Observations and reflections of a retired hydrobiologist.* Privately published, London. 44pp.

Thys van der Audenaerde, D.F.E. 1964. Révision systématique des espèces congolaises du genre *Tilapia* (Pisces, Cichlidae). *Ann. Mus. R. Afr. Centr.,* sér. in-8°, Sci. Zool., 124: 155p.

Van Dobben, W.H. & R.H. Lowe-McConnell. (ed.) 1975. *Unifying concepts in ecology.* Report of the plenary sessions of the First International Congress of Ecology, The Hague, 1974. Dr W. Junk Publishers, The Hague. 302 pp.

Worthington, E.B. 1965. The International Biological Programme. *Nature, London* 208:223-226.

Aquarium books

T.F.H. and Cichlid Press books contain superb underwater photographs of all the then known cichlids from the lakes.

Brichard, P. 1989. *Pierre Brichard's book of Cichlids and all other Fish of Lake Tanganyika.* T.F.H., Neptune City, NJ, USA. 544 pp.

Goldstein, R.J. 1973. *Cichlids of the World.* T.F.H., Neptune City, NJ, USA.

Innes, Wm. 1935 (followed by 18 editions). *The Handbook of Exotic Aquarium Fishes.* Innes Publishing Co, USA.

Konings, Ad. 1990. *Ad Konings book of Cichlids and all other Fishes of Lake Malawi.* T.F.H. Neptune City, NJ, USA. 495 pp.

Konings, Ad & Dieckhoff, H.W. 1992. *Tanganyika Secrets.* Cichlid Press El Paso, Texas. 207 pp.

Konings, Ad. 1992. *Malawi Cichlids in their natural habitat.* Cichlid Press, El Paso, Texas.

Seehausen, Ole, 1996. *Lake Victoria Rock Cichlids – taxonomy, ecology and distribution.* Verduijn Cichlids, The Netherlands.

Turner, George, 1999. *Offshore cichlids of Lake Malawi.* Cichlid Press, El Paso, Texas. 240 pp.

Chapter 8 Back to Africa

Leveque, C. 1997. *Biodiversity dynamics and conservation. The freshwater fish of tropical Africa.* Cambridge University Press. 438 pp. [A comprehensive analysis of fish communities across Africa, bringing together work done in Franco-phone and Anglo-phone countries.]

Worthington, E.B. 1983. *The Ecological Century. A personal appraisal.* Clarendon Press, Oxford. 206 pp.

Man-made lakes

Ackermann, W.C., White G. & Worthington, E.B (eds) 1973. Man-made lakes their problems and environmental effects. *Geophysical Monograph 17,* American Geophysical Union, Washington DC.

Balon, E.K. 1974. *Fishes of Lake Kariba.* T.F.H., Neptune City, NJ, USA. 144 pp.

Balon, E.K. & Coche, A.G. (eds) 1974. *Lake Kariba: a man-made Tropical Ecosystem in Central Africa.* Monongraphicae Biologicae Vol. 14. Dr W. Junk, The Hague. 764 pp.

Bruton, M.N. & Allanson, B.R. 1974. The growth of *Tilapia mossambica* in Lake Sibaya, South Africa. *J. Fish. Biol.* 6:701-716.

Crul, R.C.M. & Roest, F.C. (eds) 1995. Current status of fisheries and fish stocks of the four largest African reservoirs: Kainji, Kariba, Nasser/Nubia and Volta. *CIFA Tech Paper 30,* FAO, Rome.

Imevbore, A.M.A. 1971. The first symposium on Lake Kainji, Nigeria's man-made lake. *Afr. J. Trop. Hydrobiol. Fish.* 1:67-68.

Machena, C., Kolding, J. and Sanyanga, R.A. 1993. A preliminary assessment of the trophic structure of Lake Kariba, Africa. pp 130-137 in: Christensen, V. & Pauly, D. *Trophic models of aquatic ecosystems.* ICLARM Conf. Proc. 26, 390pp.

Marshall, Brian, 1995. Why is *Limnothrissa miodon* such a successful introduced species and is there anywhere else we should put it? pp. 527-545 In: Pitcher & Hart (eds) *The Impact of Species Changes in African Lakes.* Chapman & Hall, London. Fish & Fisheries Series 18.

Obeng, L.E. (ed.) 1969. *Man-Made Lakes: the Accra Symposium.* Ghana Universities Press, Accra. 398 pp.

Obeng, L.E. 1973. Volta Lake: Physical and biological aspects. *Geophysical Monograph* (American Geophysical Union) 17:87-98.

Petr, T. 1967. Fish population changes in the Volta Lake in Ghana during its first sixteen months. *Hydrobiologia* 30:193-320.

Petr, T. 1975. On some factors associated with the initial high fish catches in new African man-made lakes. *Arch. Hydrobiol.* 81:32-49.

White, E. (ed) *First Scientific report of the Lake Kainji Biological Research Team,* University of Liverpool, U.K.

Whyte, S.A. 1975. Distribution, trophic relationships and breeding habits of the fish population in a tropical lake basin (Lake Bosumtwi, Ghana). *J. Zool. Lond.* 176:77-81.

Great Lake updates

De Vos, L., Snoeks, J. and van den Audenaerde, D.T. 2001. An annotated checklist of the fishes of Rwanda (east central Africa), with historical data on introductions of commercially important species. *J. East Afr. Nat. Hist.* 90:41-68.

Pitcher, T.J. & Hart, P.J.B. (eds) *The Impact of Species Changes in African Lakes.* Chapman & Hall, London. Fish & Fisheries Series 18. [A symposium stimulated by the introduction of Nile perch into Lake Victoria, this book has many useful chapters on Lakes Victoria, Malawi, Kariba and other lakes.]

Turner, G.F. 2000. The nature of species in ancient lakes: perspectives from the fishes of Lake Malawi. pp. 39-60 In: Rossiter, A. & Kawanabe, H. (eds) *Ancient Lakes: Biodiversity, Ecology and Evolution.* Academic Press.

Turner, G.F., & Robinson, R.L. 2000. Reproductive biology, mating systems and parental care. pp 33-58 In: Beveridge, M.C.M. & McAndrew, B.J. (eds) *Tilapias: Biology and Exploitation,* Kluwer Academic Publishers.

Malawi:

FAO, 1993. Fisheries management in the Southeast Arm of Lake Malawi, the Upper Shire and Lake Malombe, with reference to Chambo (*Oreochromis*) fisheries. *CIFA Technical Paper 21,* FAO, Rome. 113 pp.

Irvine, K. *et al.* (9 authors) 2002. The trophic ecology of the demersal fish communities of Lake Malawi, Nyasa. *INCO/DC Report to the European Commission No: ERBIC18CT 970195,* 157 pp.

Lewis, L.D., Reinthal, P. & Trendall, J. 1988. *Guide to the fishes of Lake Malawi National Park,* WWF.

McKaye, K.R. 1991. Sexual selection and the evolution of cichlid fishes in Lake Malawi, pp 241-247 In Keenleyside, M.H.A. (ed), *Cichlid Fishes: Behaviour, Ecology and Evolution.* Fish & Fisheries 2, Chapman & Hall.

Menz, A. (ed) 1995. The fishery potential and productivity of the pelagic zone of Lake Malawi/Niassa. *Scientific Report of the UK/SADC Pelagic Fish Resource Assessment Project.* Natural Resources Institute, Chatham. (ODA, London.)

Ribbink, A.J., Marsh, A.C., Marsh, B.A. & Sharp, B.J. 1983. A preliminary survey of the cichlid fishes of rocky habitats in Lake Malawi. *S. Afr. J. Zool.* 18: 160 pp.

Ribbink, T. *et al.* (10 authors) (ed) 2001. The Lake Malawi/Niassa/Nyasa biodiversity conservation programme: science in a socio-economic context. *Annal. Mus. Roy. Afrique centrale. (Tervuren)* 288:28-59.

Turner, G.F. 1995. Management, conservation and species changes of exploited fish stocks in Lake Malawi, pp 365-396 in: T.J. Pitcher & P.J.B. Hart, *The Impact of Species Changes in African Lakes,* Fish & Fisheries No 18 Chapman & Hall London

Duponchelle, F., Ribbink. A.J, Msukwa, A., Mafuka, J., Mandere, D. & Bootsma H. 2005. Food partitioning within the species-rich benthic fish community of Lake Malawi, East Africa. *Can. J. Fish. Sci. Aquat.* 62:1651-1664.

Snoeks, J. (ed.) 2004. *The cichlid diversity of Lake Malawi/Nyasa/Niassa: Identification, distribution and taxonomy.* Cichlid Press, El Paso, Texas. 360 pp.

Stauffer, J., Kellogg, K. & McKaye, K. 2005. Experimental evidence of female choice in Lake Malawi cichlids. *Copeia,* 3:657-660.

Tweddle, D. 1991. Twenty years of fisheries research in Malawi. *Fisheries Bulletin* No 7, Fisheries Dept., Ministry Forestry & Natural Resources, Malawi.

Tweddle, D. 1991. A limnological bibliography of Malawi. *FAO/CIFA Occasional Paper 13, Supplement 1.* FAO, Rome. 18 pp.

Lake Tanganyika

Coulter, G.W. (ed) 1991. *Lake Tanganyika and its Life*. Oxford University Press, Oxford. 354 pp.

Hori, M., Gashagasa, M.M., Nshombo, M. & Kawanabe, H. 1993. Littoral fish communities in Lake Tanganyika: irreplaceable diversity supported by intricate interactions among species. *Conservation Biology* 7(3):657-666.

Kawanabe, H., Horie, M. & Nagoshi, M. 1997. *Fish Communities in Lake Tanganyika*. Kyoto University Press, Japan.

Lindqvist, O.V., Molsa, H., Salonen, K. & Sarvala, J. 1999. From Limnology to Fisheries: Lake Tanganyika and other large lakes. *Hydrobiologia*, 407 [Reprinted as *Developments in Hydrobiology* 141, Kluwer Academic Publishers, Dordrecht, 218 pp.]

Lake Victoria :

Balirwa, J.S. 1995. The Lake Victoria environment: Its fisheries and wetlands – a review. *Wetlands Ecology and Management*, 3(4):209-224.

Balirwa, J.S. 1998. Lake Victoria Wetlands and the Ecology of the Nile Tilapia *O. niloticus*. PhD dissertation, Agricultural University, Wageningen, Netherlands.

Balirwa, J.S., Chapman, C.A., Chapman, L.J., Cowx, I.G., Geheb, K., Kaufman, L., Lowe-McConnell, R.H., Seehausen, O., Wanink, J.H., Welcomme, R.L. and Witte, F. 2003. Biodiversity and fishery sustainability in the Lake Victoria Basin: an unexpected marriage? *BioScience* 53(8):703-715.

Barel, C.D.N., Ligtvoet, W., Goldschmidt, T., Witte, F. & Goudswaard, P.C. 1991. The haplochromine cichlids in Lake Victoria: an assessment of biological and fisheries interests. pp 258-279 In: M.H.A. Keenleyside, *Cichlid Fishes Behaviour, Ecology and Evolution*. Chapman & Hall, London.

Goudswaard, P.C., Witte, F. & Katunzi, E.F.B. 2002. The tilapiine fish stock of Lake Victoria before and after the Nile perch upsurge. *J. Fish Biol.* 60:838-856.

HEST = Haplochromis Ecology Study Group, which has produced a huge number of papers under many names [see references in papers by Barel, Witte, Goldschmidt et al.]

Kaufman, L. 1992. Catastrophic change in species-rich freshwater ecosystems; the lesson of L.Victoria. *BioScience* 42: 846-858.

Ogutu-Ohwayo, R. 1990. The decline of the native fishes of lakes Victoria and Kyoga and the impact of introduced species, especially the Nile perch (*Lates niloticus*) and the Nile tilapia *Oreochromis niloticus*. *Environmental Biology of Fish* 27: 81-96

Twongo, T. 1995. Impact of fish species introductions on the tilapias of Lake Victoria and Kyoga. pp 45-58 in Pitcher, T.J. & Hart, P.J.B. (eds) *The Impact of Species Changes in African Lakes*. Chapman & Hall, London. Fish & Fisheries Series 18.

Witte, F. et al. 2005. Eutrophication and its influence on the fish fauna of Lake Victoria, pp 301-338, in: M.V. Reddy (ed). *Restoration and Management of Tropical Eutrophic Lakes*. Science Publishers, Inc. Enfield (NH) USA.

Chapter 9: S. America revisited

Barluenga, M., Stolting, K.N., Salzburger, W., Muschick, M. & Meyer, A. 2006. Sympatric speciation in Nicaraguan crater lake cichlid fish. *Nature,* 439: 719-723.

Cox-Fernandes, C., Podos, J. & Lundberg, J.G. 2004. Amazonian ecology: tributaries enhance the diversity of electric fishes. *Science,* 305:1960-1962.

Gery, J. 1977. *Characoids of the World.* T.F.H. Pubs. Neptune City, New Jersey.

Goulding, M. 1980. *The Fishes and the Forest: Explorations in Amazonian Natural History.* University of California Press, Los Angeles.

Goulding, M., Carvalho, M.L. & Ferreira, E.G. 1988. *Rio Negro: Rich Life in Poor Water.* SPB Academic Publishing, The Hague.

Goulding, M., Smith, N.J.H. & Mahar, D.J. 1996. *Floods of Fortune: Ecology and Economy along the Amazon.* Columbia University Press, New York.

Malabarba, L.M., Reis, E.R., Vari, R.P., Lucena, Z.M.S. & Lucena, C.A.S. (eds) 1998 *Phylogeny and Classification of Neotropical Fishes.* Porto Alegre, Brazil, 603 pp

Reis, R.E, Kullander, S.O. & Ferraris Jr, C.J. (Organisers) 2003. *Check List of the Freshwater Fishes of South and Central America.* Porto Alegre, Brasil, 729 pp.

Petrere, M. 1989. River fisheries in Brazil: a review. *Regulated Rivers; research and Management,* 4:1-16.

Smith, Anthony, 1971. *Mato Grosso, Last Virgin Land. An account of the Mato Grosso based on the Royal Society and Royal Geographical Society expedition to Central Brazil 1967-69.* Michael Joseph, 288pp.

Zaret, T.M. & Paine, R.T. 1973 Species introduction in a tropical lake. *Science*, New York 182:449-55

Brazil SIL

Agostinho, A.A., Thomaz, S.M., Gomes, L.C. 2004. Threats for biodiversity in the floodplain of the Upper Parana River: effects of hydrological regulation by dams. *Ecohydrology & Hydrobiology* 4(3):267-280.

Agostinho, A.A. *et al*, 2004. Flood regime, dam regulation and fish in the Upper Parana River: effects on assemblage attributes, reproduction and recruitment. *Rev. Fish. Biol. & Fisheries* 14:11-19.

Junk, W.J. (ed). 1997. *The Central Amazon Floodplain: Ecology of a Pulsating System.* Ecological Series 126 Springer, Berlin. 525 pp.

Junk, W.J. et al (eds) (2000) . *The Central Amazon Floodplain: Actual Use and Options for a Sustainable Management.* Backhuys Publishers, Leiden, 584 pp.

Godoy, M.P. de, 1967. Dez anos de observações sôbre periodicidade migratoria de peixes do Rio Mogi Guassu. *Revta bras. Biol.* 27:1-12.

Gurgel, J.S. and Fernando, C.H. 1994. Fisheries in the semi-arid NE Brazil with special reference to the role of Tilapias. *Int. Rev. ges. Hydrobiol.* 79(1):77-94.

Okada, E.K., Agostinho, A.A. & Gomes, L.C. 2005. Spatial and temporal gradients in artisanal fisheries of a large Neotropical reservoir, The Itaipu Reservoir, Brazil. *Can. J. Fish. Aquat. Sci.,* 62:714-724.

Thomaz, S.M., Agostinho, A.A. & Hahn, N.S. (eds) 2004. *The Upper Parana River and its Floodplain; physical aspects, ecology and conservation.* Backhuys Publishers Leiden, pp 393 pp.

Tundisi, G. Bicudo, C.E.M. & Tundisi, T.M. (eds) *Limnology in Brazil.* ABC/SBL, Rio de Janeiro, 384 pp.

Chapter 10: Aquatic chicken

Coe, M.J. 1966. The biology of *Tilapia grahami* in Lake Magadi in Kenya. *Acta Tropica* 23:146-177.

Fishelson, L. 1983. Social behaviour of adult tilapia fish in nature and captivity. pp, 48-58, in: *Proc. Internat. Symposium on Tilapia in Aquaculture (ISTA I)*, held in Nazareth, Israel May 1983. Tel Aviv University, Israel.

Gupta, M.V. & Acosta, B.O. 2004. From drawing board to dining table: the success story of the GIFT project. pp 4-14 in *NAGA WorldFish Center Quarterly*, 27(3&4):4-14.

Hickling, C.F. 1962. *Fish Culture*. Faber & Faber, London 295 pp.

Iles, T.D. 1973. Dwarfing or stunting in the genus *Tilapia*: a possible unique recruiting mechanism. *Rapp. P-v. Reun. Cons. perm. int. Explor. Mer.*, 164:246-254.

Lever, C. 1996. *Naturalized Fishes of the World*. Academic Press, London.

Man, H.S.H & Hodgkiss, I., 1977. Studies on the ichthyofauna in Plover Cove Reservoir, Hong Kong. *J. Fish Biol.* 10:493-503 & 11:1-13.

Pauly, D, 1976. The biology, fishery and potential for aquaculture of *Tilapia melanotheron* in a small West African lagoon. *Aquaculture*, 7:33-49. [This *Sarotherodon* species is useful in brackish ponds, and was also studied in aquaria by Aronson (and others) under the names *Tilapia macrocephala* or *T. heudeloti*].

Pauly, D. 1984. A mechanism for the juvenile-to-adult transition in fishes. *J. Cons. Int. Explor. Mer.*, 41:280-284.

Petr, T. 2004. Inland Fisheries – The Global Situation. *Acta Universitatis Carolinae Environmentalica* 18:7-34.

Pillay, T.V.R. (ed) *Proceedings of the World Symposium on Warm-water pond Fish Culture*. FAO Fisheries Reports No 44 (5 vols of FRI/R44), Rome

Pullin, R.S.V. & Lowe-McConnell, R.H. (eds) 1982. The Biology and Culture of Tilapias. *ICLARM Conf. Proceedings* 7, Manila 432 pp [The Bellagio meeting.]

Pullin, R.S.V. (ed.) 1988. Tilapia Genetic Resources for Aquaculture. *ICLARM Conference Proceedings 16*, Manila. [The Bellagio meeting.]

Pullin, R. 1991. Cichlids in aquaculture, pp 280-310, in: Keenleyside, M.H.A. (ed.) *Cichlid Fishes; behaviour, ecology and evolution*. Chapman and Hall, London.

Seegers, L. 1996. The Fishes of the Lake Rukwa Drainage. *Ann. Mus. Afr. Cent, Sci. Zool.* 278:1- 407 [p. 146 records other Tanzanian waters now inhabited by *O. esculentus*, including L. Rukwa (stocked 1969) where it now far outnumbers the endemic *O. rukwaensis*.]

Seegers, L. & Tichy, H. 1999. The *Oreochromis alcalicus* flock from Lakes Natron and Magadi, Tanzania and Kenya, with a description of two new species. *Ichthyol. Explor. Freshwaters*, 10:97-146.

Sparks, J.S. & Smith, W.L. 2004. Phylogeny and biogeography of cichlid fishes (Teleostei: Perciformes: Cichlidae). *Cladistics*, 20:501-517.

Stiassny, M., Schliewen, U.K. & Dominey, W. 1992. A new species flock of cichlid fishes from Lake Bermin, Cameroon, with a description of eight new species of *Tilapia. Ichthol. Explor. Freshwaters* 3:311-346.

Trewavas, E., Green, J. & Corbet, S.A. 1972. Ecological studies on crater lakes in West Cameroon. Fishes of Barombi Mbo. *J. Zool. Lond.* 167:41-95.

van Someren, V.D. and P.J. Whitehead, 1960. The culture of *Tilapia nigra* in ponds. IV. The seasonal growth of male *T. nigra. East Afr. Agric. For. J.* 26:79-86.

Publications of R.H. Lowe-McConnell

1. Lowe, R.H. 1951. Factors influencing the runs of elvers in the River Bann, Northern Ireland. *J. Cons. Int. Explor. Mer.* 17:299-315.

2. Lowe, R.H. 1952. The influence of light and other factors on the seaward migration of the silver eel *(Anguilla anguilla* L.). *J. Anim. Ecol.* 21:275-309.

3. Lowe, R.H. 1952. Report on the *Tilapia* and other fish and fisheries of Lake Nyasa, 1945-47. Fishery Publ. Colon. Off. 1(2):1-126.

4. Lowe, R.H. 1953. Notes on the ecology and evolution of Nyasa fishes of the genus *Tilapia* with a description of T. *saka,* Lowe. *Proc. zool. Soc. Lond.* 122:1035-1041.

5. Lowe, R.H. 1955. New species of *Tilapia* (Pisces, Cichlidae) from Lake Jipe and the Pangani River, East Africa. *Bull. Br. Mus. (Nat. Hist.), Zool.* 2:349-368.

6. Lowe (McConnell), R.H. 1955. Species of *Tilapia* in East African dams, with a key for their identification. *E. Afr. Agric. J.* 20:256-262.

7. Lowe (McConnell), R.H. 1955. The fecundity of *Tilapia* species. *E. Afr. Agric. J.* 21:45-52.

8. Lowe (McConnell), R.H. 1956. Observations on the biology of *Tilapia* (Pisces-Cichlidae) in Lake Victoria, East Africa. *E. Afr. Fish. Res. Org. Suppl. Publ.* 1:1-72.

9. Lowe (McConnell), R.H. 1956. The breeding behaviour of *Tilapia* species (Pisces: Cichlidae) in natural waters: observations on *T. karomo* Poll and *T. variabilis* Boulenger. *Behaviour* (Leiden) 9:141-163.

10. Lowe (McConnell), R.H. 1957. Observations on the diagnosis and biology of *Tilapia leucosticta* Trewavas in East Africa. *Rev. Zool. Bot. Afr.* 55:353-373.

11. Lowe (McConnell), R.H. 1958. Observations on the biology of *Tilapia nilotica* Linne in East African waters. *Rev. Zool. Bot. Afr.* 57:129-170.

12. McConnell (Lowe), R.H. 1958. Introduction to the fish fauna of British Guiana. Timehri, *Journal of the Guyana Museum and Zoo of the Royal Agricultural and Commercial Society of British Guiana* 34:1-11.

13. Lowe (McConnell), R.H. 1959. Breeding behaviour patterns and ecological differences between *Tilapia* species and their significance for evolution within the genus *Tilapia* (Pisces: Cichlidae). *Proc. zool. Soc. Lond.* 132:1-30.

14. Mitchell, W.G. & R.H. McConnell. 1960. The trawl survey carried out by the R.V. 'Cape St Mary' off British Guiana 1957-59. Part II. The interpretation of the catch records. *Bulletin* No. 2, Fisheries Division, Department of Agriculture, Georgetown. 53 pp.

15. Lowe (McConnell), R.H. & A.R. Longhurst. 1961. Trawl fishing in the tropical Atlantic. *Nature* 192:620-623.

16. Lowe (McConnell), R.H. 1962. Notes on the fishes in Georgetown fish markets and their seasonal fluctuations. *Fisheries Bulletin* No. 4, Department of Agriculture, Georgetown. 31 pp.

17. Lowe-McConnell, R.H. 1962. The fishes of the British Guiana continental shelf, Atlantic coast of South Africa, with notes on their natural history. *J. Linn. Soc. (Zool.)* 44:669- 700.

18. Springer, S. & R.H. Lowe. 1963. A new smooth dogshark, *Mustelus higmani,* from the Equatorial Atlantic coast of South America. *Copeia* 1963:241-251.

19. Lowe (McConnell), R.H. 1964. The fishes of the Rupununi savanna district of British Guiana, South America. Part 1. Ecological groupings of fish species and effects of the seasonal cycle on the fish. *J. Linn. Soc. (Zool.)* 45:103-144.

20. McConnell (Lowe), R.H. 1964. Tropical fishery problems and research. *Ann. appl. Biol.* 53:502-503.

21. McConnell, R.H. & E.B. Worthington. 1965. Man-made lakes. *Nature* 208:1039-1042.

22. Banks, J. W., M.J. Holden & R.H. McConnell. 1966. Fishery report. pp. 21-31. *In:* E. White (ed.) *The First Scientific Report of the Kainji Biological Research Team,* Liverpool University, Liverpool.

23. Lowe-McConnell, R.H. 1966. The sciaenid fishes of British Guiana. *Bull. mar. Sci.* 16:20-57.

24. Lowe-McConnell, R.H. (ed.). 1966. *Man-made lakes.* Symposia of the Institute of Biology no. 15, Academic Press, London. 218 pp.

25. Lowe-McConnell. R.H. 1967. Biology of the immigrant cattle egret *Ardeola ibis* in Guyana, South America. *Ibis* 109:168-179.

26. Lowe (McConnell), R.H. 1967. Some factors affecting fish populations in Amazonian waters. *Atas do Simposio sobre a Biota Amazonica (Conservação da Natureza e Recursos Naturais)* 7:177-186.

27. McConnell, R.H. 1967. The fish fauna of the Rupununi District. Guyana. Timehri, *Journal of the Guyana Museum and Zoo of the Royal Agricultural and Commercial Society of British Guiana* 43:57-72.

28. Lowe-McConnell, R.H. 1968. Identification of freshwater fishes. pp. 46-77. *In:* W.E. Ricker (ed.) *Methods for Assessment of Fish Production in Fresh Waters,* IBP Handbook no. 3, Blackwell Scientific Publications, Oxford.

29. Lowe-McConnell, R.H. 1969. Speciation in tropical freshwater fishes, pp, 51-75, *In:* R.H. Lowe-McConnell (ed.) *Speciation in Tropical Environments,* Academic Press, London. (also in *Biol. J. Linn. Soc. Lond.* 1:51-75).

30. Lowe-McConnell, R.H. (ed.) 1969. *Speciation in tropical environments.* Academic Press, London. 246 pp.

31. Lowe-McConnell, R.H.1969. The cichlid fishes of Guyana, S. America. with notes on their ecology and breeding behaviour. *J. Linn. Soc. (Zool.)* 48:255-302.

32. Lowe-McConnell, R.H. & A.A. Wuddah. 1972. *Freshwater fishes of the Volta and Kainji Lakes.* Keys for the field identification of freshwater fishes likely to occur in or above the new man-made lakes, Lake Volta in Ghana and the Kainji Lake on the River Niger in Nigeria. Ghana Universities Press. Accra. 22 pp.

33. Lowe-McConnell, R.H. 1973. Summary: reservoirs in relation to man – fisheries. pp. 641- 654. *In:* W.C. Ackermann, G.F. White & E.B. Worthington (ed.) *Man-made Lakes: Their Problems and Environmental Effects,* Geophysical Monograph 17, American Geophysical Union, Washington, D.C.

34. Lowe-McConnell, R.H. 1975. *Fish communities in tropical freshwaters: their distribution, ecology and evolution.* Longman, London. 337 pp.

35. Lowe-McConnell, R.H. 1975. Freshwater life on the move. Man and the changing wildscape IX. *Geographical Magazine* 57:768-775.

36. Van Dobben, W.H. & R.H. Lowe-McConnell. (ed.) 1975. *Unifying concepts in ecology.* Report of the plenary sessions of the First International Congress of Ecology, The Hague, 1974. Dr W. Junk Publishers, The Hague. 302 pp.

37. Lowe-McConnell, R.H. 1976. Review of 'Lake Kariba: a man-made tropical ecosystem in Central Africa'. *J. Fish. Res. Board Can.* 33:2142-2144.

38. Lowe-McConnell, R.H. 1977. *Ecology of fishes in tropical waters.* Studies in Biology no. 76. Edward Arnold, London. 64pp.

39. Lowe-McConnell, R.H. 1977. On environmental stability and its effects on fish populations in tropical freshwaters. Actas del IV Simposium Internacional de Ecologia tropical, Marzo 7-11 1977, Panama, Organizacione Patrocianadoras, Panama 2:695-710.

40. McConnell, R.H. 1978. *The Amazon. Rivers of the World.* Wayland Publishers Ltd., Howe. 65 pp. (Translated into German in 1979 as Der Amazonas, Schwager & Steinlein, Nurnberg).

41. Lowe-McConnell, R.H. 1978. Identification of freshwater fishes. pp.48-83. *In:* T. Bagenal (ed.) *Methods for Assessment of Fish Production in Fresh Waters,* 3rd edition, IBP Handbook no. 3, Blackwell Scientific Publications, Oxford.

42. Lowe-McConnell, R.H. 1979. Ecological aspects of seasonality in fishes of tropical waters. pp. 219-241. *In:* P.J. Miller (ed.) Fish Phenology: Anabolic Adaptiveness in Teleosts, *Symposia of the Zoological Society of London* 44, Academic Press, London.

43. Le Cren, E.D. & R.H. Lowe-McConnell (ed.) 1980. *The functioning of freshwater ecosystems.* International Biological Programme no. 22. Cambridge University Press, Cambridge. 588 pp.

44. Lowe-McConnell, R.H. & G.J. Howes. 1981. Pisces. pp. 218- 229. *In:* S.H. Hurlbert, G. Rodriguez & N.D. Santos (ed.) *Aquatic Biota of Tropical South America, Part 2: Anarthropoda,* San Diego State University, San Diego.

45. Lowe-McConnell, R.H. 1982. Tilapias in fish communities. pp. 83-113. *In:* R.S.V. Pullin & R.H. Lowe-McConnell (ed.) *The Biology and Culture of Tilapias,* ICLARM Conference Proceedings 7, Manila.

46. Pullin, R.S.V. & R.H. Lowe-McConnell. (ed.) 1982. *The biology and culture of tilapias.* International Center for Living Aquatic Resources Management (ICLARM) Conference Proceedings 7, Manila. 432 pp.

47. Lowe-McConnell, R.H. 1984. The status of studies on South American freshwater food fishes. pp.139-156. *In:* T.M. Zaret (ed.) Evolutionary Ecology of Neotropical Freshwater Fishes, *Developments in Environmental Biology of Fishes* 3, Dr W. Junk Publishers, The Hague.

48. Barel, C.D.N., R. Dorit, P.H. Greenwood, G. Fryer, N. Hughes, P.B.N. Jackson, H. Kawanabe, R.H. Lowe-McConnell, M. Nagoshi, A.J. Ribbink, E. Trewavas, F. Witte & K. Yamaoka. 1985. Destruction of fisheries in Africa's lakes. *Nature* 315: 9-20.

49. Lowe-McConnell, R.H. 1985. The biology of the river systems with particular reference to the fishes. pp. 101-140. *In:* A.T. Grove (ed.) *The Niger and its Neighbours. Environmental History and Hydrobiology, Human Use and Health Hazards of the Major West African Rivers.* Balkema, Rotterdam.

50. Lowe-McConnell, R.H. 1987. *Ecological studies in tropical fish communities.* Cambridge University Press, Cambridge. 382 pp. (Translated into Portuguese in 1992 as, *Estudos Ecológicos de Comunidades de Peixes Tropicais,* with additional chapters on Brazilian fishes, 535 pp.)

51. Benke, A.C., C.A.S. Hall, C.P. Hawkins, R.H. Lowe- McConnell, J.A. Stanford, K. Suberkropp & J.V. Ward. 1988. Bioenergetic considerations in the analysis of stream ecosystems. *Journal of the North American Benthological Society* 7:480-502.

52. Lowe-McConnell, R.H. 1988. Broad characteristics of the ichthyofauna. pp. 93-110. *In:* C. Levêque, M.N. Bruton & G.W. Ssentongo (ed.) *Biology and Ecology of African Freshwater Fishes,* Travaux et Documents ORSTOM 216, Paris.

53. Lowe-McConnell, R.H. 1988. Ecology and distribution of tilapias in Africa that are important for aquaculture. pp. 12- 18. *In:* R.S.V. Pullin (ed.) *Tilapia Genetic Resources for Aquaculture,* ICLARM Conference Proceedings 16, Manila.

54. Lowe-McConnell, R.H. 1988. Fish of the Amazon system. pp. 339-351. *In:* B.R. Davies & K.F. Walker (ed.) *The Ecology of River Systems,* Dr W. Junk Publishers, The Hague.

55. Lowe-McConnell, R.H. 1988. Concluding remarks II: tropical perspectives for future research in river ecology. *Journal of the North American Benthological Society* 7:527-529.

56. Lowe-McConnell, R.H. 1989. Review of 'Rio Negro, rich life in poor water: Amazonian diversity and foodchain ecology as seen through fish communities'. *Trends in Ecology and Evolution* 4:120-121.

57. Lowe-McConnell, R.H. 1990. Summary address: rare fish, problems, progress and prospects for conservation. *J. Fish Biol.* 37 (Suppl. A):263-269.

58. Lowe-McConnell, R.H. 1990. The changing ecosystem of Lake Victoria. *Freshwater Forum* 4:76-88, Freshwater Biological Association.

59. Lowe-McConnell, R.H. 1991. Ecology of cichlids in South American waters and African rivers. pp. 60-85. In: M.H.A. Keenleyside (ed.) *Cichlid Fishes: Behaviour, Ecology and Evolution.* Chapman and Hall, London.

60. Lowe-McConnell, R.H. 1991. Natural history of fishes in Araguaia and Xingu Amazonian tributaries. Serra do Roncador, Mato Grosso, Brazil. *Ichthyol. Explor. Freshwaters* 2:63-82.

61. Lowe-McConnell, R.H. 1991. Evolution in tropical lakes: review of 'Lake Tanganyika and its life' by G.W. Coulter (ed.). *Trends in Ecology and Evolution* 6: 72-273.

62. Lowe-McConnell, R.H. 1991. Ecological roles of littoral fishes in Tanganyika and other African lakes. pp. 39-41. *In:* H. Molsa (ed.) *Proceedings of the International Symposium on Limnology and Fisheries of Lake Tanganyika,* Kuopio. Finland. (abstract).

63. Lowe-McConnell, R.H., R.C.M. Crul & F.C. Roest. 1992. Symposium on resource use and conservation of the African Great Lakes, Bujumbura, 1989. *Mitt. internat. Verein. Limnol.* 23:1-128.

64. Lowe-McConnell, R.H. 1993. Fish faunas of the African Great Lakes: origins, diversity and vulnerability. *Conservation Biology* 7(3):1-10.

65. Lowe-McConnell, R.H. 1994. The roles of ecological and behaviour studies in understanding fish biodiversity and speciation in African Great Lakes: a review. *Arch. Hydrobiol. Beih. Ergebn. Limnol.* 44:335-345.

66. Lowe-McConnell, R.H. 1993. Workshop on Biodiversity, Fisheries and the Future of Lake Victoria. *Rev. Fish Biol. Fish.* 3:201-3.

67. Lowe-McConnell, R.H., F.C. Roest, G. Ntakimaizi & L. Risch. 1994. The African Great Lakes. Geographical Overview. In Biological Diversity in African Fresh and Brackish Fishes. Symposium PARADI, Teugals *et al* (eds) *Ann. Mus. Roy. Afr. Centr. Zool.,* 275:87-94 [The Senegal meeting.]

68. Lowe-McConnell, R.H. 1994. Threats to, and conservation of, tropical freshwater fishes. *Mitt. Internat. Verein. Limnol.,* 24:47-52.

69. Lowe-McConnell, R. 1996. Fish communities in the African Great Lakes. *Env. Biol. Fish* 45:219-235.

70. Lowe-McConnell, R. 1996. Views from the Bridge: a memoir of the freshwater fishes of Trinidad by J.S. Kenny (book review) *Rev. Fish Biol. & Fisheries* 6(4):473-5.

71. Lowe-McConnell, R.H. 1996. Review of 'The Impact of Species Changes in African Lakes' (ed T. Pitcher & P.J.B. Hart). Chapman & Hall, London (Fish & Fisheries No 18) *Rev. Fish Biol. & Fisheries,* 6:363-372.

72. Lowe-McConnell, R.H. 1997. EAFRO and after: a guide to key events affecting fish communities in L. Victoria (East Africa). *S. African J. Science* 93:570-574 [the Greenwood Festschrift]

73. Lowe-McConnell, R.H. 1997. Review of 'Biodiversity, Dynamics & Conservation. The freshwater fish of Tropical Africa' by Christian Lévêque (Cambridge University Press, 434 pp.). *J. Fish Biol.* 51:864-5.

74. Lowe-McConnell, R.H. 1998. Freshwater fishes of northern South America: a need for field guides. *Env. Biol. Fish* 53:11-115 (Review of T. Boujard, M. Pacal, J.F. Meunier & P.Y. Le Bail, 1997. Poissons de Guyane - guide ecologique de l'Approuague et de la reserve des Nouragues INRA Paris, with mention of Atlas des Poissons d'eau douce de Guyane vol 1, P. Planquette, P. Keith & P.-Y. Le Bail 1996 Mus. National d'Histoire Naturelle Paris & INRA).

75. Lowe-McConnell, R.H. 1998. Reviews of 'So Fruitful a Fish. Ecology, Conservation and Aquaculture of the Amazon's Tambaqui', by Carlos Araujo-Lima & Michael Goulding. & 'The Catfish Connection' by Ronaldo Barthem & Michael Goulding 1997, both Columbia University Press, Biology & Resource Management in the Tropics Series. *J. Fish Biology* 53:230-233.

76. Lowe-McConnell, R.H. 1999. Lacustrine fish communities in Africa. pp 29-48 In: W.L.T. van Densen & M.J. Morris (eds) *Fish and Fisheries of Lakes and Rivers in SE Asia and Africa*, Westbury Publishing, Otley, UK.

77. Lowe-McConnell, R.H. 1999. The history of aquatic biodiversity. [Keynote talk in: Setting the Theme, in Sustainable use of Aquatic Diversity: Data, Tools & Cooperation. EXPO 98, Lisbon Sept 1998.] *ACP-EU Fisheries Research Report* No. 6.

78. Lowe-McConnell, R.H. 2000. The role of tilapias in ecosystems, pp 129-162 in M.C.M. Beveridge & B.J. McAndrew, *Tilapias: Biology & Exploitation.* Kluwer Academic Publishers, Dordrecht.

79. Lowe-McConnell, R.H. 2000. Foreword in *Ancient Lakes: Biodiversity, Ecology and Evolution.* Advances in Ecology vol 31, Academic Press.

80. Lowe-McConnell, R.H. 2002. Cichlids all! With an ecological view of African cichlids. [Based on requested critique of G.W. Barlow (2002) The Cichlid Fishes Nature's Grand Experiment in Evolution. Perseus Publishing, Cambridge, Mass.] *Env. Biol. Fish.* 63:459-463.

81. Lowe-McConnell, R.H. 2000. *Land of Waters: Explorations in the Natural History of Guyana, South America.* The Book Guild, Lewes, Sussex.

82. Lowe-McConnell, R.H. 2003. Recent research in the African Great Lakes: fisheries, biodiversity and cichlid evolution. *Freshwater Forum* vol. 20. Freshwater Biological Association.